The Good Rider

by David L. Hough

Mixed *MEDIA*

PUBLISHING
Seattle, WA

Lead Editor: Tom Mehren

Copy & Consulting Editors: Levi Stroppel, Connie Adams

Photography: David Hough, Tom Mehren except where noted

Illustrations: David Hough

Graphic Design & Layout: Tom Mehren, Levi Stroppel

Printing: Gorham Printing, Centralia WA

Text Copyright © 2013 Mixed *MEDIA*®

All rights reserved. No part of this book may be reproduced, stored in a retrieval system, or transmitted in any form or by any means electronic mechanical, photocopying, recording, or otherwise, without prior written permission by Mixed MEDIA, except for brief quotations in an acknowledged review. The author and publisher assume no liability for any errors or omissions that may exist and the damages that may result from the use of this information.

Disclaimer: Both the author and the publisher of The Good Rider disclaim any and all responsibility for the incursion of, personal or other than personal, liabilities and risks from the application or direct or indirect use of any of the contents of this book.

Mixed *MEDIA* publishing®

10115 Greenwood Ave N, #123

Seattle, WA 98133

www.mm411.com

CONTENTS

INTRODUCTION 10

Controlling the Situation 13
Adult Learning Styles 15
Feel Free to Disagree 17

CHAPTER 1: BALANCING AND STEERING 19

Balancing 20
Steering 27
Wheels as Gyroscopes 30

CHAPTER 2: BRAKING BASICS 34

The Tires Stop the Bike 35
Traction is a Function of Weight 35
Weight Transfer 36
Braking Technique 40
Getting Off the Brakes 40
Practice Makes Perfect 41
Rear Wheel Skids 43
Front Wheel Skids 43

CHAPTER 3: SPECIAL BRAKING SITUATIONS 45

Braking with a Passenger 46
Braking in Curves 48
Converting to a Straight-Line Stop 53
Braking Downhill 55
Braking on Loose Surfaces 57

CHAPTER 4: CORNERING CONTROL 59

Smarter Cornering Lines 61

THE APEX 66

CHAPTER 5: THE THROTTLE 70

CHAPTER 6: WEIGHT AND BALANCE 79

HANGING OFF 83
MANAGING THE SITUATION 88

CHAPTER 7: WANDERING RIDERS 90

THE PACE MAY BE THE PROBLEM 94
ROLLING THE DICE 97
FOUR STEPS TO STACK THE ODDS 98

CHAPTER 8: MENTAL SKILLS 101

TEACHING THE "MISSING" EMERGENCY SKILLS 109
UG VS. AG 112

CHAPTER 9: HOW DANGEROUS IS MOTORCYCLING, ANYWAY? 114

A LITTLE MOTORCYCLING HISTORY 116
FATALITY RATES 118
BIKES VS. CARS 121
VMT FATALITY RATE 123
FATALITIES VS. POPULATION 125
MORBID CRASHES 126
WHAT DO YOU DO WITH THE NUMBERS? 127

CHAPTER 10: WHY SHOULD I CARE ABOUT MOTORCYCLE FATALITIES? 128

AVOIDING FATALITIES 132
FEWER CRASHES 134

CHAPTER 11: STUPID HURTS 138

SKILLFUL IN CONTROLLING A WIDE VARIETY OF MOTORCYCLES 139

Proficient at Negotiating Traffic on Public Roads 140
Knowledgeable About Appropriate Riding Gear 141
Knowledgeable About the Human Body 142
Stupid Decisions 143

CHAPTER 12: EXPANDING YOUR RIDE 148

CHAPTER 13: GETTING NOTICED IN TRAFFIC 159

Olson Report Conclusions 161
Foveal vs. Peripheral Vision 161
Seeing = Focusing On the Details 162
Visual Priorities 164
Conspicuity Tactics 165
Positioning 167
Tacking 168
Lights On 169
Judging Speed 170
Night Riding 173

CHAPTER 14: MANAGING THE RISKS 174

Four Main Causes of Crashes 176
Control Skills 176
Matching Speed to Conditions 178
Impairment 179
Situational Awareness 180

CHAPTER 15: FOREIGN TRAVEL 185

CHAPTER 16: RIDING UNPAVED ROADS 200

CHAPTER 17: ARE YOU FIT FOR DUTY? 210

Vision 210

    Hearing 213

    Familiarity with the Machine 218

    Average Age: 49 and Increasing 219

CHAPTER 18: RIDING GEAR 222

    Body Armor 225

    The Helmet 231

    Neck Protection 233

    Gloves and Boots 236

    Practicality 236

CHAPTER 19: DEALING WITH THE ENVIRONMENT 239

    Hot Weather 243

    Dang Winds 245

    Higher Altitudes 251

CHAPTER 20: RIDING IN COLD WEATHER 254

    Turning Back, or Not 255

    Staving off Hypothermia 257

    Insulate the Neck 257

    Survival Tactics 258

    Rehydrating 259

    Cold Weather Riding On Purpose 260

    Getting Prepared 261

    Keeping the Shiny Side Up 263

    The Third Wheel 268

CHAPTER 21: SURFACE HAZARDS 271

    Rails 272

    Edge Traps 275

    Steel Plates 279

Slick Pavement 280
  Tar Snakes 282
  Slippery Pavement Blends 283
  Grated Bridge Decks 285

CHAPTER 22: DAZZLED BY FARKLES 287

  Distracted Driving 290
  The Myth of Multitasking 293
  Reaction Time 294
  The Distracted Brain 296
  Suggestions 298

CHAPTER 23: BREAKDOWNS 300

  How People Handle Breakdowns 301
  When the Bike Goes Bonk 305
  The King is a FINK 306
  What's the problem, anyway? 308
  Pick a Comfortable Place to Work 309
  Remember Where You Left It 310
  Now what? 311
  Being Prepared 313
  Emergency Roadside Service 318
  Medical Emergencies 318

CHAPTER 24: MECHANICAL SKILLS 323

  Tools 332
  The Workspace 332
  The Mentor 333
  Practical Advice 334
  Tires 335

Fuel	337
Battery	338
Getting More Information	343

CHAPTER 25: GROUP RIDES 344

Aggressive Riding	345
Thinking Alike	346
Group Leadership	348
Hey, It's Only Another 300 Miles!	349
The Ride Captain	351
Newbies to the Front, Please	352
The Formation	352
When it's Time to Go, GO!	354
Getting Through the Green Light	355
Signals	356
Getting Stopped	356
Back in the Pack	358
Alternate Ways to Move a Group	359
Try It, You Might Like It	360

CHAPTER 26: THE SECOND RIDER 361

The Safety Briefing	362
Expect Handling Changes	363
Carrying Children	371

CHAPTER 27: LET'S GET LOADED 374

Gross Vehicle Weight Restriction	376
Carrying Capacity	376
How Much Can I Overload?	378
Staying Within the Limits	379

Prioritize, Downsize	380
Packing the Bike	381
Tie One On	382
Luggage	383
Wind Turbulence	385

CHAPTER 28: SIDECARS AND TRIKES 387

Yeah, but it doesn't lean around corners!	391
Trikes	393
Building an Outfit	397
Sidecar Attachment	397
Learning to Drive	398
What about rider training courses?	400
"Driving a Sidecar Outfit" Textbook	401
Not the Bottom Line	401

SUMMARY 402

RESOURCES 405

BIOGRAPHY 407

THE GOOD RIDER

Introduction

What's your idea of a good rider?

Several years ago I participated in an organized tour in New Zealand. During dinner on the final night of the tour, I raised the question, "What's a "good rider?" One of the participants immediately responded, "Valentino Rossi." Obviously, this rider equated "good" with "fast on the track." Of course Rossi has been a very competitive road racer, but my view of motorcycling includes activities other than racing.

To stimulate a little thought about this, I asked whether or not Rossi would have made a good tour leader, or whether he would have been fun to ride with—or for that matter, what sort of dinnertime conversationalist he might have been. My point was that each of us has our own definition of "good rider." If you are focused on racetrack wins, the latest and greatest race winner might fit your definition of "good rider." If speed and absolute traction control on a racetrack are the only criteria, then I'd nominate Reuben Xaus.

Reuben Xaus demonstrates absolute traction control, which for a race fan might qualify him as a "good rider." (Reprinted from Proficient Motorcycling, 2nd ed., Bowtie Press)

Let's be clear that I am impressed with the skills required to negotiate a racetrack at winning speeds, but with due respect for racers, I see racing as only one narrow part of motorcycling. For those of us who are focused more on riding public roads, our definition of "good rider" might be quite different, because the skills are different for commuting to work every day in urban traffic, or participating in an organized tour, or heading off to a rally thousands of miles from home.

Maybe you'd value a tour guide who can show you the way at a pace more in tune with your riding style or lead you to out-of-the-way sights and experiences that you would otherwise miss, or maybe just someone with whom you would enjoy traveling. Wouldn't stacking up a million miles of riding be some indication of a good rider?

Speaking for myself, I am more impressed with riders who can function in the real world of public roads, traveling far and wide, and surviving the inherent risks of aggressive traffic, strange cultures, and unbelievable surface hazards or weather conditions. I don't know Rossi or Reuben personally— I've never ridden with either one. But my guess is that a professional road racer probably wouldn't be my first choice as a tour leader or dinnertime conversationalist. Negotiating public roads requires a hefty dose of control skill *plus* an even heftier dose of street smarts, knowledge born of experience, and a few social skills, such as being able to control aggression.

Controlling the Situation

Moto-journalist Ken Condon put this in perspective for me. Ken not only commutes to his day job by motorcycle, he is an amateur road racer, a leader in an east coast sport bike association, a dirt rider, and current author of the "Proficient Motorcycling" and "Street Strategies" columns in *Motorcycle Consumer News*.

After one typically stimulating ride with the sport bike guys, Ken returned home and announced to his wife that he would no longer lead group rides.

"Why not? Did you have a close call?"

"No, it was a perfect ride. We were riding aggressively but we were all in complete control of our bikes."

"So what's the problem?"

"As we were rounding a blind curve at a good clip, it suddenly dawned on me that while I was in control of the bike and the group, I wasn't in control of the situation. If a farm truck had pulled out of a driveway just around the curve, we would all have been toast."

I suppose that's a big part of my image of a good rider—someone who is not only in control of the motorcycle, but in control of the situation. If it's a commute to work, a good rider is not only skillful enough to avoid collisions, but also clever enough to manage surface hazards such as spilled diesel oil, tar snakes, and "edge traps;" and equipped for comfort and protection in whatever weather conditions occur. If it's a cross-country journey, a good rider would not only be in control of the machine and the potential traffic, surface, and weather hazards--but also manage navigation, fuel, food, communication, and security. If it's a group ride, a good leader controls the pace so that everyone enjoys the event, but no one is pressured to take unnecessary risks.

Ron Ayres might not win any professional road races, but he has an impressive resume of motorcycling experience, including endurance rides, authorship of several motorcycling books, and management of organized tours in different parts of the world. Would he qualify as a "good rider?"

Don't get me wrong. "Being in control" doesn't mean we don't take any risks. I don't know about you, but I ride motorcycles for pleasure, not safety. I enjoy the whole package of motorcycling, and a big part of the package is managing the inherent risks. I find it satisfying to challenge potentially nasty situations and survive. I took up motorcycling in 1965, and I'm still riding, more than a million miles and 40 years later. Perhaps sharing my knowledge will help you to become (or remain) a good rider.

Adult Learning Styles

I've done quite a few seminars at big motorcycle rallies. At one big BMW rally, my plan was to ask what the participants wanted to talk about, and deal with whatever subjects came up. The very first question was a serious one, and that encouraged other serious questions. At the conclusion of the seminar one of the riders made an interesting observation:

"Dave, there have been a lot of really interesting questions, and you answered all of them very well. But you know, there wasn't one question asked that you haven't already covered in your book."

He was referring to my book, *Proficient Motorcycling: The Ultimate Guide to Riding Well*. And he was correct. His point was that those riders who had asked questions could have saved us all time by reading the book. But I understand that different people have very different learning styles. Some can learn by reading. Others just aren't in the habit of reading, or find reading boring. Many of us learn best by face-to-face dialogue—which is exactly what we were doing in the seminar. Another learning approach is scanning through Internet sites at your own pace. In that regard, I sincerely hope that columns on websites such as *http://www.soundrider.com* will help you to increase your skills and knowledge. Perhaps some small detail will make the difference between a crash and a close call in your own riding.

To get us started on this adventure, I'd like to propose a more comprehensive description of "good rider" that I think would be applicable to a wide variety of motorcyclists and machines.

A good rider is a motorcyclist who is:

- Skillful in controlling a wide variety of motorcycles.
- Proficient at negotiating traffic on public roads without causing or being involved in collisions.
- Able to negotiate whatever surface hazards are encountered without losing control, including both paved and unpaved roads.
- Skilled at managing different environmental conditions, including hot, cold, wet, dry, windy, and high or low altitude.
- Knowledgeable about appropriate riding gear to provide protection from both the elements and accidental crashes.
- Knowledgeable enough about the human body to maintain health and fitness under a variety of traveling conditions, and to administer first aid to self or others in the event of illness or injury.
- Knowledgeable enough in mechanics to maintain a motorcycle independently of a professional technician, and to diagnose and make simple field repairs on the road.
- Capable of riding in a group, and leading group rides when called upon to do so.

You may notice that I haven't mentioned competition as part of being a good rider. That's because of the tremendous differences between a competition environment and riding public roads. I don't downplay the technical advances in motorcycles as a result of competition, but I don't see more than a few racing skills that add real value to street riding.

Additional "points"

I would add "points" for the following experiences, which I believe all contribute something to the repertoire of a good rider:

- 200,000 or more miles of motorcycling in a wide variety of climates and geography.
- Foreign travel, especially by motorcycle on continents other than North America.
- 5,000 or more miles of dirt riding experience.
- Study of magazines that includes riding skills, such as *Motorcycle Consumer News*; and skills books such as *Proficient Motorcycling*, *Total Control*, and *Sport Riding Techniques*.
- Successful completion of one or more road or off-road training courses.
- 5,000 or more miles of driving three-wheeled motorcycles such as a sidecar combination or motorcycle-based trike.
- Certification as a trained motorcycle instructor/coach—MSF, S/TEP, or other recognized training program.

Feel Free to Disagree

You're welcome to disagree with my suggestions. Feel free to develop your own list of qualities that you think make a good rider. The point is to paint a target at which we might point our efforts to become smarter and more skilled.

Does the size or performance of the motorcycle have any bearing on a rider's skill level or knowledge? Would you rate a rider as being less skilled if he or she is riding a smaller, lighter machine?

Do we automatically assume that the rider of a larger or more aggressive motorcycle is better than a rider on a scooter or sidecar rig?

THE GOOD RIDER

Chapter 1: Balancing and Steering

I started this discussion with the idea that a good rider is more than someone who can go fast on the track, and I suggested a list of characteristics that I think would help define my ideal good rider, starting with, "A good rider is a motorcyclist who is skillful in control of a wide variety of motorcycles."

Of course, different machines balance, accelerate, corner, and stop differently. And I hope that you haven't developed a bigotry that prevents you from appreciating different machines, including smaller bikes and motorcycles that have more than two wheels. First, let's review some basic control techniques that are common to all two-wheeled motorcycles. I will frequently refer to two-wheeled motorcycles as "bikes."

For a novice rider, balancing a bike is a bit tricky. Think back to when you first started riding. What you needed to do with the grips wasn't intuitive. The machine may have suddenly decided to head off in some direction you hadn't intended, and it wasn't clear what you needed to do to get it pointed where you wanted it to go. For most riders, something clicks after a few months, and balance suddenly becomes easier. For others, even after decades of riding, balancing and steering is a continuous struggle. I've seen more than a few apparently experienced riders who can't make a right turn without crossing the centerline, or can't ride up to a stop sign without dragging their feet on the ground.

Let's think through why bikes do what they do, and suggest some techniques for becoming boss of the bike rather than letting the bike boss you around. First, how does a bike balance? What forces hold it up? And what forces do we have to get it to steer into a turn?

Balancing

Let's imagine three different ways a bike balances in relation to the tire contact patches. Think of a bike in motion, as viewed from the front. If there were a strong gust of wind, the tire contact patches might continue in a more-or-less straight line, but the top of the bike would be blown downwind (Roll A).

Roll A: One way a bike can lean is at the top, say from a strong wind gust. The tire contact patches continue straight ahead, but the top of the bike is pushed over.

The flip side of that would be if something forced the tire contact patches away from center, perhaps a groove in the road, or pavement that's not level. The rider's head would continue straight, but the wheels and rest of the bike would roll sideways (Roll B).

Roll B: Another way a bike can lean is with the front wheel being steered away from center. The top of the bike continues straight ahead, but the contact patches move away from center. An example would be a rider recovering from a wind gust.

Another possible way the bike could roll is that the mass of the machine and rider continue straight ahead, but the contact patches move one way, and the top of the bike rolls in the opposite direction (Roll C).

Roll C: The motorcycle may roll (lean) around its Center of Mass (CoM). The inertia of the motorcycle makes it want to continue straight ahead, so when the contact patches are steered one way, the top of the bike rolls the other way. For most bikes the CoM is approximately between the rider's knees. This is the most typical way a motorcycle leans, with the rider leaning slightly toward the curve, while steering the front tire away from the curve.

Why does it make any difference how a bike rolls to one side or the other? Well, in order to control a bike proficiently, it helps to understand how it works. What's more, there are some situations where you absolutely need to know what to do. A novice rider can get away with lack of skill most of the time, but when a non-normal situation develops you need proficient skills.

Let's note that the rider doesn't have much control over Roll A. A crosswind gust might push the bike sideways, but it's not within the rider's control. A heavy motorcycle will be reluctant to roll as in Roll B because the bike wants to move straight ahead, not sideways. The most typical way a motorcycle rolls is Roll C, with the "hinge point" being the CoM, represented by the little round symbol.

Normally a bike keeps itself balanced. But let's say the bike starts leaning toward the left. What can you do to get it rebalanced? It's not intuitive, but you can steer the front wheel more toward the left, forcing the bike to roll more toward the right. It's the action we talked about in Roll C. Of course, steering the front wheel will result in the bike being in a slightly different position on the road when you get it rebalanced.

If the bike becomes unbalanced and starts to lean left, the rider can correct the lean by steering toward the left to force the bike to roll upright.

It's important to understand that the rider momentarily steers the front wheel opposite the way he or she wants the bike to roll. If it's a matter of recovering from a crosswind or negative road camber, the bike will recover balance in a slightly different position on the road. If just a gentle correction is needed on a level road, the geometry of the front end does this automatically. Tire drag off-center (and other forces) steers the front wheel toward the direction of lean, rebalancing the bike. Even in what you might swear is a "straight line," the front wheel makes a very slight weave from side to side as the bike rebalances itself.

Let's note that a bike doesn't always roll exactly around its CoM. The bike is carving an arc through space, and the actual geometric center of the roll/curve can be far away from the motorcycle, even below ground level. But you might find it useful to imagine a bike rolling around an imaginary CoM that's approximately centered between your knees, with bike roll controlled by how you steer the front wheel.

Steering

To get the bike to roll toward a turn, you steer the front wheel opposite the way you want to go. When you want to turn left, you momentarily steer toward the right until the bike is rolled over to an angle you think is about right for the curve.

Bikes steer differently from other vehicles, because to get a bike to turn, it must first be leaned. Once the bike is rolled into a nice lean, you can steer the front wheel toward the direction you want to go without falling over or rolling upright. You can position the front wheel contact patch to balance centrifugal force against gravity.

To get the bike to roll toward a turn, the rider momentarily steers the front wheel opposite the intended direction. In other words, to roll left, the rider momentarily steers slightly toward the right. The wheel tracks away from center, forcing the top of the bike to roll toward the left. As the bike rolls over to an angle appropriate to the turn, the rider eases up on the grips, allowing the front wheel to return to center, and then to point slightly toward the curve.

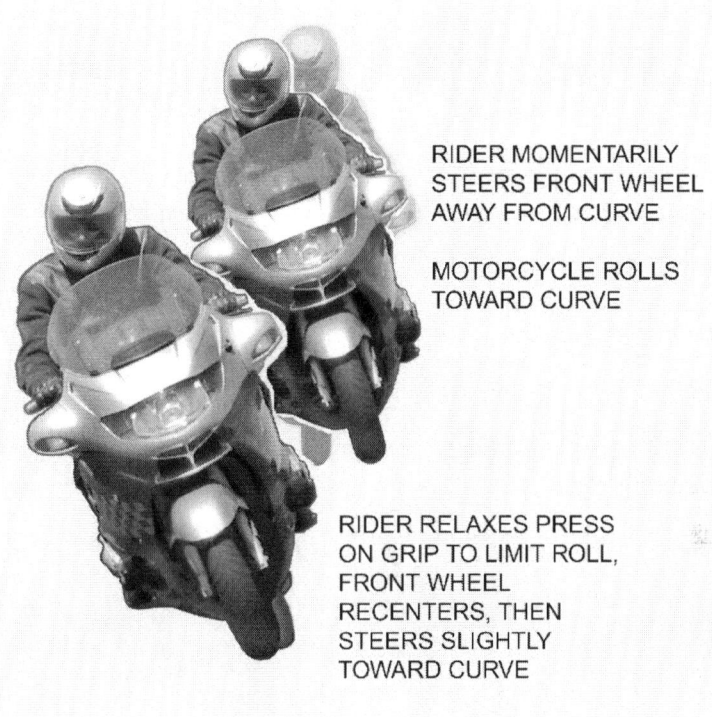

RIDER MOMENTARILY STEERS FRONT WHEEL AWAY FROM CURVE

MOTORCYCLE ROLLS TOWARD CURVE

RIDER RELAXES PRESS ON GRIP TO LIMIT ROLL, FRONT WHEEL RECENTERS, THEN STEERS SLIGHTLY TOWARD CURVE

To get the bike leaned toward a curve, the rider momentarily steers the front wheel opposite the intended curve. For instance, approaching a right turn, the rider momentarily steers slightly left. The front wheel tracking toward the left causes the bike to roll right. When the bike is leaned at an appropriate angle for the curve, the rider eases up on the grips and allows the front wheel to re-center and steer toward the curve.

Lots of riders are confused about this because the front wheel doesn't have to steer very far to cause the bike to roll, and because the view of the bike from the front is different from the view in the saddle. The steering movement is so slight you might suspect that the bike rolls toward the turn without the front end steering at all, but for a typical turn at road speed the front wheel does steer away from center a tiny amount, perhaps 1 or 2 degrees. At highway speed, just a slight nudge on the grips results in the front wheel out-tracking quickly and with considerable force. The more aggressively you attempt to roll the bike toward a curve, the more obvious it will be that you first steer to get the bike rolled over, and then steer toward the curve.

Wheels as Gyroscopes

The spinning wheels (and engine) generate gyroscopic stability that helps hold the bike vertical and pointed generally in a straight-ahead direction. That's why it is possible for a bike to motor down the road with the rider's hands off the grips, at least for a well-balanced machine and load. Of course, machines that are heavier on one side than the other will not balance easily in a straight line.

More than a few riders have theorized that the gyroscopic action (precession) of the front wheel is what causes the bike to roll toward the curve. After all, if you hold a spinning bicycle wheel by its axle and "steer" it toward the left, it leans right. But let's note that this experiment is with the wheel in the air, not in contact with the ground like a motorcycle front tire, and that it takes lots of steering to cause much roll. What's more, if gyroscopic precession were the dominant force causing the bike to roll, then as the front wheel is returned to center at the desired angle of lean, precession would just roll the bike back to vertical. So we must conclude that gyroscopic precession isn't what causes the bike to roll.

Actually, the gyroscopic stability of the wheels is very important, because it *resists* roll. Gyroscopic stability allows the rider to make predictable steering inputs that aren't so quick or forceful the bike would be uncontrollable. Think of the gyroscopic behavior of the wheels as a centering spring the rider must overcome to make steering inputs.

As it happens, front wheel traction is much more powerful than the gyroscopic forces. This is very obvious when your front tire contacts a raised pavement edge. The edge steers the front wheel, but gyroscopic stability isn't sufficient to hold the bike upright. Imagine easing your bike parallel to a raised edge on your left. As the front tire snuggles up to the edge, you can suddenly lose control of steering. And without steering control, you will find it difficult, perhaps impossible, to keep the bike balanced. The lesson in this is that it's steering the contact patch that controls balance and steering. Later on we'll talk about tactics for crossing edge traps.

If you allow your front tire to snuggle up to the raised edge at the left side of this lane, the front wheel will be steered straight, and it's almost impossible to control balance when you lose control of steering.

If your brain is reeling from this business of steering to control roll and direction, it's time for some homework. Take your bike for a spin. Find a vacant road or empty parking lot for an experiment. Get the bike up to say, 35 mph, and nudge the right grip—making a point to not resist the nudge with your other hand. You'll notice the bike rolls toward the right, and wants to steer right. Press on the left grip, and the bike will roll left and steer left. Experiment with this enough to convince yourself that steering the front wheel controls a bike's balance and direction— at least on pavement.

At 35 mph or so, pressing momentarily on the right grip will roll the bike toward the right. Pressing on the left grip will roll the bike left.

THE GOOD RIDER

Chapter 2: Braking Basics

Riding on public roads exposes us to all sorts of hazards. The key to avoiding crashes is to maintain your awareness of what's happening ahead, so that you can make simple corrections to not be at the wrong place at the wrong time or the wrong speed. In city traffic, braking gives you options for quickly getting out of the way of other vehicles. Out in the country, braking gives you options for avoiding hazards such as stalled vehicles or wandering animals. Once in a while, you need to brake very aggressively to avoid a hazard that suddenly pops into view. For such situations, it's important to have developed the correct muscle memory to brake without losing control.

Novice riders in training courses are often reminded of concepts such as "The front wheel does 70% of the braking." That's good advice for novices, but at some point a rider needs to move beyond novice techniques. A good rider needs to be able to brake at any time, even in curves, or on loose gravel, without spilling. More than a few riders embarrass themselves by demonstrating that they haven't developed their braking skill. Even if your bike has linked or Anti-lock Brakes (ABS), you're not excused from braking practice. There are lots of situations where the brake system can't save you from bad habits or undeveloped skills. So, let's work on it.

The Tires Stop the Bike

We might come to believe that it's the brakes that stop the bike, but really it's the tires. Brakes can stop the wheel from turning, but its tire traction against the road surface that overcomes the forward energy of the motorcycle, and slows it down. That means we need to be aware of the condition of the road surface as well as our tires. The situation determines our braking technique.

For what follows, let's define "braking force" as the deceleration force applied by the tires, not the force pressing the brake pads against the disc.

Traction is a Function of Weight

The braking force that a tire can supply is directly proportional to the weight pressing the tire onto the roadway. Let's imagine a motorcycle and rider with a combined weight of 800 pounds, equally supported on both wheels. The load on each wheel would be 400 pounds, so each tire could provide 400 pounds of braking force to slow the bike. That's the braking force available at the start of braking, but the situation changes quickly.

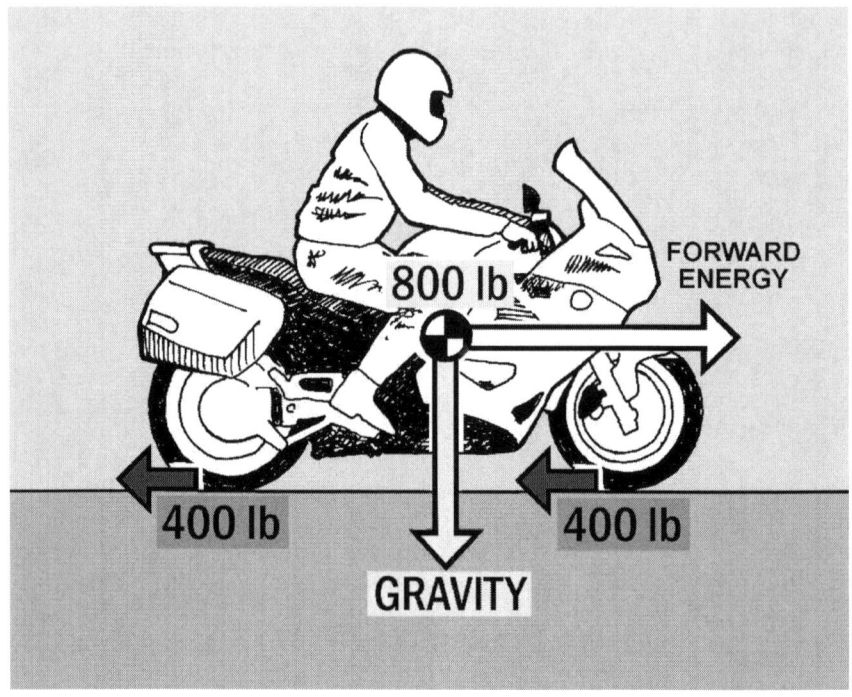

With a total weight of 800 pounds and rear/front weight bias of 50/50, brake force on either tire would be 400 pounds. Of course, weight bias changes quickly once the brakes are applied.

Weight Transfer

At rest, a motorcycle's inertia resists movement. It doesn't want to move. To accelerate a motorcycle up to highway speed, engine power is required to overcome inertia, plus wind resistance, bearing friction, etc.

The flip side of inertia is that once up to speed, the motorcycle wants to keep moving straight ahead at the same speed. So, to decelerate the motorcycle, the brakes must overcome the machine's inertia. The kinetic energy of the speeding motorcycle is converted to heat as the brakes are applied. The brakes on most contemporary motorcycles are as powerful as the engine.

Although the motorcycle, rider, and load are composed of many bits and pieces, we can pretend that the whole collection has a Center of Mass (CoM), and that gravity and inertia act on that single point. The CoM will probably be somewhere in the middle of the heaviest parts, perhaps midway between the rider's knees.

Now, when the brakes are applied, the braking force is way down at the contact patch of the tires, while kinetic energy ("forward energy") is acting much higher on the bike. The result is that under braking, everything pitches forward, applying more weight onto the front tire. This is sometimes called "weight transfer," although it should be obvious that the mass or "weight" doesn't move around—it's that forward energy is loading more of the mass onto the front tire.

As the front tire is pressed more onto the surface, it gains traction, so it's capable of more braking force. If the front tire has sufficient traction, aggressive front braking can lift the rear tire off the surface (a "stoppie"). In that situation, 100% of brake force would be on the front tire with nothing on the rear. The rear brake could be fully applied with the wheel locked, but with the tire waving in the air it can't apply any braking force.

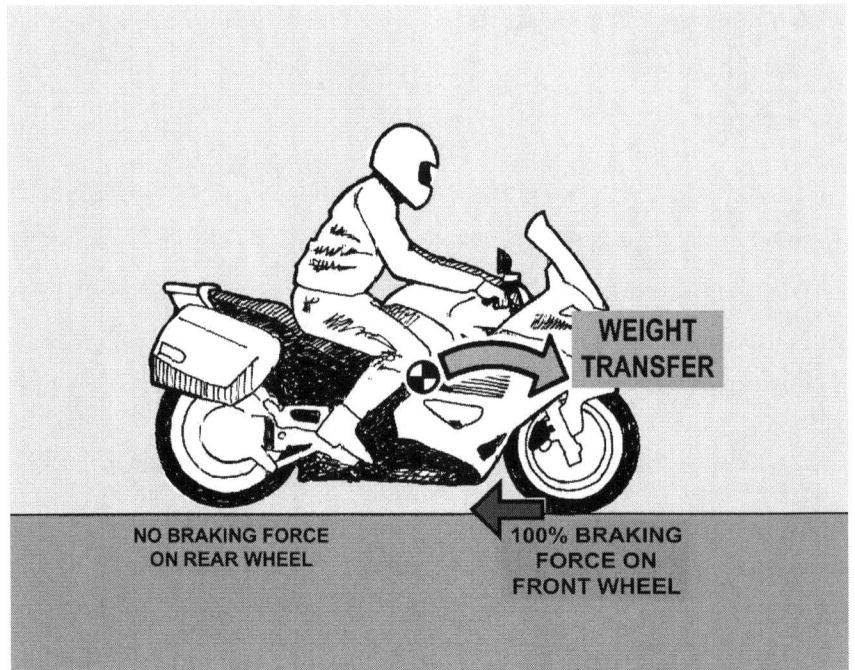

If the rider applies the front brake sufficient to lift the rear tire off the surface (a "stoppie"), braking force at the front tire would be 100% of the weight of bike and rider.

So, with our theoretical 800 pound motorcycle, under hard braking we could have all 800 pounds perched on the front tire, in which case we could have 800 pounds of braking force on the front.

However, in the interests of keeping the bike pointed straight ahead, it would be good to have some weight on the rear tire. So, a more realistic "maximum" braking situation for an 800 pound motorcycle would be something like 680 pounds of braking force on the front, and 120 pounds on the rear.

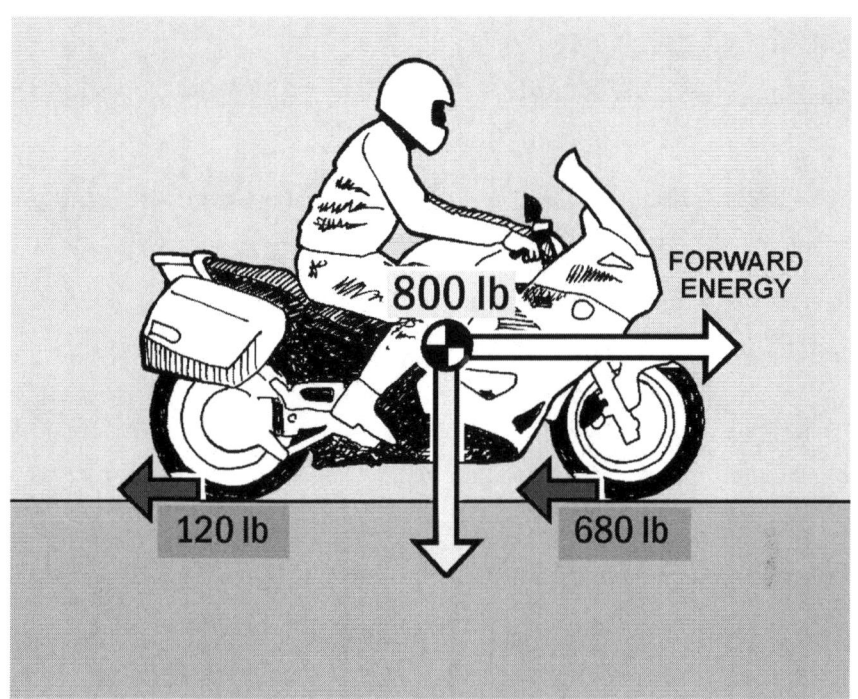

In a realistic quick stop, assuming an 800 pound machine and 85% of braking on the front wheel, there might be 680 pounds of braking force on the front tire.

There have been some serious real-world motorcycle braking tests in the past few years, and the results suggest that more aggressive braking is possible. You can get on the front brake very quickly without skidding the tire—if you squeeze the lever smoothly and progressively to match weight transfer. If you haven't practiced aggressive stops for a while, I suggest you practice squeezing the lever over one second, the time it takes to say, *"one-thousand-and-one."* As you gain skill, you can gradually get that time down to a half-second. The goal is to be fully on the brakes as quickly as possible without skidding either tire.

Braking Technique

Regardless of the brake system on the machine you're riding, the same general techniques will apply. First, squeeze the clutch when braking aggressively, to separate engine compression braking from the equation. If you just roll off the throttle without using the clutch, engine braking may exceed available traction and cause a rear wheel skid. Squeezing the clutch lever as you brake makes it easier to control the rear wheel.

I suggest applying both front and rear brakes simultaneously, then immediately easing up on the rear brake pedal as you squeeze harder on the front lever. If you can't seem to avoid skidding the rear tire, ignore the rear pedal and concentrate on the front brake. Sport bikes, because of the short wheelbase and powerful front brakes, make it much easier to loft the rear wheel. ABS won't help prevent a stoppie, since the front tire isn't skidding. Cruisers and Sport Touring bikes, with longer wheelbases, have more of a rearward weight bias that helps keep the rear wheel on the ground.

Getting Off the Brakes

It's also important that when you get off the brakes, you ease off rather than just let go of the lever. That's especially important if you are braking aggressively to slow down, but you're not making a complete stop. Remember that during hard braking, the front tire is loaded more, and that compresses the suspension. Suddenly popping off the brake lever will cause the suspension to unload, reducing traction. So, smooth *on* the brakes, smooth *off* the brakes.

Practice Makes Perfect

You can't expect to be skillful just by reading about it. The only way to improve your skills is to practice. The point is to make braking so familiar that you do it automatically without having to think much about it. To put this another way, you want to develop the muscle memory to brake correctly for any situation. The way to develop muscle memory is to practice the correct skills over and over.

I suggest finding a quiet area away from traffic and making a series of quick stops, preferably at the start of every riding season. Perhaps you can borrow a vacant portion of a parking lot early on a Sunday morning. If it's your first time practicing quick stops, expect to spend two or three hours honing your braking skills.

Lay out a straight "braking chute" about 100 feet long, with lots of run-out room at the end. You can mark the chute with small cones or tennis balls cut in half, with double markers for the point where you will start to brake. Be cautious at first, making your first run at no faster than 18 mph. If you slide the rear tire at that speed, you need to correct that problem before bumping your speed up. As you get it right, bump up your approach speed by an additional 2 mph, with an eventual target of 35 mph. That may not sound fast, but forward energy builds rapidly, and you really need skill to manage an aggressive stop from 35 mph. Of course, if you ride at 70 mph, shouldn't you eventually work up to initiating an aggressive stop from 70 mph?

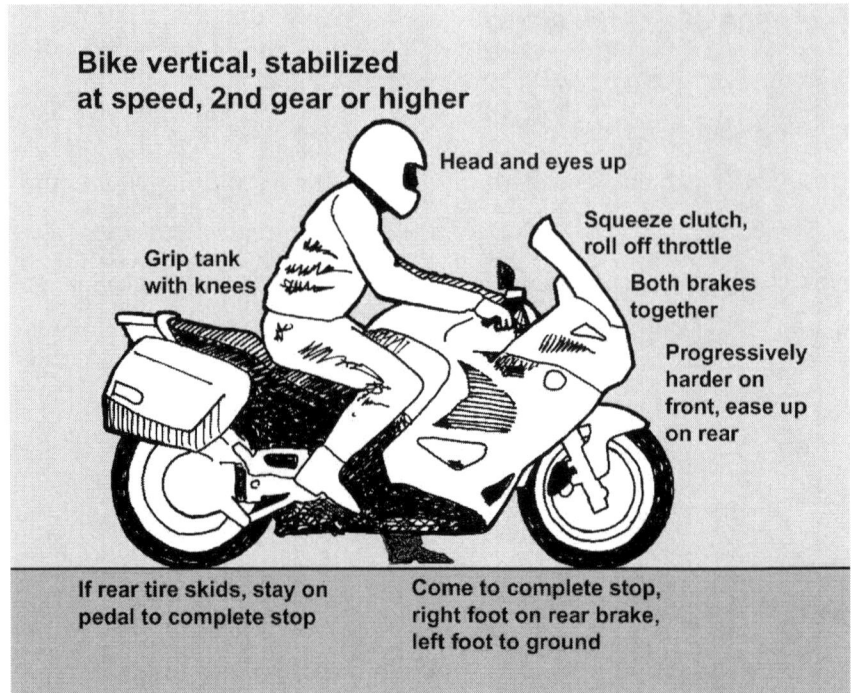

The whole point of braking practice is to develop the muscle memory to brake correctly in any situation.

Regardless of your experience level or the braking system on your bike, there is a big difference between slowing from 70 to 40 mph, and making a controlled stop from 40 to 0 mph. Later on we'll need to think about aggressive braking in corners.

Do us both a favor and wear your best abrasion-resistant riding gear—just in case you make a little boo-boo. I've seen more than a few experienced riders who crashed while attempting their first quick stop—typically a result of an inflated image of their not-so-good braking skills. Even if you think you're very good at braking, I advise you to start conservatively and gradually work up to higher approach speeds as you demonstrate to yourself that you have the techniques down.

Rear Wheel Skids

Be aware that as your approach speeds increase, forward energy increases, and that tends to decrease rear wheel traction during an aggressive stop. The danger is that if you skid the rear tire into a slideout and then panic and pop off the pedal, the bike is very likely to snap back to center and throw you over the high side. To avoid a high-side crash, you need to know if you're sliding the rear tire, and that's not easy to detect from the saddle. I advise you to find a riding partner who can take turns practicing and observing stops, and provide some feedback to each other on what's happening.

Front Wheel Skids

Front wheel skids result from grabbing the lever too quickly, or holding a death grip on the lever even as the tire begins to slide. An impending front tire skid causes steering to feel light and unresponsive. If steering suddenly feels "rubbery" under aggressive braking, you should ease up slightly on the lever. And if the front tire suddenly begins to slide, ease off the brake lever to restore traction, then squeeze again—more smoothly.

If the mere thought of practicing quick stops makes you break out in a cold sweat, I suggest signing up for a training course where you can build skill under the watchful eye of an instructor.

The big advantage of practicing braking at a training course is getting immediate feedback from an instructor who knows what to watch for.

Chapter 3: Special Braking Situations

We've covered some of the basics of straight-line braking on a level surface, but what about braking with a passenger, or braking in a curve, or on a hill, or in the dirt?

Braking with a Passenger

Braking technique needs to change as the load on the bike changes. Extra weight on the bike, whether traveling gear or a passenger, adds forward energy to the bike, which means more braking is needed to decelerate the increased mass. Most importantly, additional weight on the rear moves the combined CoG rearward, increasing the load on the rear tire. That increases rear tire traction, so you can use much more rear brake than when riding solo.

Imagine a motorcycle with two riders plus gear weighing a total of 1000 pounds, with a rear/front weight bias of say, 60/40.

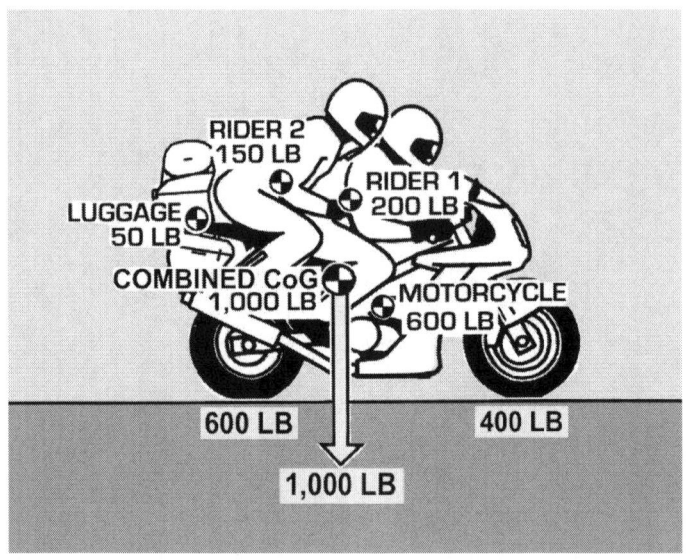

When carrying a passenger and gear, weight bias might be 60/40 rear/front.

At the start of braking, rear tire braking could be up to 600 pounds and front braking 400 pounds. But as braking increases to around 80% of available traction, the braking forces would change to say, 200/600 rear/front, requiring the rider to modulate more pressure to the front brakes. It's much less likely the bike will lift the rear end off, but there are other considerations when carrying a passenger.

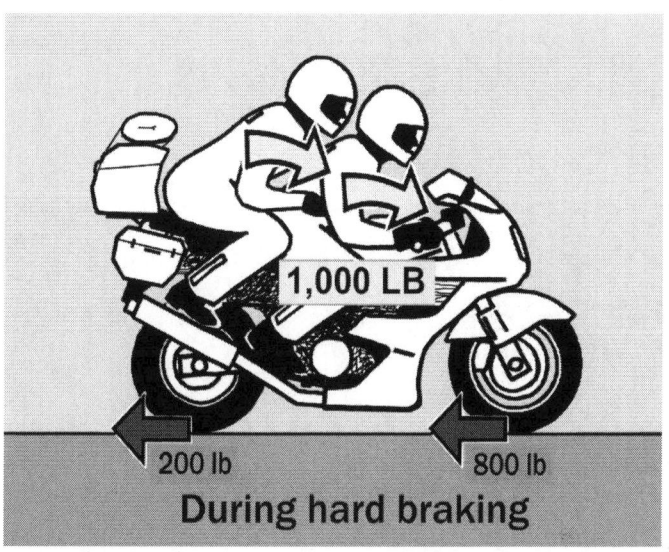

Carrying a passenger, there will be more weight on the rear, and therefore more traction on the rear. Even during aggressive braking, it's less likely the rear tire will lose traction.

The forward energy of the passengers and gear needs to be managed. The gear is secured to the bike, and the rider can brace against the handlebars and tank. But the passenger has little to hang onto other than the rider. A passenger's weight adds significantly to the mass that needs to be stopped, and the passenger is typically seated high on the bike. As the rider applies the brakes aggressively, the passenger slams forward into the rider's back. Or more correctly, the bike pushes the rider back into the passenger.

There is little to brace against even if the passenger is aware of the situation. At the point where the rider is being pushed up onto the tank by the passenger's weight, the rider must ease off on braking in order to maintain control of the bike. So, the limiting factor in aggressive braking with a passenger isn't the brakes or traction, but how well the passenger and rider are able to decelerate with the bike.

Since quick stops are more difficult when carrying a passenger, if you often carry a passenger you should consider practice braking with your passenger aboard. On-road solutions include riding at a more conservative pace, and scrutinizing the situation farther ahead to provide more time to deal with hazards.

Braking in Curves

When the bike is leaned over into a curve, the tires are consuming a lot of the available traction forcing the bike to turn. Depending upon the risk acceptance level of the rider, the bike could be leaned over to the point where there is little or no extra traction available for braking. In such a situation, if the rider applies too much brake, or grabs the brakes too suddenly, the likely result will be a low-side crash with the bike sliding off the road.

Cornering forces can use up all of the available traction in a curve, leaving nothing for braking. Although it might seem safer to avoid using any front brake while leaned over, there's a real risk of the rear tire sliding first, as a result of either engine braking or rolling on too much throttle too soon. Braking while leaned over requires considerable skill, but hazards are just as likely to appear in corners as on the straights.

To avoid a slideout while braking in a curve, the rider must transition to the brakes smoothly and then brake progressively harder as the bike slows and the lean angle is reduced. In other words, cornering traction can be traded for braking traction as the bike is lifted up.

Let's say you're riding a narrow backroad somewhat aggressively, when you suddenly realize there is a farm tractor backing a load of hay into the barn ahead. To avoid a spill, you transition smoothly to the brake lever as you roll the bike more vertical, and brake progressively harder as you get the bike more upright.

If you need to brake while leaned into a curve, should you use both brakes, or just the rear brake, or only the front?

When the bike is leaned way over in a curve, the tires may be close to the limits of traction. It's best to use both brakes to share the braking traction between both tires, and also to squeeze the clutch. Just rolling off the throttle can cause a rear wheel skid. Definitely you should use the front brake, not just the rear. If you roll off the gas, that applies engine compression braking to the rear wheel, transferring some weight onto the front tire. So, rear tire traction can be even more limited than front tire traction. The technique for avoiding a front wheel slideout is to avoid any sudden changes in traction, so the transition from throttle to brakes must be very smooth.

To prepare for braking while leaned over into a curve, it helps to practice throttle-to-brake transitions, which you can do in a straight line. You'll need to manage the throttle and front brake lever simultaneously so that you can start to squeeze the brake lever while you're still easing off the throttle. Some riders prefer to hold the throttle with the thumb and outside fingers, and brake with the first two fingers. Two fingers may be adequate for a sport bike with powerful front brakes, even if you are carrying a passenger. You're less likely to lift the rear tire off and slide out.

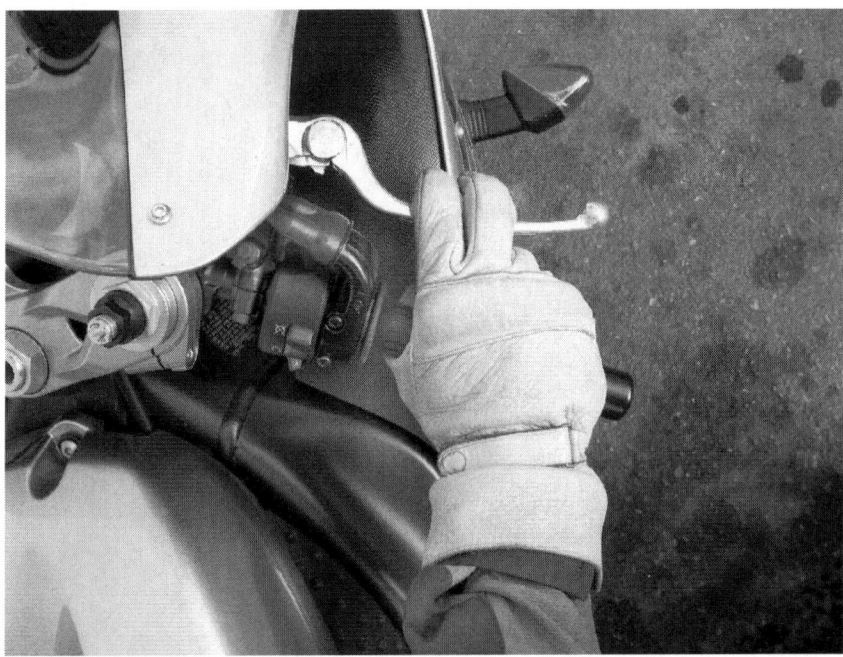

If you're riding a heavier machine, you might prefer to hold the throttle with the thumb and first finger, and brake with the outer three fingers. This allows a more precise brake squeeze, and works better for heavier bikes because you'll have more pressure squeezing on the end of the lever. It's important to find a technique that works for you, so that you can transition smoothly from throttle to brake.

I suggest practicing throttle-to-brake transitions first in a straight line at slower speeds. The skill is to smoothly squeeze the front brake lever as you are rolling off the throttle, then ease back on the throttle as you smoothly release the brakes. You want to avoid snapping the throttle off first and then grabbing the brake lever. It's also important to ease off the brakes as you ease back on the gas. Suddenly popping off the brakes can cause the front tire to lose traction. Practicing throttle-to-brake transitions in a straight line can help build the correct muscle memory to do the right thing when the bike is leaned over.

Inexperienced riders tend to think of the brake lever as a switch—on or off. More skillful riders realize the brake lever can be squeezed in small increments. Imagine a brake lever with 5 positions. Each position is an increase of 20%. Make an imaginary brake lever out of your left hand, and try squeezing just hard enough to go from position three to position four. That's the sort of smooth control we're talking about.

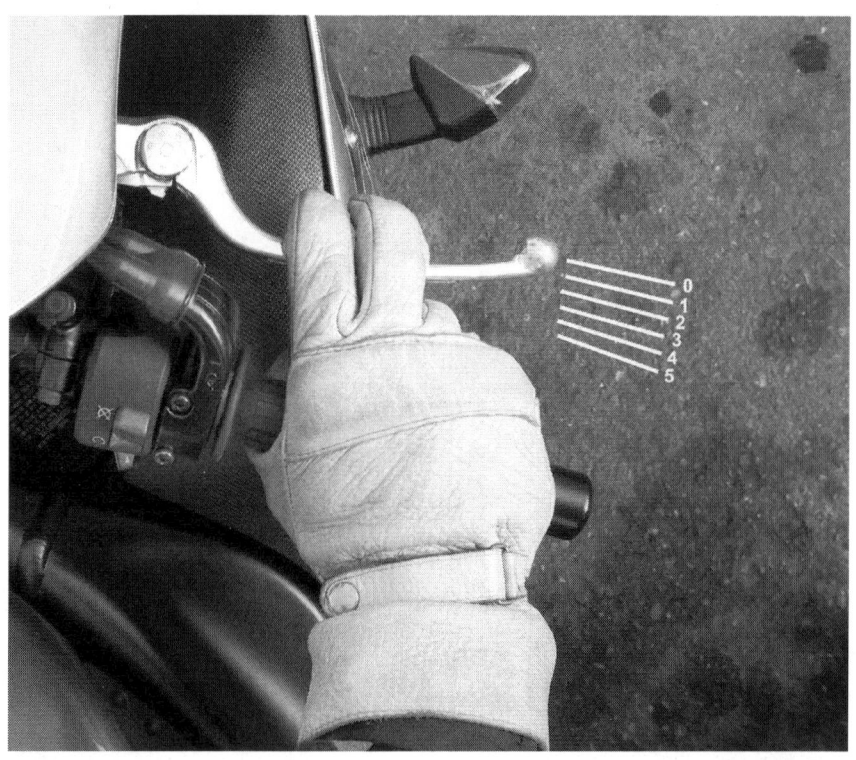

Converting to a Straight-Line Stop

An alternate method of doing a maximum effort stop in a curve is to quickly straighten the bike to vertical, then brake hard in a straight line. That allows all of the available traction to be used for braking. And, since you would normally squeeze the clutch during a straight-line stop, it's unnecessary to smoothly roll off the throttle. The technique is the same as for a straight-line stop. This straight-line technique favors braking systems such as ABS, integrated, and linked.

The issue with attempting a straight-line stop from a curve is that if you are riding aggressively you need a longer distance to stop, and the road curvature might not allow that. For instance, consider attempts to make straight-line stops from speeds of 70 mph and 50 mph. From 50 mph, a skilled rider should be able to lift the bike up and brake to a stop within about 150 feet. But from 70 mph, stopping distance for that same machine in the same situation would be more than 250 feet, due to the increased forward energy. So from the higher speed, the bike might still be decelerating through 30 mph when it runs out of road.

By the way, if you're wondering what that little blob in the road is, it's a brown bear with a fish, and you probably don't want to hit it.

If you enjoy cruising the back roads at more aggressive speeds, you need to be much more skilled at braking while leaned over.

The message in this is that if you enjoy riding curvy roads at more aggressive speeds, you need to be very proficient at braking while leaned over. You'll need to smoothly ease on the brakes at first, then brake progressively harder as the tires reduce their demand for cornering traction. As you scrub off some speed, you will have other options, such as lifting the bike up and doing a maximum effort straight-line stop, or swerving around the hazard.

Braking Downhill

Up to this point, we've discussed braking on a level road. Obviously, braking dynamics change on hills. Braking heading uphill is easy, because gravity helps slow the bike, and because the weight bias is moved toward the rear. However, braking heading downhill is more difficult, because there is a "downslope" pull of gravity adding to the forward energy. The result is that braking distances are increased, and more weight is transferred onto the front wheel.

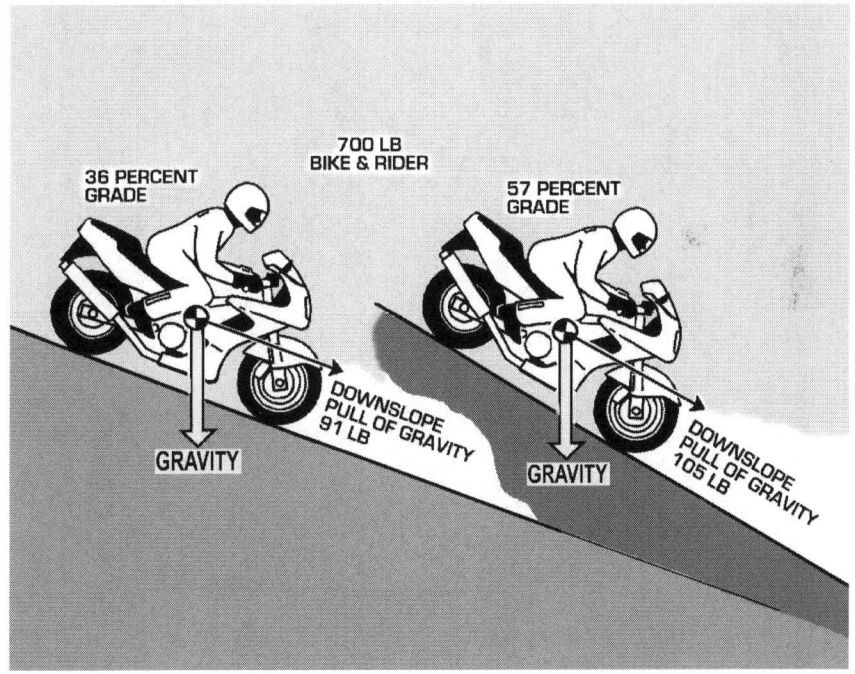

Riding downhill, the downslope pull of gravity is added to forward energy, requiring much more brake energy to decelerate the bike and load.

When riding downhill, it's important to keep speed under control, especially on a curvy road. The downslope pull of gravity adds to the forward energy, and it takes a lot of traction to get the bike slowed or stopped. Approaching a downhill curve, use the front brake and brake early. Engine braking is less effective descending a steep grade because traction on the rear tire will be reduced. Even in a downhill right turn, it may be necessary to trail the front brake all the way around the curve to keep speed from increasing. Downhill left turns are especially hazardous because the pavement typically cambers to the right, reducing both traction and lean-over clearance. And if the pavement is wet, it's especially important to keep speed under control.

Downhill left-hand curves are especially hazardous because the surface typically cambers to the right, reducing lean-over clearance. If the surface is slippery, it's essential to get your speed under control well before you need to lean the bike.

Braking on Loose Surfaces

How you brake on slick or loose surfaces depends greatly on your tires. The tread patterns on street tires don't have the aggressive blocks and grooves to maintain traction. You can still brake on dirt or gravel, but it won't be as easy as with dirt tires. Since you won't have nearly as much tire traction as on pavement, there will be much less weight transfer to the front wheel, and therefore much less front wheel braking. So, when braking on a loose surface such as gravel, you can use compression braking to help slow the bike, plus rear brake up to the point of sliding. You can also ease on some front brake, but short of skidding.

On a downhill slope, just a modest increase in speed can increase forward energy to the point where your tires don't have enough traction to slow the bike, so it's essential to keep speed in check. On a steep downhill gravel road you may have to allow the bike to increase speed because there just isn't enough traction to keep speed in check. If it's a short downhill followed by an uphill section, you want to keep the bike rolling fast enough that its inertia carries it up the hill. But if it's a continuous steep downhill, it's absolutely essential to prevent the bike from accelerating. You don't want to allow speed to increase and not be able to slow for a corner or brake for a stop sign. Shift to a lower gear at the top, and apply enough rear brake to hold speed. If the rear tire begins to slide, just stay on it. A sliding rear tire is controllable. And if you slide the rear tire on a loose surface, it's less likely to cause a high-side flip.

If riding on gravel makes you break out in a cold sweat, the answer is to borrow a dirt bike and gain some experience. Riding on dirt with knobby tires involves lots of sliding around, and maybe a few fall-downs while you're learning. There are also a number of training courses where you can learn to handle a big dual-sport off pavement. We'll discuss riding on unpaved roads a little further on.

THE GOOD RIDER

Chapter 4: Cornering Control

A few years ago I was hired as an expert witness in a court case involving a rider who had crashed his overloaded machine, and was looking for some deep pockets to pick up the bills. He didn't think he had done anything wrong, until he heard me explaining it to the jury.

This bloke had made a navigational error, and was riding fast downhill to get back to the right road. He was considerably overweight, and riding a heavy six-cylinder bike carrying his girlfriend and all their gear. This wasn't a really nasty corner, just a sweeping left-hander. But it was downhill, the bike was overloaded, and it was pointed toward a very early apex.

Approaching the corner at maybe 50 mph, the rider apparently snapped the throttle off and jammed on the rear brake, but of course it couldn't decelerate as quickly as he expected. The skid marks indicated that the bike was toward the left side of the lane and had dropped onto its left side when the highway peg mounted low on the left crash bar dug into the asphalt, flipping the bike over onto its right side, where it slid straight into a rock wall.

This crash serves as an example of several bad tactics. There are lots of earmarks that make it very typical of what's happening today. About half of motorcycle crashes in the Northwest are "single vehicle" and a majority of them are the fault of the rider.

Let's think through some cornering habits and suggest a few tactics to avoid crashing in similar situations. First, let's consider cornering lines.

Smarter Cornering Lines

This rider is approaching a tight right-hander from close to the centerline, allowing him to follow a straighter cornering line, and giving him a better view of what's ahead.

One of the advantages of a narrow 2-wheeler is that you can follow lines through corners that not only provide better traction, but also decrease the risks of a collision. Yes, you can just follow one of the "car" wheel tracks through a corner, but that doesn't give you any advantages. Riding a motorcycle, you can use the entire lane, "straightening out" curves. The straighter your line through a corner, the less the demand on tire traction, which helps avoid a slide-out.

It's also important to improve the view ahead, because what you can see is a big factor in how fast you can corner. To avoid sticking your neck out too far, you always need to be able to bring the bike to a stop within the roadway you can see. And when you're rounding a right-hand corner, your sight distance typically gets shortened by the shape of the landscape.

The best way to straighten out your line and also maximize the view is to enter corners from the "outside" of the turn. That is, approaching a right-hander, make your turn-in from a position closer to the centerline. For a left-hander, make your turn-in closer to the right edge of the pavement. You have to assume that there will be hazards in the road halfway around, even if you can't see them yet.

The best way to straighten out your line and also maximize the view is to enter corners from the "outside" of the turn. That is, approaching a right-hander, make your turn-in from a position closer to the centerline.

For a left-hander, make your turn-in closer to the right edge of the pavement. You have to assume that there will be hazards in the road halfway around, even if you can't see them yet. Entering a curve from the outside helps you see farther ahead.

It's also a high priority to avoid getting sideswiped by oncoming vehicles. It might seem prudent to just stay away from the centerline all the time, but that's not necessary.

Drivers tend to wander over the line in specific areas, and it's only necessary to avoid those areas. Consider how an oncoming driver sees the road. There is a tendency to enter curves too fast, cut toward the inside too early, then drift wider in the last half of the curve. You don't need to avoid the centerline all the time, you only need to avoid those "sideswipe" areas. As it happens, entering a curve from the outside allows you to increase your distance from potentially wandering drivers.

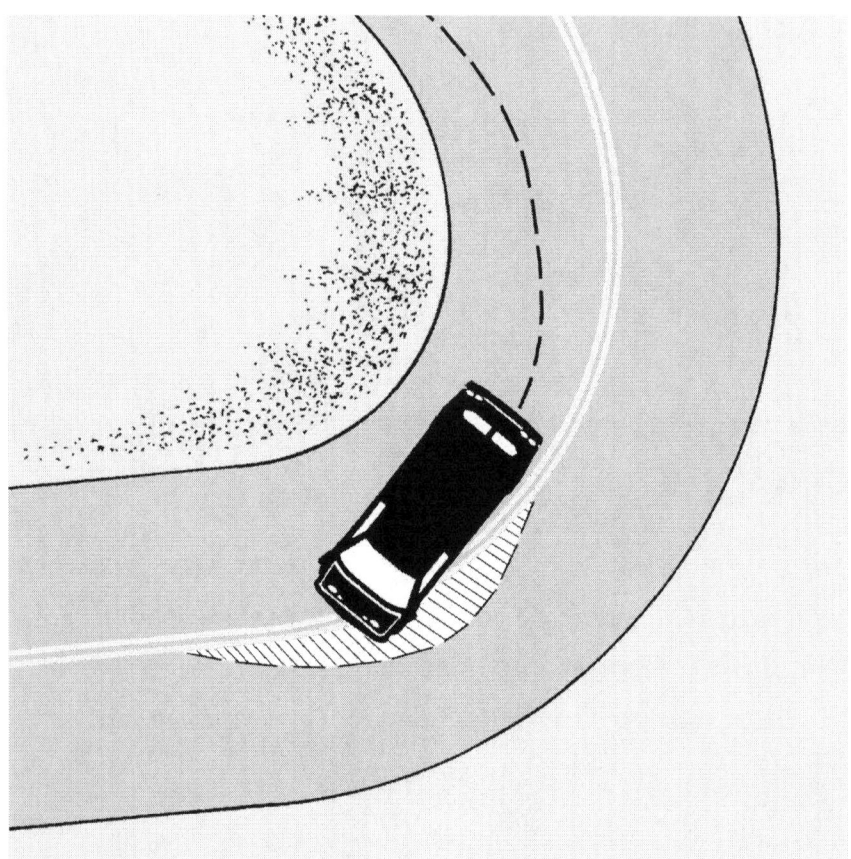

You don't need to avoid the centerline all the time. You only need to avoid those "sideswipe" areas.

Those twisty secondary roads we enjoy typically have lots of crown in the center, with the pavement on either side slanting off ("cambered") toward the edges of the road. A steep camber in a right-hander works to your advantage, but a steep camber in a left-hander works against you, decreasing traction and eating up lean-over clearance.

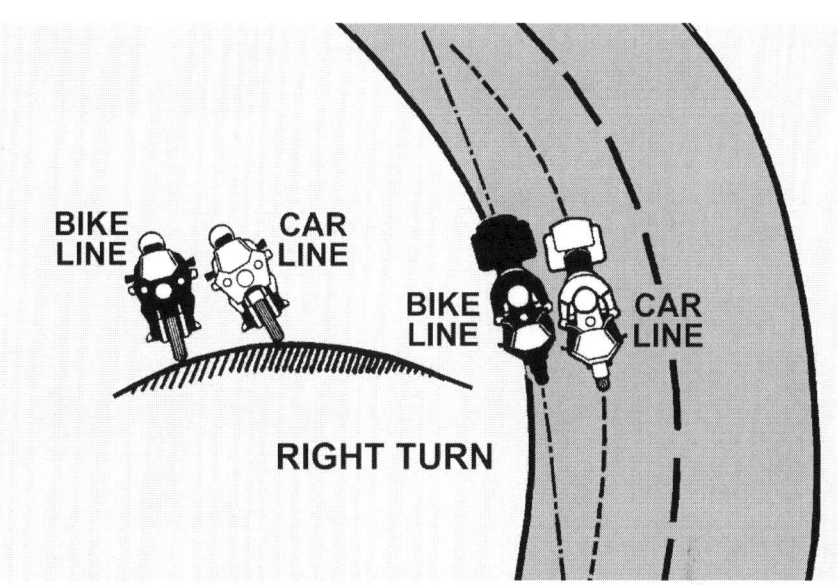

The "bike" line takes advantage of road crown to maximize traction and lean-over clearance.

In a left-hander, riding in the left wheel track puts you in danger of collisions with oncoming vehicles.

Consider one motorcyclist following the center of the lane (the "car" line) compared to another motorcyclist following a straighter line (the "bike" line). The bike line takes advantage of road crown to maximize traction and lean-over clearance.

Entering a turn from the outside helps make the best of a well-cambered surface. Entering a right-hander, you can carve over toward the right edge of the pavement where the camber is steepest. Halfway through a left-hander, you can ease over toward the center of the road where it's more level.

The Apex

We usually describe cornering lines in terms of the apex—the imaginary point where the motorcycle passes closest to the inside of the curve. The location of the apex determines the shape of your line. If you turn in early and point the bike toward the inside of the curve too soon, you'll pass by an early apex. The problem with an early apex is that you're tempted to carry too much speed into the turn, and then halfway around, realize you're too fast and running wide.

A delayed or late apex requires that you turn in later and closer to the outside edge of the curve. The delayed apex provides a better view ahead, conserves traction during the last half of the turn, keeps you away from those sideswipe zones, and points the bike more around the curve.

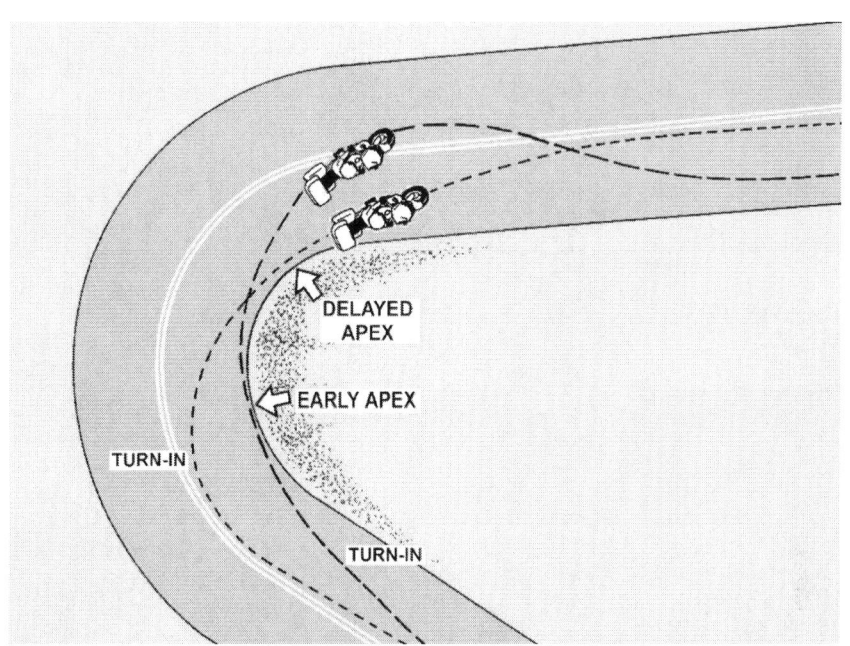

An early turn in leads to an early apex, which tends to point the bike wide in the last half of the turn. A delayed apex requires you to turn in later, and then point the bike toward the inside.

You don't actually need to see the position of your delayed apex. Just imagine that it's a little farther around the curve than the road apex.

A delayed apex line is a good idea for riding public roads where anything can happen. Even if you can't see the actual location of your delayed apex, you can imagine that it's somewhat farther around the turn. In a right-hander you'll need to make your turn-in closer to the centerline, and a bit later.

A delayed apex line works just as well in a left turn, with your imagined apex along the centerline, a little farther around the turn.

In a left-hander, the turn-in point should be close to the outside edge of the road. The delayed apex will then be closer to the centerline, but avoid the collision zone. If the road happens to have a steep camber tilting toward the outside, the delayed apex line will help maximize both lean-over clearance and traction.

THE GOOD RIDER

Chapter 5: The Throttle

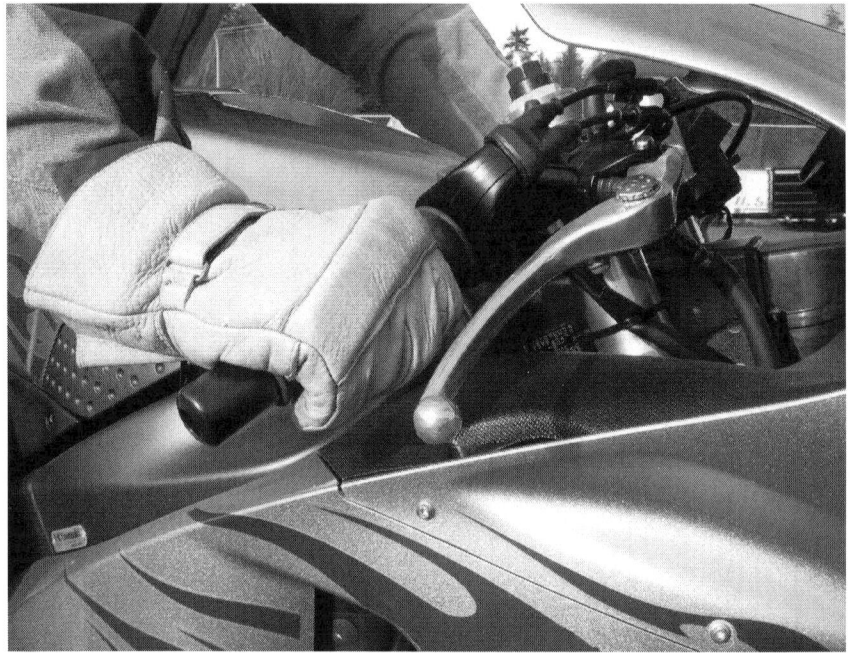

When and how you roll on the throttle—or roll *off* the throttle—has a lot to do with cornering control. For instance, imagine leaning a 150 hp bike into a tight turn, and then suddenly rolling on a big handful of throttle. You shouldn't be surprised when a sudden burst of power slides the rear end out. Obviously, engine thrust has a lot to do with both balance and steering.

Even with the bike in a straight line, rolling on the throttle transfers weight to the rear wheel. Enough power will lift the front wheel off the ground. Rolling off the throttle transfers weight toward the front wheel. The point here is that rolling on or off the throttle changes the traction bias, whether in a straight line or when leaned over in a corner. To maintain traction, it would be best to maintain weight distribution while leaned over.

Even if the bike is in a straight line, rolling on the throttle tends to shift weight from the front wheel onto the rear wheel.

Rolling off the throttle shifts weight toward the front. That same front-rear weight shift can occur in a corner.

Let's note that even if the tires seem to be tracking a perfect arc in a curve, the flexible tire rubber allows the bike to move in a slightly different path from where the wheels are pointed. It's called slip angle. Easing on a bit more throttle tends to increase the slip angle of the rear tire, pointing the bike more toward the curve. The front tire and the rear tire may be moving in two different directions.

Engine thrust can cause the tires to slip in a different direction from where they are pointed, even on tractable pavement.

Rolling on more throttle also increases centrifugal force, which limits roll, or even rolls the bike toward vertical. Put all of this together, and you can see that throttle control affects balance and steering, whether accelerating or decelerating. As it happens, throttle control and cornering lines can work together.

If you're following a nice delayed apex line, you can ease on the throttle as you turn the bike in, and then gradually roll on more throttle through the rest of the curve. Engine thrust can be used to control the roll, both stabilizing the bike when it's at the correct lean, and lifting it up as you exit the corner. That eliminates the wobble that would occur if you decelerate toward a mid-curve apex on a trailing throttle, and then get back on the throttle in the middle of the turn.

It's not just being on the gas that causes slide-outs: sudden *changes* in throttle momentarily change traction and roll. If you were to snap the throttle closed while leaned over, it's not difficult to visualize the rear tire sliding out, dropping the bike on its low side. That's enough of a problem for sport bikes that some manufacturers include back-torque clutches, to prevent engine compression from braking the rear wheel.

With the bike leaned into a turn, snapping the throttle closed would have the same effect as stomping on the rear brake pedal.

If your bike doesn't have back-torque limitation, then snapping the throttle closed has an effect similar to stomping on the rear brake pedal. To help maintain traction, steering, throttle, and braking, input should be as smooth as possible. When rolling on the throttle, it should be progressive, not sudden. It's just as important to roll off the throttle smoothly.

You can brake while leaned over. Just transition smoothly from throttle to brakes and squeeze the lever progressively harder as the bike lifts up. How you get *off* the brakes is just as important. When releasing the brakes, you should ease them off, not just let go of the lever. The correct rate for transitioning between throttle and brakes is approximately two seconds.

You can practice smooth throttle and brake application in a straight-line exercise. At a speed of say, 40 mph, ease the throttle closed as you progressively squeeze on the front brake. Don't clutch or shift down. As the bike decelerates to about 20 mph, ease off the brake as you smoothly roll back on the throttle. The goal is to transition from throttle to brakes and back to throttle so smoothly that the bike stays level.

Controlling the throttle and brakes simultaneously requires some right hand dexterity. You'll have to find a technique that works for you. Some riders prefer to hold the throttle with thumb and outer two fingers, and brake with the two inner fingers.

You can expect surface hazards to appear in corners. You may feel a momentary slip of the tires. But if you expect to make it around the corner without falling, you need to resist the urge to snap the throttle closed.

You can expect surface traction to change, even during a corner. A patch of sand or dribble of diesel oil will reduce traction, and you can feel a momentary slip of either or both tires. For a road rider who has learned to depend upon good traction, the feel of a tire slipping can cause panic. The typical survival reaction when a tire slips is to snap the throttle closed, but that can turn a short slide into a major crash. It's difficult to resist the urge to snap off the throttle, but it's important to hold a steady throttle and steer toward the direction of the skid. If the tire can regain traction, it will.

It's important to not overlook the road surface while you're cornering. Given a choice, put your tires on the most tractable surface, even if that means a less-than-desirable cornering line.

THE GOOD RIDER

Chapter 6: Weight and Balance

The design of the bike determines how it wants to corner. How you place your weight on the bike during a corner affects lean-over clearance, traction, and steering feedback.

Motorcycle engineers are constantly trying to improve the cornering habits of machines. The geometry of the front end helps stabilize the bike in a straight line. And a good match of geometry to tire profiles can produce almost neutral steering with the bike leaned over on a level surface. If the surface isn't level, you can expect some strange behavior.

A curve with positive camber allows the tires to be almost perpendicular to the road surface with the bike leaned over. For example, let's say the road cambers off toward the right in a right turn. Obviously, that provides good lean-over clearance, and also relatively neutral steering. However, if the surface slants the wrong way for the curve, not only will lean-over clearance be reduced, but the steering will feel very strange. The bike may want to straighten up, or even steer itself downhill.

Most machines are happiest when cornering on a surface that's level or cambered slightly toward the curve.

An "off camber" surface can cause strange steering feedback.

What's happening is that the contact ring of the front tire shifts sideways as the bike's angle changes in relation to the surface. When the surface cambers the wrong way—say, slanting off to the left in a right-hander— the bike may require a much stronger push on the "uphill" grip to keep it turning.

Hanging Off

A rider can adjust the lean angle of the bike in relation to the road surface by shifting weight in the saddle. Shifting body weight toward the curve is called "hanging off." Hanging off not only increases lean-over clearance, but keeps the tire contact rings closer to the centerline of the bike, which helps neutralize steering feedback.

Hanging off can improve lean-over clearance, and also keep the tire contact rings closer to the centerline of the bike, which helps neutralize steering feedback.

For machines with limited lean-over clearance, hanging off can help prevent touchdowns. And even if your bike has more than adequate lean-over clearance, hanging off may result in less steering effort needed to keep the bike turning.

Shifting weight away from the turn is called "counter leaning." Counter leaning is appropriate for very tight turns at slow speeds, such as a U-turn on a narrow road. Counter leaning allows the bike to turn tighter because the farther over you lean the bike, the smaller the radius of turn.

Counter leaning is appropriate for very tight turns at slow speeds, such as a U-turn on a narrow road.

You don't have to hang way off the bike in every curve to achieve better cornering control. Just sliding to the edge of the saddle, or weighting one foot peg more than the other will have an effect. But when you do need to hang off for strange camber situations, or you want to ride more aggressively, here are some pointers:

Hang Off Early

Shift your weight before you lean the bike into the curve. Get your entire upper torso to the "turn" side of the bike centerline two or three seconds before your turn-in point. You may have to hold some pressure on the "up" grip to keep the bike from turning until you're ready. At the turn-in point, simply relax your steering input to allow the bike to roll toward the curve.

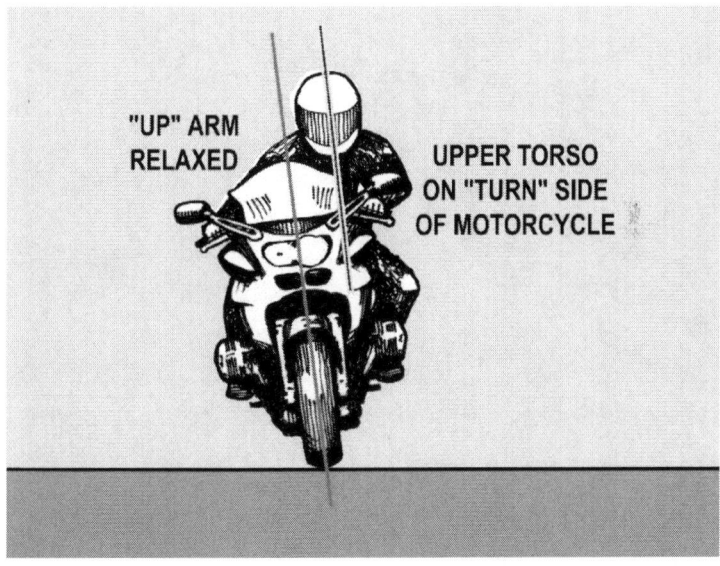

If you're going to hang off, it's best to shift your weight two or three seconds prior to the turn-in. Your spine should be parallel to the bike centerline, but off center toward the "turn" side.

Chapter 6: Weight and Balance

Get Tucked In

Wedge your "up" knee against the tank to prevent sliding off too far. Brace your "up" leg against the foot peg. And tuck your "down" toe in to prevent snagging it on the ground. You don't want to get your foot caught between the peg and the pavement. At the turn-in point, relax your pressure on the grips to allow the bike to roll toward the curve. If it doesn't roll quickly enough, press both grips toward the turn to achieve the desired lean angle.

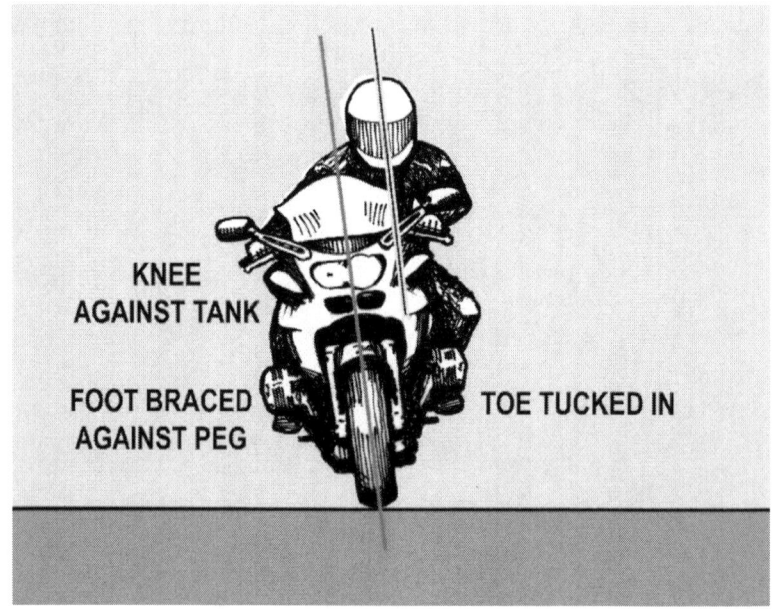

Just before the turn-in, brace your "up" leg against the tank and foot peg, and get your "down" toe tucked in so it won't get caught between the peg and the pavement.

Keep Your Eyes Level

As you lean the bike, tilt your head to keep your eyes level with the horizon. You get better triangulation of the curve ahead with your eyes level. That makes it easier to plan your cornering line, whether you're hanging off or sitting straight in the saddle.

When the bike rolls over to the appropriate angle, you can steer toward the curve and sneak on some throttle. It always helps to keep your head tilted so your eyes are level with the horizon. It's best to keep your "down" toe tucked in, although some riders use the side of their boot sole to gauge the lean angle.

Managing the Situation

Whatever the bike you're riding, or however aggressively you are riding it, it's very important to get your eyes up and looking as far ahead as possible. At a road speed of 60 mph, you're covering 88 feet per second. Even if you notice a hazard and try to take some evasive action, it takes time to make it happen. For those of us over age 50, our reaction times are probably greater than one second. But even if you are able to react within a second, you will have covered almost 88 feet at 60 mph before anything happens. In other words, at 60 mph, that next 88 feet ahead of the bike is history. There's absolutely nothing you can do about it. The message is: there's no point in looking down at the pavement 40 or 50 feet in front of the bike.

Looking farther ahead gives you more time to react to what you see. So, get your eyes up and scrutinize what's happening as far down the road as you can see details. Use the vanishing point, the point farthest from you that the road disappears on the horizon, to determine your speed. When the vanishing point closes up, transition to the brakes and get your speed down. When the vanishing point stretches out, get back on the gas.

A big part of being able to finish the ride in one piece is getting your eyes up and scanning as far ahead as you can see details. Let the vanishing point determine your speed. When the vanishing point is closing up, the clever rider transitions to the brakes to allow stopping within the available sight distance.

THE GOOD RIDER

Chapter 7: Wandering Riders

Back in the 1980s and 1990s it was sort of comforting to be able to lay the blame for motorcycle crashes on car drivers. A typical motorcycle crash was a collision with a car driver who turned into the bike without warning. We could feel victimized by errant motorists not seeing us or not yielding the right of way. *"Damn blind cager!"* we could mutter, when some driver made a quick left turn across the path of the motorcycle. Well, the situation has changed: today about half of motorcycle crashes are car/bike collisions, which means the other half are motorcycle crashes where the rider lost control.

Motorcycles have been getting better and more powerful, and apparently more dangerous. Over the past few years, U.S. motorcycle fatalities have been hovering above 5,000 per year. Due perhaps to the recession, bike sales dropped in 2009, and fatalities were also down to somewhere around 4,500. However, by 2012 bike sales were up again, and preliminary data hints that fatalities for 2012 will be close to 5,000. We can assume that half of those, about 2,500, were single-vehicle crashes. In addition to the fatalities, there were more than 55,000 "morbid" single-vehicle crashes that left riders with serious injuries. That's just half the totals for one year, the ones where the rider did something dumb. It's getting very obvious that too many riders are unable to control their bikes.

One scary scenario is with the motorcyclist going wide in a right-hand curve and colliding with an oncoming vehicle. An example of this occurred a couple of years ago on the Olympic Peninsula northwest of Seattle, where a novice rider was out with some friends on a group ride. She had just taken basic rider training a couple of months before.

According to newspaper reports, "The motorcycle failed to negotiate a right curve. The motorcycle crossed the centerline and struck the right-front bumper of a southbound pickup truck that was towing a boat trailer. The rider was pronounced dead at the scene by a deputy coroner."

Crossing the centerline in a right-hand curve is a good way to shorten your riding career.

This isn't an isolated incident. There have been a huge number of motorcycle crashes where the rider crossed the centerline. There was one situation in Marin County, California (north of San Francisco) in which a Sunday rider crossed the centerline in a curve just as an SUV was approaching. The rider sideswiped the SUV with considerable force and fatal results. What I found appalling was a San Francisco motorcycle paper wagging an emotional finger at the SUV driver for failing to get out of the way of the motorcyclist. The writer apparently felt that a motorist in Marin County on a Sunday morning should know that bikers use the twisty back roads for high speed shenanigans.

I say the motorcyclist did it to himself! It's pretty lame to attempt to pass off the blame for bad riding on others. Even when another motorist does something dumb, a motorcyclist needs to be prepared to get out of the way. In my view, the responsible party for any motorcycle crash is whoever was holding onto the handlebar grips at the moment.

There are lots of motorcycle crash videos online. One of the most somber is a brief ride in an eastern European country, ending in a high speed collision with an oncoming rider. The whole thing was recorded by a camera taped to the fuel tank. It's worth watching because once you've overcome the shock of the crash, you can replay it and observe the rider of the camera bike making minor mistakes, including increasing speed when another rider passes him. The minor mistakes eventually lead to an excursion across the centerline and a high speed collision. It seems obvious to me that the camera bike rider just didn't know how to make his motorcycle lean and turn. See if you agree: http://www.ebaumsworld.com/video/watch/80503216/.

Let's take a few moments to consider why a rider might cross the centerline. First, there is the temptation to use the other side of the road to gain a faster cornering line, as if the public roads were somehow a legitimate race track. The temptation to go faster is almost irresistible when riding a high performance sport bike.

At a rally, I overheard a famous road racer/journalist giving a seminar in which he was attempting to convey the message that riding really fast on public roads was not as enjoyable as riding a brisk but reasonable pace. He described the previous day's ride with some companions, and emphasized that they had not exceeded 85 mph all day. For a veteran road racer, 85 mph may seem like dawdling along. But in many states, more than 20 mph over the posted speed limit is defined as "reckless driving," with hefty fines and the potential for confiscating the motorcycle. I respect this famous rider for his skills, but I have a much different attitude about riding fast on public roads.

The Pace May Be the Problem

I suspect that one prime reason for corner crashes is failure to decelerate quickly enough to get the bike down to an appropriate speed for conditions. It's fun to ride a steady pace with speed controlled only with the throttle, but when sight distance closes up, you can't see the hazards, and it's easy to ride into trouble way too fast to allow for avoidance maneuvers. More and more, I'm braking when the vanishing point of the road suddenly retracts. Not just rolling off the gas and hoping for the best, but easing on the front brake to scrub off speed quickly.

I'll admit to having cruised the back roads at an aggressive pace once in a while, but for me 85 mph on a public road is way too fast. It's not just an issue of being able to control the bike to avoid running off the road. We face a number of potential hazards out there, including wild animals, gawking tourists, wandering drivers, spilled gravel, and edge traps. If you want to avoid running into such things, you need to be able to get the bike slowed within the roadway you can see. To put this another way, you need to be in control of the bike, but you also need to be in control of the situation. Even a veteran road racer with quick responses can't outmaneuver the rules of physics.

Let's say you are approaching the crest of this hill at 60 mph. Would you be able to stop short of a collision with that stalled truck on the other side? Hint: stopping distance from 60 mph is around 195 feet for a skilled road racer.

For example, let's say you are riding a nice curvy back road. The surface is clean and dry, the curves are nicely cambered, and traffic is light. You're cruising along at about 60 mph, just a little over the posted limit. You can't see over the crest, but it appears the road curves to the left and descends. You're maybe 150 feet from the crest, doing 60 mph. What would you do?

- Hold a steady throttle, but watch the situation ahead for possible hazards.
- Roll off the throttle to reduce speed, and cover the brakes.
- Transition from throttle to front brake to reduce speed quickly.

If this road were a closed track, you would already know where the pavement goes over the hill, and you could be confident there are no hidden hazards such as a wandering elk or stalled tanker truck. There would be no need to slow down, because you know how fast your bike will take the corner without sliding out. If you were racing, you would probably be looking north of 130 mph.

But this isn't a closed track, it's a public road, and there could be a hazard just over the hill. Most of us would roll off the throttle and cover the brakes. But at 60 mph, you are covering 88 feet/second. Rolling off the gas would have about the same effect as stepping on the rear brake, which would possibly slow the bike to 50 mph by the crest of the hill.

If you then crested the hill and realized there was a stalled truck blocking the road, would you have enough distance left to stop? Assuming you have a very quick reaction time of 0.75 seconds, you would eat up 55 feet just getting on the brakes. And even if you are skilled enough to brake aggressively, your braking distance from 50 mph would be around 90 feet. Total stopping distance would be at least 144 feet. That's if you're really quick and really skilled, your new tires are warmed up, and the road surface is clean and dry.

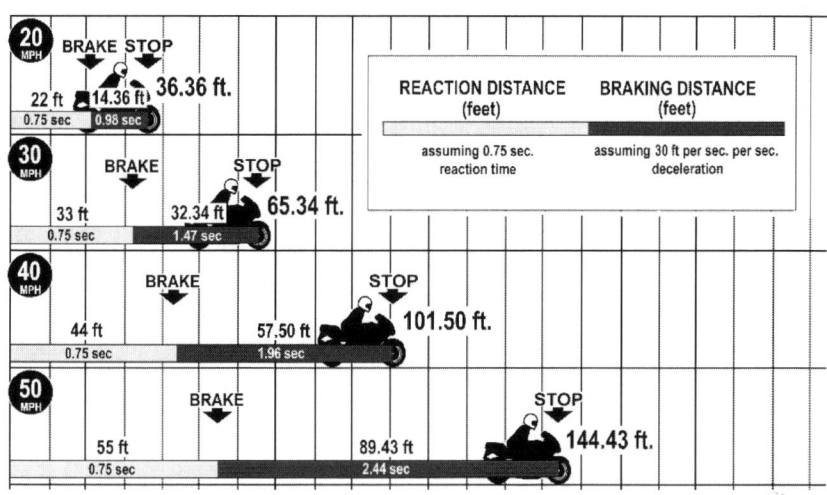

If you want to check my figures, there's a handy braking computer at *http://hyperphysics.phy-astr.gsu.edu/hbase/crstp.html.*

What these stopping distances suggest is that if you're not already on the brakes as you crest the hill, it's questionable whether or not you could stop short of a hazard (such as an elk herd crossing the road, or a wrecker pulling a car out of the ditch).

Rolling the Dice

Of course, the odds are good that the road goes where you think, and that there isn't a hazard blocking the lane today. Many riders gamble their lives that there won't be a hidden hazard in a blind situation. But, according to the fatality statistics, more than a few riders are losing that gamble.

Are you willing to gamble your life that the road is clear around this blind corner? The odds vary greatly with your speed.

Four Steps to Stack the Odds

If you want to stack the odds in your favor, I have four suggestions.

Hone your balancing/steering/braking skills.

You must be proficient at controlling the bike so that you can put it exactly where it needs to go without a lot of wasted thought. And you should be skilled enough to brake aggressively, even when leaned over. Your goal should be to develop the muscle memory to control the bike as easily as you walk or blink your eyes.

Separate alcohol from riding

Somewhere around half of motorcyclists involved in fatal crashes had alcohol in their systems. That's about 58,000 serious crashes and 2,500 fatalities per year in the U.S. You don't have to be drunk to crash, a beer or two is enough to degrade your judgment and precipitate a crash.

Plan your cornering line entirely within your own lane, even if that means a speed reduction

Frequently borrowing the opposing side of a public road is unwise, because other vehicles can appear suddenly. Make a habit of delayed apexing, even when you have a good view through the corner. Some day when you suddenly find yourself in an unexpected off-camber or decreasing-radius turn, or an oncoming vehicle crosses the centerline, you'll be more likely to handle it without a lot of drama.

When emergencies arise, there's little time to think about your options. You're very likely to react subconsciously, and only think about it later. That's why it's important to practice the right skills over and over to make them habits.

When sight distance closes up, immediately transition from throttle to front brake and get the bike slowed smoothly and quickly, to enable a quick stop within your sight distance

When the view opens up and the road is clear, it doesn't take long to get back up to speed. Use the vanishing point to determine your speed.

THE

Chapter 8: Mental Skills

When anyone talks about motorcycle safety, the conversation almost always revolves around physical riding skills such as counter-steering, shifting, braking, balancing, and throttle. Most of us realize that there are mental skills too, such as planning cornering lines, or looking ahead for surface hazards. But the riders I've talked with are often a lot fuzzier about what the important mental skills might be or how to learn them, other than just continuing to ride and hoping the lessons will present themselves in a way that provides an education without a lot of pain.

A couple of decades ago I was visiting a gentleman friend in England who had, in his youth, raced a Vincent on the Isle of Man. This is a way of noting that Jim was very skillful, even at racing speeds. And since he had ridden for many years, he also had learned many important lessons about negotiating public roads. For me, it was a quick lesson in riding in a foreign country, on the left side of the road.

As it happened, there was a Sunday BMW rally in the Birmingham area, and Jim invited me to join him for a ride to the afternoon rally. We were both on BMW airheads then, and I was eager to observe his techniques, as well as have the opportunity to rub elbows with some veteran English BMW riders.

"A" roads in England are the equivalent of our state highways in the U.S.

As we set out from the south coast, it quickly became apparent that Jim's concept of "appropriate" speed was different from mine. Jim navigated our way via the main "A" roads. At that time the national speed limit was 70 mph. Jim would typically cruise at 80 or 85 mph, sometimes ticking the hedgerows alongside the road. It was not uncommon for an oncoming car to pass a slower car in a corner, straddling the centerline, when only a motorcycle was approaching. I remember being a bit panicked at those speeds, given my experiences in North America. Here, when a car approaches on a side road, I watch carefully, and if the driver doesn't seem to be stopping at the white line, I'm ready to squeeze on the brakes to avoid a collision.

Over there, the side roads are typically hidden. The first thing you might see is the bumper of a car poking out over the white line, between the trees and bushes. Since you can't see the windshield yet, you know the driver can't see you coming. While I was panicking at cars about to pull out, Jim didn't flinch. He simply cruised along at 75 or 80 mph.

"B" roads in England are the secondary highways, often narrow lanes between villages, crisscrossing the countryside like spider webs. However, traffic is two-way, and drivers typically zip along at 70 mph.

Once in a while, we'd take one of the narrower "B" roads connecting village to village. And when I say narrow, I mean that the pavement is only about one car wide, and the hedgerows often extend right up to the edge of the road. Not only are there no shoulders, but you need to watch for oncoming cars, who may also be blasting along at 60 or 70 mph. Somehow, it's realistic for drivers in England to know how to pull out of hidden driveways and cruise down the "B" roads at greater-than-U.S. speeds, without too many collisions.

However, when approaching a village, Jim would immediately decelerate, and I would often need to brake aggressively to avoid running up his tail light. Speeds through the villages were typically posted at 25 mph, right at the edge of town. You don't slow down a mile in advance; you maintain speed right up to the sign and then quickly decelerate. Once through a village, there would be an "end speed limit" symbol, and Jim would immediately wick it back up to his cruising speed.

Highway junctions are typically roundabouts (traffic circles). Imagine yourself approaching a roundabout (remember, you're in the left lane). Vehicles are entering the roundabout from your right. Jim's tactic for roundabouts was to decelerate quickly on the approach, looking for a gap in vehicles where a motorcycle could slip through. He would adjust position so he could merge between two cars, signaling right when he was going past the first exit. When he reached his desired exit he would quickly signal left to indicate he was turning off. Then he banked off and was back up to speed. I remember being amazed at how quickly we could negotiate the road, barely slowing for roundabouts, and never having to stop.

One big advantage with roundabouts in the UK are the huge signs just before the entry, to give you a heads up depicting the exact shape of the roundabout, and which spoke you'd want to take to get where you were headed. Including the graphic really helps give motorists situational awareness.

Although traffic in the UK is aggressive, the roads are well marked and every roundabout has a sign depicting the various turnoffs. The circle actually goes all the way around. That break on the sign is symbolic, reminding you to enter to the left.

As we progressed north toward Birmingham, we were passed by bikers, most of whom wore gear and rode like the bad guys in the movie "*Mad Max:*" the motorcycle would be a grotty, unadorned Japanese multi; the rider would be wearing a nasty-looking leather jacket with metal studs and spikes, and tall boots with buckles; and his passenger would be wearing similar biker garb, but with tight-fitting jeans to show off her curves. Think of Ogri from the Paul Sample cartoons.

The bikers who passed us reminded me very much of the lead character Ogri, featured in Paul Sample's cartoon strips.

The bikers would ride by at a race pace, passing everyone else on the road. Approaching one roundabout, a gaggle of three bikers couldn't squeeze past Jim and me, so they went around the center dividers on the wrong side--what the Brits call the "off side." The dividers are often stone walls and concrete pillars, not just painted lines, so a little mistake could be costly. The gaggle barely managed to swerve back into the left lane at the roundabout, scant inches from disaster, and left us in their dust.

Now, it appeared to me that those Road Warriors were really hanging it out, but then I wasn't very familiar with traffic in the UK, nor the crash statistics for motorcyclists. I wondered whether the bikers simply appeared to be taking big risks, or if it was just my overactive imagination.

When we arrived at the BMW event, I was introduced to a member who explained that he was a motorcycle officer in the Birmingham district, but he had access to all the crash statistics for the entire UK. I asked him about the bikers, explaining that their riding looked very risky to me, but I could have misinterpreted the situation.

The policeman affirmed that aggressive riders had an awful fatality record. They didn't crash frequently, but when they did crash it was always serious. Let's face it: if a rider collides with another vehicle or a stone wall at 100 mph, the forces will literally turn flesh to porridge. So, when a British biker did crash, it was most often fatal to both rider and passenger.

Ever since that experience, I've realized that a lack of physical control skills may not be the biggest factor in motorcycle crashes. Sure, we have lots of very unskilled riders in the U.S. who cross the centerline in curves, demonstrating that they don't know how to make the bike lean. But the serious crashes that have come to my awareness seem to be related to inadequate mental skills. For instance, those bikers in England were skillful enough at making their machines do what they wanted, but no one can manage the situation if something goes wrong at higher speeds. If any of those bikers on the wrong side of the center divider had suddenly encountered a truck or bus leaving the roundabout, the results would have been instantly fatal.

Teaching the "Missing" Emergency Skills

Rider training courses in the U.S. today are still based to a great extent on the "Hurt Report" from 1981. When the Motorcycle Safety Foundation (MSF) was in the process of deciding what to teach, they looked at the errors that led to crashes, and then designed practice exercises to teach riders the missing skills. For instance, the Hurt Report shows that riders who crashed only realized a crash was happening about 2 seconds prior to impact. And the majority of those riders who did crash apparently didn't take any evasive action at all. So, the first MSF courses included exercises in emergency braking and swerving, and all subsequent courses have followed suit.

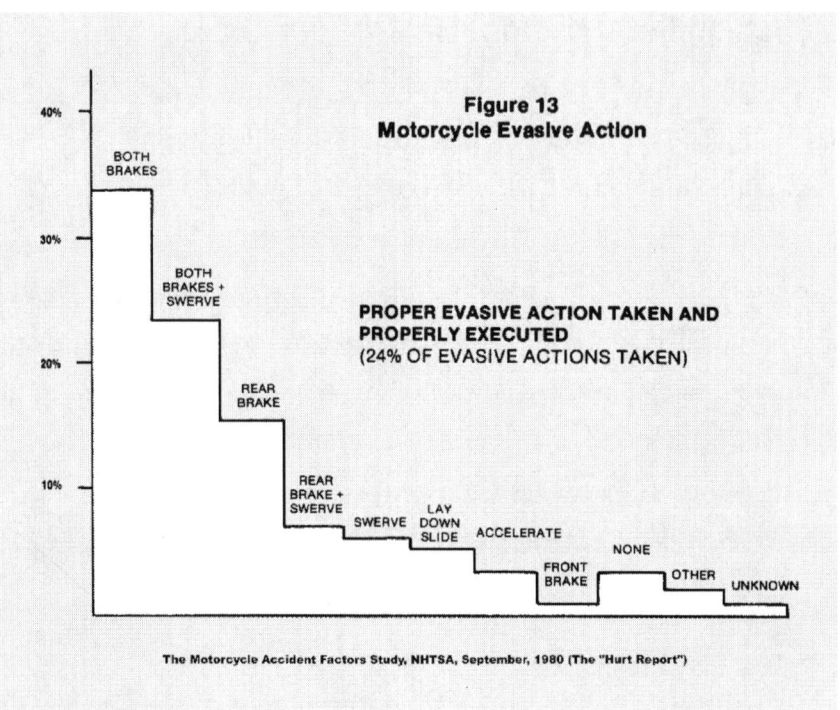

The famous Hurt Report from 1981 lists evasive actions they considered proper. However, today we might wonder how evasive actions such as "lay down and slide" or "rear brake and swerve" could be considered appropriate.

Teaching emergency evasive skills sounded like a good approach when I was an instructor in the 1980s. Besides, it's fun to teach swerving and quick stops. But in retrospect, the logic was faulty. As I gained experience, I realized that a rider who is aware of the situation typically has several seconds to avoid a crash, without any spectacular maneuvers. If you don't spot the problem until two seconds prior to impact, it's too late to take evasive action, even if you are very skilled at swerving or braking.

As an example, let's say a rider is following a van in traffic at 35 mph, when suddenly the van driver brakes to avoid a left turning truck. If the rider doesn't comprehend what's happening until the van's brake lights come on, there aren't many emergency actions that can prevent a collision. Even if the rider is very skilled at making quick stops, there will be a loss of time while the rider's brain reacts to the brake lights. At 35 mph, a reaction time of 0.75 seconds means the bike will be doing 35 mph for 51 feet before the rider gets on the brakes.

By comparison, a proficient rider who sees the pickup slowing three or four seconds in advance could just brake normally to open up some space. The difference between a crash and no crash is primarily in looking farther ahead, not in emergency skills.

So is there any good news to go along with this chilling analysis? Well, the good news is that veteran riders seem to have developed mental skills to spot potential hazards well in advance so that they don't allow emergencies to happen. Let's say you are scrutinizing the unfolding situation eight or ten seconds ahead. You spot an oncoming car that potentially could turn left across your path. You simply increase speed to get through the intersection before the car gets there. Or, you spot the bumper of a car about to emerge from an alley, and you brake and move left to make more room, several seconds before the car pulls out.

In either situation you figure out what's happening, assume the other driver doesn't see you, and take evasive action earlier in the process to stay out of the way. That's the situational awareness I'm talking about.

There is another reason why practicing emergency skills may be a waste of time. The controlling factor may be our human thinking processes. Our brains developed over thousands of years of survival tactics. When a hazard suddenly appears, the human brain seems to be hardwired to take immediate action, and only think consciously about the situation after the fact.

Ug vs. Ag

Here's the way I explain this in seminars: Ug the caveman steps out of his abode to have his morning stretch, and suddenly looks up to see a hungry T-rex. Ug thinks this over: *"Should I go back into the cave and get my club? Should I run?"* Unfortunately, several seconds of thinking wastes just enough time that T-rex has Ug for breakfast, and Ug's genes are deleted from the pool.

Meanwhile, Ug's cousin Ag steps out of his cave and notices the shadow of a saber-tooth tiger on the rocks overhead. Ag doesn't pause to think about evasive action. His feet have the muscle memory to dash back into the cave, a microsecond ahead of the tiger's sharp claws and teeth. Afterward, Ag thinks about the close call. And since Ag survived, he passed on his genes to the pool, of which we are the recipients. We inherited Ag's "run first, think later" brain wiring.

How does this relate to motorcycling? When faced with a sudden emergency, we're very likely to take evasive action subconsciously, without wasting any time mulling it over. We just escape without any conscious decision. So, even if you have a few emergency maneuvers stashed in your bag of tricks, it's unlikely you'll access them.

But if you can increase your awareness of the situation far enough in advance, you won't need to pull any quick emergency maneuvers out of your brain, and you'll have time to deal with the situation without panic.

THE GOOD RIDER

Chapter 9: How Dangerous is Motorcycling, Anyway?

When you first took up riding, you probably got an earful about the dangers of motorcycling from your spouse, your family doctor, and your mother. But you rolled your eyes and went riding anyway. And perhaps you've been successful at managing the dangers, so you can feel vindicated that motorcycling hasn't been as risky as your family and friends thought it would be.

You probably realize that riding a motorcycle is somewhat more hazardous than riding in an automobile, but it's difficult to comprehend just how dangerous motorcycling is, because those who get seriously injured or killed tend to drop out of the conversation. We have to depend on the statistics to get some feeling for the relative danger.

What's your risk tolerance? If you knew that motorcycling was five times as dangerous as driving a car, would you accept that risk? What if the risk was twenty times greater than driving a car? Would you still ride a bike? Would the joys of riding be worth the extra danger? And how do we calculate the relative danger? If a motorcycle salesman told you that it's not really dangerous, he was just doing what salesmen do. If your mother warned you that motorcycling is dangerous, she was honest, and right. Just between us motorcyclists, how dangerous is motorcycling, anyway? You're probably not too keen on discussing the dangers of motorcycling, but occasionally someone blathers on about motorcycle fatalities, and that tends to get us thinking.

The Governors Highway Safety Association made a big splash two years ago, when the preliminary data for 2009 showed a decrease in U.S. motorcyclist fatalities for the first time in more than ten years. There was some optimism that finally something was working to reduce motorcyclist fatalities, which had soared to an all-time high of 5,290 in 2008. The Motorcycle Safety Foundation and many state programs were quick to take credit, but the self-congratulations were short-lived. On May 22 of 2012, the GHSA issued another press release quietly noting that fatalities had leveled out and looked like they might be increasing. What the GHSA (and a number of other agencies) have been trying to measure is the relative danger of motorcycling, and whether the risks are going down or up. This is an uncomfortable subject, but if we really want to manage our risk of riding, it's unhelpful to ignore what's happening. So just between us motorcyclists, let's share a little information about fatalities.

A Little Motorcycling History

There was a sales boom in the 1970s that put an additional million bikes on the road. In 1980 I flew my BMW R80 to England, and went to the Tourist Trophy (TT) races on the Isle of Man. The TT is actually two weeks, and between races the spectators get out and ride the course. I remember feeling that riding the Island during TT week among 40,000 semi-crazed race fans was pretty dangerous. But the truth was that motorcycling back in the U.S. was at the peak of danger. The surge of new U.S. riders resulted in a huge increase in fatalities.

The worst year of that surge was 1980, with 5,144 fatalities. The feds ordered a study which we know today as the Hurt Report. That got us started on the path of rider training and licensing. Then, after the 1980 boom, motorcycle registrations fell off. The fatality total bounced up and down a bit, but eventually dropped to a low of around 2,000 in 1996-1997. Everyone was pleased at that, because it seemed to prove that motorcycling was gradually getting safer, just as automobiles and trucks had been getting safer. Rider training and licensing appeared to be solving the motorcycle fatality problem.

When we talk about the risks, the most common measure is fatalities. The federal government tracks vehicle fatalities very accurately through the Fatal Accident Reporting System (FARS). Almost all modes of transportation have seen a gradual decrease in fatalities over the years, with the single exception of motorcycling. Whether it's airplanes, trains, or commercial trucks, the fatality rates have gone down year after year as safer vehicles and safer roads have been developed. Motorcycling did see a decrease in fatalities from 1980 through 1997. But around 1998, the bubble burst. Motorcycle sales surged again, and there was another dramatic increase in fatalities. By 2008, there were 7.7 million motorcycles registered nationwide, and 5,290 fatalities.

What happened to the dream that motorcycles could be made safer? Rider training must be a good deal, right? Well, more people are being introduced to motorcycling through training courses, but the result is an increase in fatalities, not a decrease. Riding a motorcycle has always been more dangerous than driving a car, but the spread is getting wider because cars are getting safer while bikes are getting more dangerous. To see how that's happening, we need to think about fatality rates.

Fatality Rates

There are several different ways to measure the relative dangers of different vehicles. The total number of motorcyclist fatalities can be misleading, because it doesn't take into account the number of riders on the road. Fatalities more than doubled between 1998 and 2008, but so did motorcycle registrations. To get a clearer picture, we need to look at the *rate* of fatalities: comparing the number of fatalities to a base such as motorcycle registrations or miles traveled, or population.

What do we mean by "fatality rate?" Let's say there were a total of 100,000 motorcyclists in Washington, and 52 died in one year. That would be a rate of 52 per 100,000. What if there were say, 7 million motorcyclists in the U.S. and 5,000 of them died? That would be a fatality rate of around 71 per 100,000.

For years I've tracked the U.S. fatality rate based on motorcycle registrations. I realize that's not very scientific, since the number of *motorcycles* registered is only an approximation of the number of *riders*. For instance, let's say Tom owns five bikes, while Dave only owns one. If Tom crashes, his rate is only one crash per five registered bikes. If Dave crashes, his rate is one crash per registered bike. And, of course, registrations don't show Tom's or Dave's exposure—say, in terms of miles traveled, or numbers of trips. Tom might have one or other of his machines on the road for thousands of miles each year, while Dave might only fire up his scoot three or four times each summer. So, there can be a huge difference in exposure.

Historically, the rate of motorcyclist fatalities per 100,000 motorcycle registrations in the U.S. peaked at 94.02 in 1978, then eased down to 55.30 by 1997, and then bumped back up to 73.48 in 2005, and dropped down to 53.79 in 2010.

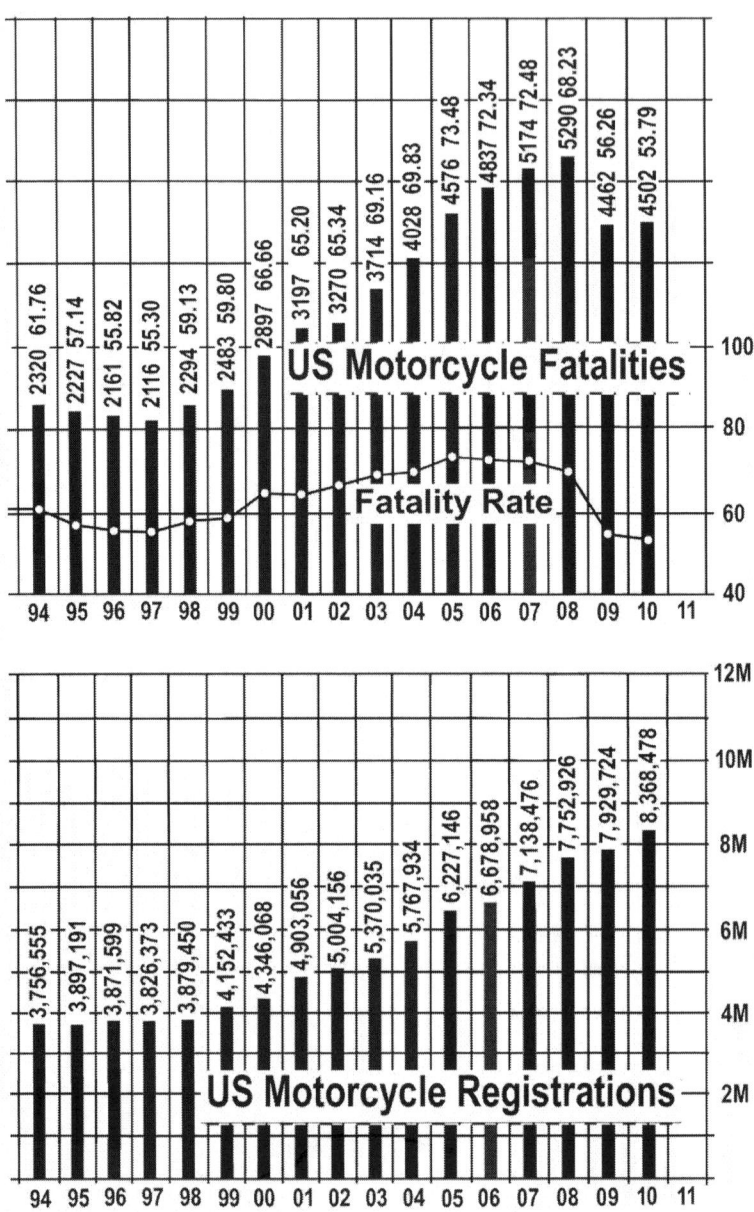

Motorcycle fatalities were climbing from 1997 to 2008, but so were motorcycle registrations. Comparing fatalities against

registrations gives us a rate. When new bike sales tapered off after 2008, the fatality rate dropped lower than it was in 1997. There are still lots of bikes registered, but perhaps fewer new riders on the road.

Bikes vs. Cars

As a reality check, let's just compare total U.S. motorcyclist fatalities to U.S. passenger vehicle driver fatalities, based on vehicle registrations. "Passenger vehicles" for this purpose include automobiles, pickup trucks, vans, and SUVs. We'll compare drivers only. According to NHTSA registration numbers, there were more than 196 million "light" four-wheelers (cars, SUVs and pickups) registered in the U.S. in 2008, and just under 8 million registered motorcycles. That makes it approximately one registered motorcycle per 25 registered passenger vehicles—about 4 percent.

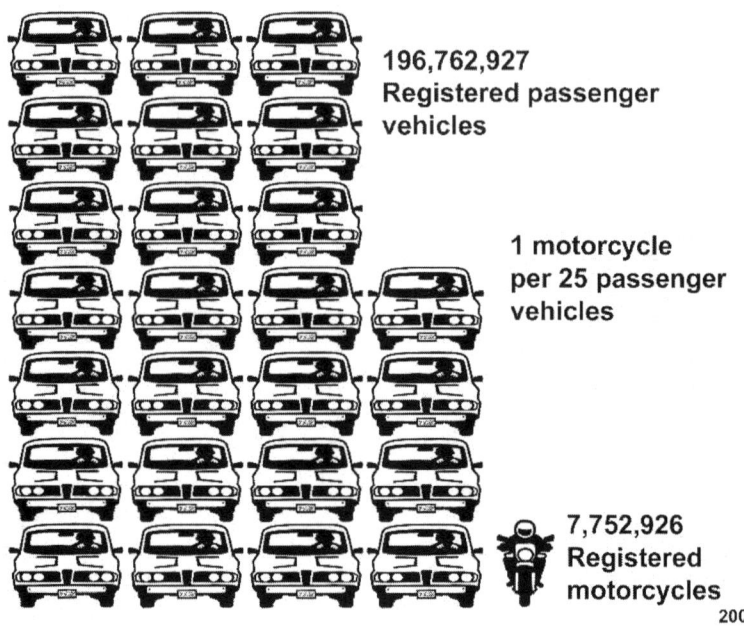

In 2008, the ratio of bikes to cars in the U.S. was 1 to 25, or about 4%.

OK, here's the rub: there were just over 16,000 car driver fatalities in 2008, and more than 5,000 motorcyclist fatalities. If the dangers of riding a bike were exactly equal to the dangers of driving a car, we would expect motorcyclist fatalities to be around four percent of passenger vehicle driver fatalities—say, 640 motorcyclists killed. But in 2008 motorcyclists racked up 5,290 fatalities—a whopping 32% of passenger vehicle driver fatalities. You read that right: motorcycles are fewer than 4 out of every 100 passenger vehicles on the road, but in 2008 we generated 32 out of every 100 fatalities.

16,753 fatalities to passenger car drivers

5,290 fatalities to motorcyclists

The number of registered motorcycles in the U.S. is less than 4% of motor vehicles, but motorcyclist fatalities are way out of proportion to all drivers killed. 32% of all passenger vehicle driver fatalities were motorcyclists.

So, comparing motorcycles to passenger vehicles, based solely on registrations, the current odds are roughly 54 to 10, making the risks of riding a bike around 6 times greater than driving a car. Unlike motorcycles, the weight of the motor vehicle you're driving has a huge impact on who gets hurt. The heavier your vehicle, the better your chances. That's probably why the motorcyclist so often gets injured in a car/bike collision.

VMT Fatality Rate

NHTSA is moving toward a fatality rate based on Vehicle Miles Traveled (VMT). Comparing fatalities to VMT is potentially more realistic, because it paints a clearer picture of a motorcyclist's relative exposure. Frankly, I've been skeptical of VMT for motorcycles because I haven't had much faith that anyone knows how to measure the cumulative miles motorcyclists rack up in any given year. Passenger vehicles are easier to count by means such as compression strips across highways. But can a pressure strip differentiate between a Smart Car, a Gold Wing, and a Spyder?

I've been assured by my scientist mole that NHTSA is working hard to develop foolproof systems for accurately counting motorcycle VMTs. I sure hope they get it right.

HTSA releases a *Traffic Safety Facts* bulletin every year (with about a two year lag). They chart the fatality rate for motor vehicles per 100 million VMT. Back in the 1950s, the passenger vehicle rate was above five per 100 million VMT, but dropped to 2.48 by 1978, and has steadily declined since then, thanks to such advances as crash barriers, safety glass, ABS, airbags, shoulder belts, and frontal crush zones. The rate was down to 0.87 fatalities per 100 million VMT in 2009, while motorcycles have been consistently up in the range of 20-30. That's probably where NHTSA gets their statistic that the average motorcyclist is 30 times more likely to die in a motorcycle crash than the average motorist. That may be a lot more depressing than the rate based on registrations, but I don't have any reason to believe it's not realistic.

Fatalities vs. Population

There's another way of looking at the relative dangers of motorcycling. We can just compare the total number of motorcyclist fatalities in a given geographical area to the total population of that area. The usefulness of the rate per population is reliability: it's very realistic because both motorcyclist fatalities and population are accurately tracked. It doesn't make any difference how many of the citizens actually ride motorcycles. We're measuring the relative danger to society from motorcycling.

We can look at what has happened over time in one geographical area, and we can also compare one area to another. For example, let's compare Washington to Oregon, California, and Alaska. The numbers are motorcyclist fatalities per million state population:

State	Best	Current
WA	6.0	10.4
OR	6.5	10.8
CA	7.1	11.6
AK	7.1	10.4

If you'd like to compare WA or any other state year-by-year, or see how the rate in any state has changed over time, the data is available at *http://www.nmcti.org/fatality_rate.php.*

What's clear from the various fatality rates is that although all vehicles are less dangerous than they used to be, passenger vehicles are getting safer at a much faster rate than motorcycles. It could also be a hint that our motorcycle training/licensing programs are less than successful at getting new riders up to speed for today's hectic traffic.

If you enjoy being seen as a risk-taker, you can now quantify that, and maybe hang a sign on your bike: *"I'm 30 times more dangerous than you are!"* (Make that *40 times* if you're under age 40.)

Morbid Crashes

The national Fatal Accident Reporting System (FARS) focuses on vehicle crashes that resulted in fatalities. With all of today's safety features, car drivers often escape a crash with just bruises. When a motorcycle is involved in a crash, it's much more likely the rider will be injured. Serious ("morbid") injuries often put riders in the hospital for surgery and sometimes long term care. We're not talking scraped shins from gas station tip-overs here, we're talking broken backs, compound fractures, punctured lungs, ruptured spleens, and brain injuries.

So how many motorcycle crashes result in morbid injuries, anyway? As it happens, there is an almost constant ratio of 20 morbid motorcycle crashes to each fatal crash. Some crashes are less serious, some very serious, but every major injury is a big problem for the rider and his or her family. Want a number? For 2008, there were right around 107,000 morbid motorcycle crashes nationwide.

What Do You Do With the Numbers?

I've tried to give you reasonably correct statistics, but what you do with the knowledge is up to you. If you choose to ride, you'll need to be exceptionally clever about managing the risks to survive the odds. And I know several people who have racked up a million or more motorcycling miles crash-free. If you're disturbed by the numbers, you might decide to ride less, or even hang up your helmet. Either way, it's your life, and your decision.

THE GOOD RIDER

Chapter 10: Why Should I Care About Motorcycle Fatalities?

For the past several years, motorcycle fatalities in the US have been frighteningly high. According to NHTSA Traffic Safety Facts, there were 4,612 motorcyclist fatalities in 2011. However you crunch the numbers, it's obvious that riding a bike is much more dangerous than driving a car, at least for the average motorcyclist.

But aren't you and I smarter than average, and skilled enough to avoid most crashes? Well, I've had a few crashes and racked up some jaw-dropping medical bills, but I'm not riding nearly as much as I used to, so my crash exposure is lower. I wear armored riding gear, so even if I do crash, I'm theoretically more likely to escape with only minor injuries, right? So why should I care that the national motorcycle carnage has been so high?

Well, what happens in motorcycling affects me personally. For instance, my insurance rates are determined not just by my personal risks, but by what happens to millions of other motorcyclists. I get lumped in with others based on age, family situation, motorcycle type, and even credit score. So, if there are many riders who are crashing big time, my rates will go up to allow the insurance company to continue making a profit after they pay out claims.

It's not just insurance rates that affect me personally, but also community attitudes about the risks of riding. For example, a few years ago some doctors at Harborview hospital in Seattle announced that injured motorcyclists were not paying their medical bills. That quickly got picked up by the news media. The doctors didn't seem to remember that lots of people—including car drivers and street bums—didn't pay their medical bills. They just decided to focus the spotlight on motorcyclists. And the news media gobbled it up.

In the minds of the general public, motorcyclists were not paying their bills, so society had good reason to step in and force us to reduce our risky behavior. Without much scientific study, the doctors decided that a mandatory helmet law would work wonders. And sure enough, within months a mandatory helmet law had been passed.

What's really curious about all this is that helmets work against the doctors' concern about paying the bills. The rider who dies quickly doesn't rack up millions of dollars in critical care, and often serves as an organ donor. The seriously injured rider who survives but needs years of care costs the system big bucks and doesn't contribute any good used body parts. So, from the standpoint of saving Harborview money, it would have made more sense to discourage helmet use.

I choose to wear protective riding gear when I ride, including a good helmet. My problem with a mandatory helmet law is when it's a knee-jerk reaction to questionable claims of a few medical professionals, rather than a well-thought-out response to a problem, with some chance of success.

**I've always been an ATGATT kind of rider:
"All The Gear All the Time."**

If we take a deeper look into the doctors' claims that injured motorcyclists are cheating the system, let's ask the hospital bean counters about who were responsible for the crashes. Let's note that about one-fourth of motorcycle crashes in the Northwest are the fault of car drivers. If auto drivers were at fault, shouldn't the blame for failing to pay the medical bills be directed toward the auto insurance industry?

Trouble is, motorcyclists are responsible for more and more of our crashes. These days, about three out of four motorcycle crashes are the fault of the rider. So, in terms of who is or isn't paying the medical bills, it's fair to ask, did the rider have adequate medical insurance? Are the insurance companies dragging their feet on paying legitimate medical bills? Are states allowing insurance companies to exclude medical coverage for crashes involving a motorcycle? Are we getting a fair shake?

That gets us full circle back to reasons why I must care about motorcycle crashes and fatalities. The bad press from motorcycling gives society reasons to come down on motorcyclists, and that includes me. It's not only injuries and fatalities that drive a concern to limit motorcycling; we have lots of scofflaw "brothers" who ride around making unnecessary noise or pulling antisocial stunts. Apparently society can forgive riders for feeling their oats, but there is much less tolerance for paying the costs of their folly.

The Harborview situation is a good example of how society deals with minorities. We're demonized, and then laws are created theoretically to solve the problem, although the real purpose may be simply to take us to the woodshed and give us a whuppin.'

Beyond my own selfish concerns about medical bills, insurance, and laws, I also feel some empathy toward for my fellow motorcyclists. I feel some sort of bond because of our mutual choices of vehicles and lifestyles. And I hate to see my fellow riders get injured or killed. Personally, I've devoted a big part of my life to helping other riders manage the risks.

Avoiding Fatalities

Showing some empathy toward my fellow riders doesn't prevent me from observing some really dumb riding. The sad truth is that the majority of motorcycle crashes are precipitated by rider errors. In the Northwest today, about half of motorcycle crashes are "single vehicle," meaning the rider crashed without hitting another vehicle.

These days, at least in the Northwest, motorcyclists precipitate about three out of four motorcycle crashes.

One big difference between bikes and cars is that car occupants are protected by roll cages, crumple zones, restraint belts, and airbags. Riding a bike, we must wear our crash padding. Various inventors have attempted to build crash protection into motorcycles, similar to the automobile approach.

Honda has devised a motorcycle airbag system, with the logic that the majority of bike crashes are frontal. Similar to the air bag system in a car, the airbag on the motorcycle inflates upon impact, giving the rider something softer to bounce into. There are also jacket designs with inflatable bags. I'm a little leery of motorcycle airbags. I certainly wouldn't want an airbag to suddenly inflate on a bike due to a pothole or an electrical fault.

Inventive people are always dreaming up ways to prevent injury. In the UK, a scheme was proposed to require mandatory leg protectors ("crash bars") to prevent lower extremity injuries. That might have resulted in fewer leg injuries in sideswipe situations, but the majority of bike crashes are frontal. And in frontal crashes the "leg protectors" actually increase injuries as riders are thrown forward into the bars.

Helmets appear to be somewhere between 13% and 35% effective in reducing brain injury, depending on the agenda of who's telling the story. Certainly, the crushable EPS liner inside the helmet shell is capable of reducing brain sloshing. But the reality is that helmets just can't do much to prevent the brain from being injured.

But wait! Aren't helmets tested to make sure they work? Yes, but the impact speed in helmet tests are only about 12 mph. In ideal conditions, a crushable EPS liner might cushion the brain at impact speeds of maybe 18 mph. But it turns out that rotational injuries are more prevalent than anyone suspected. The head gets snapped around, and the brain sloshes around inside the skull. Helmets are now being designed with dual liners, one to allow the head to rotate inside the shell and one to soften the blow.

I've crashed three or four times in my million-some miles of riding, always wearing an approved helmet. But none of those crashes were head-on into a solid object. If I had smacked my head against a rock or bridge abutment, I wouldn't be here writing this. A helmet can be useful in sliding/bouncing situations, but if you bash your head into a rock wall or dump truck at even 40 mph, it's game over, no question. So, helmets are good at preventing some injuries, but not very good at saving lives. Remember, helmets are only 13-35% effective in reducing *brain injury*.

In my opinion, the primary path to reducing motorcycle injuries (and medical bills) is to help riders to avoid crashes. I'll wear ATGATT, thank you, but I believe that the only way to ensure there are no injuries is to not allow a crash to occur. If the Harborview doctors were really as smart about saving money as they pretended to be, they would have called for more serious license testing.

Fewer Crashes

The good news is that there are a few serious riders who rack up many years and many miles of riding without mishap. For example, my BMW riding friend Voni Glaves topped a million documented miles of motorcycling without a single crash. She's done better than I have. People like Voni show that it's possible to beat the odds if you really work at it.

Long distance rider Voni Glaves topped a million miles of riding in 2011, without a single crash, proving that it's possible to beat the odds if you're serious enough.

There are some important tactics to help you avoid becoming one of the statistics. Perhaps the most important key is figuring out what's going to happen soon enough to do something about it.

Predicting the Future

Skilled riders have learned to read the situation far enough ahead to not be in the wrong place at the wrong time. The novice rider might think, *"You can't predict the future,"* but that's exactly what's needed to avoid hazards while riding a motorcycle. Okay, we can't predict exactly what's going to happen, but we can form pretty good ideas based on our past experiences and acquired knowledge.

For example, when you're approaching a curve that blocks off your view, you can mull over a few hazards that you've seen before, and consider what you'd do if something nasty was waiting for you around the corner, say a trailer with a flat tire, or a tourist turning around in the middle of the road. There's a good chance the road is clear, but once in a while there will be a serious hazard. How much of a gambler are you?

One big key to avoiding crashes is reading the situation far enough in advance to do something about it. When you're approaching a situation with a limited view, it would be smart to scrub off some speed.

Impairment

The human brain is pretty good at predicting what might happen, but only if it's not impaired. Alcohol is the most serious offender. Alcohol is involved in about 3 of every 10 fatal crashes nationwide, and that goes up to 5 of every 10 at night. That's not drunk drivers running into sober motorcyclists, that's riders who somehow assume they can ride motorcycles with alcohol in their systems. I suspect that prescription drugs are more involved in serious motorcycle crashes than might be thought, especially among older riders. But whether it's alcohol or prescription drugs, it's also something that we can control, because we have the choice of not riding if we're impaired.

If you can manage just those two tactics, you will significantly increase your odds of surviving the ride.

Chapter 11: Stupid Hurts

Back at the beginning of book, I suggested some attributes I would expect of a proficient motorcyclist, including the following:

- Skillful in controlling a wide variety of motorcycles.
- Proficient at negotiating traffic on public roads without causing or being involved in collisions.
- Knowledgeable about appropriate riding gear to provide protection from both the elements and accidental crashes.
- Knowledgeable enough about the human body to maintain health and fitness under a variety of traveling conditions, and to administer first aid to self or others in the event of illness or injury.

I'm embarrassed to admit that I didn't follow my own advice, and I crashed. I had swapped machines with another rider who was insistent I try his new Triumph Street Triple R, and I flipped it. Fortunately my gear did its job and I didn't have any missing skin or brain damage, although I bashed up both hands and fractured several bones in my right wrist. My riding season was over in the blink of an eye. I had surgery that night to put the fingers back in their sockets. And a week later I underwent a 3-hour surgery to screw the bones back together. Then the physical therapy began, to get my hands working again. I had *lots* of time to think about the crash and about my riding.

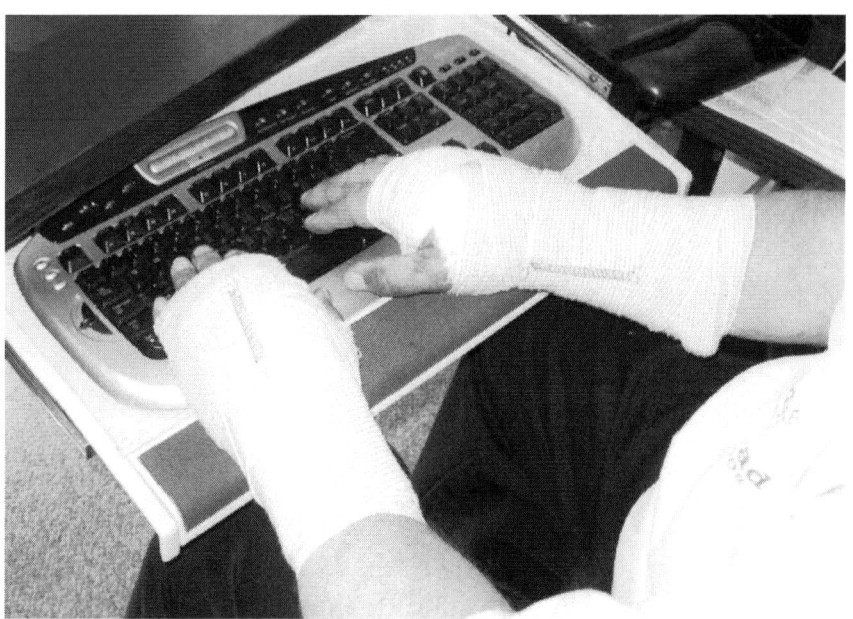

Skillful in Controlling a Wide Variety of Motorcycles

You can take away some points from me on this one. The junk truck ahead of me (with no brake lights) slowed suddenly, and I braked aggressively. Too aggressively, as it worked out. My muscle memory developed over years of riding machines with less-than-outstanding brakes had me braking too hard on the unfamiliar bike, and I flipped it end over end.

I've suggested the value of gaining experience with different machines, but let me reiterate the importance of taking the time to familiarize yourself with the machine before heading out into traffic. The flip side of that is that if you're thinking about loaning your bike to someone, make sure they get in some practice on it. Explain the controls to them, along with any quirks or limitations. If the machine they have been riding is significantly different from the one you're going to loan them, spend the time necessary to get them up to speed on the loaner before expecting them to ride off into traffic.

Proficient at Negotiating Traffic on Public Roads

I'll accept an attaboy for managing to avoid smashing into the knife-edged bed on the junk hauler. Without working brake lights to warn me the truck was slowing, it took me a second or two to realize what was happening. At first I thought the bike was accelerating: maybe it had a stuck throttle body. It was an optical illusion—I just wasn't decelerating as fast as the truck. I finally grabbed a big handful of front brake, and managed two or three stoppies before flipping the bike into a forward loop. I managed to miss the truck, but I didn't miss the pavement.

A big part of negotiating traffic is to predict what is about to happen; whether the hazard is another driver getting in your way, inoperative equipment, or a loose load; and then get out of the way.

Knowledgeable About Appropriate Riding Gear

I'll accept a good grade for wearing my protective gear. My Nolan helmet was scratched and gouged, and the side plates holding the face shield were ground away. But my brain still works, so apparently the helmet did what it could. My Aerostich Darien jacket and pants were shredded at all the usual areas, but the interior impact pads stayed put. My leather boots and elkskin gloves were seriously scuffed in spots. But the pavement didn't grind through to skin anywhere. The only bleeding was from my eye glasses being jammed into the bridge of my nose.

My point here is that wearing *All the Gear All the Time* (ATGATT) paid off big time when I went down. There have been lots of miles over the years when I've weighed the discomfort of durable riding gear against the possibility of a crash, and wondered if I really needed all the gear. But crashes happen quickly, and you never know when or where you'll get your turn to take a tumble. When my turn came up, my gear was there to protect me, and it did as good as I could expect.

Tom Mehren snapped this shot of me in my Aerostich gear about an hour prior to the crash on the borrowed Triumph. Everything was shredded, but nothing ground through to skin anywhere.

Knowledgeable About the Human Body

I've suggested that a good rider should understand enough about the human body to maintain health and fitness. That includes managing your health so that you're fit for riding. I'm diabetic, and I work to control my blood sugar with both prescription medications and daily insulin injections. One danger for a diabetic is having a drop in blood sugar that affects vision and judgment. In fact, only about an hour before the crash, I had eaten an afternoon snack to keep my blood sugar up.

Many of us take prescription medications for a variety of other conditions, and we must understand not only how our meds affect us at different times of the day, but also how the different drugs interact with each other. As we age, it's typical to be taking several prescribed drugs. It's important for a motorcyclist to think about how drugs and physical condition affect riding.

Where it went wrong for me is that in addition to my diabetic pills, I had been taking prescription meds to control back pain. I have to believe that the drugs—or a drug interaction—affected my vision, judgment, reaction time, and muscle memory. My point is that when we're on medications, we need to be aware of how they affect us, and avoid the ride if we're not fit for duty.

Stupid Decisions

A big part of this crash was accepting the offer to swap machines. Another journalist was eager to have me ride his shiny new machine. Apparently he wanted me to experience his new bike, and affirm that he had made a wise purchase. Although his confidence in my skills was flattering, I had turned down his offer the day before.

Earlier that day, I had been riding at a relaxed pace, enjoying the scenery, stopping for coffee, and buying some fresh fruit at an orchard. For my physical condition, the relaxed pace was appropriate. And had I continued the ride on my familiar motorcycle at the same relaxed pace, I suspect I would have been able to handle the truck hazard without any drama.

But I'd fallen in with the other rider, and we took a quick spin down some side roads. I was mentally jacked up and riding more aggressively.

Then during our impromptu ride, we arrived at a stop sign, and he suddenly leaned the Triumph on the side stand and shouted for me to come over. *"Let's swap,"* he called, as he trotted back to my machine, hopped on, and zoomed off down the highway.

So ready or not, I was riding an unfamiliar bike, with little time to make an intelligent decision. I suppose that in the instant when I might have shouted *"No!"* and raced him back to my machine, I was flattered by his having confidence in my skills, and also thinking, *"Okay, I can do this."*

In other words, I allowed the situation to overrule my common sense. I've had other occasions over the years where I've seen riders crash borrowed bikes, and I knew better. It's never a smart idea to swap machines in the middle of a ride. It's not that you won't be able to figure out the different controls and inputs for normal riding, but that when something happens that's not normal—like that junk truck—you'll suddenly need the correct skills for that machine.

There's also the issue of age. We're all growing older. We tend to just keep on riding the same way we used to until some disaster overtakes us. There is seldom a time when we get a sharp reminder of the limitations of our physical skills and mental abilities—until we crash. I've had a couple of those reminders over the past several years, after a million or so miles of riding. As a result, I've figured out a few rules for myself:

I need to maintain better awareness of what my body and mind are doing.

Before throwing a leg over a motorcycle, I need to consider whether I really am fit for riding duty. If I'm taking drugs for pain or allergies, I should assume they are affecting my judgment as well as my physical skills. And if I'm really not confident I'm ready, I need to have the backbone to cancel the ride, or at least make it short and relaxed.

Before throwing a leg over a motorcycle, I need to consider whether I'm fit for riding duty. I must assume that drugs will affect my judgment as well as physical skills.

I must remember the pitfalls of group riding

I seldom ride with groups, so I need to stick with some hard and fast rules. I need to have the wisdom and control to resist jacking up my speed just because my fellow riders are being more aggressive. When I find myself in a group where the ride is getting more aggressive than I prefer, I need to just back off. And if I can't control my aggressive urges, I could just make a point of never joining a group ride.

When I find myself in a group where the riding is getting more aggressive than my comfort level, I need to just back off.

As I age, I need to get smarter, not just about the risks of the road, but about my health, and about social situations

It's easy to be flattered by people pressing me to do things, and it's a strong temptation to fulfill their image of me. That's why it's very important to avoid falling for traps such as swapping bikes. Speaking for myself, I must never, ever agree to do something I don't want to do, or don't feel able to do.

It's easy to be flattered by people pressing me to do things, but I need to say no if it's something I don't feel able to do, or don't want to do.

You can adopt these rules for yourself, if you wish.

THE GOOD RIDER

Chapter 12: Expanding Your Ride

I believe that part of being a good rider is to be skillful at controlling a wide variety of motorcycles. I'm not suggesting that you should run out and buy some different machines, but I am encouraging you to gain some experience riding machines other than what you've been riding. If you've only ridden the street, you've missed a lot of lessons that can only be learned in the dirt. If you've only ridden on two wheels, you've missed out on what a three-wheeler can teach you. If you've only been riding a super-powerful sport bike, you might have missed how much fun a 250 or 400 can be. You don't have to change your current machine, just expand your skills. It's like the car driver who learns to ride a bike. It probably makes him a better driver, too.

My suggestion is to get in some seat time on a different type of motorcycle. If you've only been riding a big tourer or a high performance superbike, consider a smaller machine, perhaps a scooter. As Tom Mehren has suggested, the fun is not so much in going scary fast, but the *feeling* that you're going fast. It's handy to have big horsepower to pass creepers on a super slab upgrade against a headwind, but having all those ponies on tap can make you lazy. Small bikes have a way of encouraging you to become more skillful.

To put this another way, you might have more fun riding a 250 wide open than riding a 1400 at quarter throttle. So, think about borrowing a bike that magazine editors would derisively call an "entry level" machine. Maybe you'll enjoy it so much you'll end up adding a smaller bike to your stable.

One big lesson is that the greater the mass of the machine, the more energy is required to get it around corners. A few years ago I was in the San Francisco area for a tour reunion. Since I was just recovering from a cold, I decided to transport the 350 in the back of my pickup truck, rather than ride down the coast on one of my roadburners.

Because I was recovering from a recent cold, I hauled the 350 down the coast rather than riding one of my roadburners.

During the reunion, some local riders had been recruited to lead us through the countryside. One ride was into the redwood forest south of San Francisco. Another was across the Golden Gate Bridge into Marin County, where lots of twisty roads serve as the playground for sport bikers and police on summer weekends. The ride leader was concerned about the speed and fuel range of the 350, but I assured him could I do 80 mph, with a fuel range of over 200 miles. It would do the job. When we headed off toward the coast on some very twisty roads, I tucked in behind him, and we both ran off and left the rest of the group on their big rental machines.

The point is, a machine with much less mass is much easier to turn. Yes, it may take a bit of pedaling of the shift lever to keep the engine in the power band, but basically you can just screw on the throttle and push it through the curves. You don't have to be concerned about corners that suddenly tighten up, or lean-over clearance, or avoiding rear wheel spin.

If you take the time to peruse racetrack times, you might be amazed that the 250 class is only slightly slower than the superbikes. But speed is only half the equation. The other half is *fun*. It's really sweaty hard work to keep a fire-breathing superbike under control at full chat. Riding a 250 or a 400 can actually be more fun, without all the drama. Sure, you'll be riding at slower speeds much of the time, and maybe within the posted speed limits for a change. But if it's speed you want, take a jet!

I encourage you to learn how to drive a three-wheeled motorcycle, preferably a sidecar rig.

I also encourage you to learn how to drive a three-wheeled motorcycle, preferably a sidecar rig. Sitting in the saddle it may look and feel like a bike, but the dynamics are completely different. A sidecar combination forces you to learn many new techniques, such as steering into a corner without first having to lean the bike over, or simultaneously squeezing the front brake while rolling on the throttle. If you have so far limited your motorcycling experience to only two-wheelers, you might be reluctant to get anywhere near one of *those things* but sidecars and trikes are an extension of motorcycling, and I urge you to expand your knowledge and skills in that direction.

No, I'm not advising you to start looking for a sidecar to attach to your bike, or put the two-wheeler up for sale. But I am advising you to take the Sidecar/Trike course, where you can learn some basics on a training rig with coaching by a certified instructor.

S/TEP courses are administered nationwide by the Evergreen Safety Council in Seattle, (800) 521-0778. Three wheeler training was rolled into the Washington state motorcycle safety program several years ago, and the S/TEP course fees are subsidized similar to the two-wheeler Basic Rider Course, so you can get in some seat time on a sidecar rig or trike without having to spend a lot of money.

Be aware that Washington requires a special endorsement to operate a three-wheeler legally on public roads. If you're interested, you can get your license endorsement upgraded to include three wheelers.

I realize that the motorcyclist whose experience has been limited to two-wheelers is likely to be prejudiced against a three-wheeler. It's similar to how a car driver is likely to be biased against a motorcycle. It's natural to distrust and reject things that you don't understand. What surprises so many riders who take the sidecar course is how much fun it is. A rigid sidecar rig doesn't lean into corners, which requires the driver to do a lot of hanging off. Flying the car is not just a stunt, it's a necessary skill for learning to manage roll. Once you've mastered it, you'll very likely have a big grin on your face.

OK, I'll admit that I have a lot of experience on sidecar outfits and trikes, but I'm not a three-wheeler snob. My fleet of motorcycles has often included both two-wheelers and three-wheelers. For a run into town, I've often decided on the sidecar rig instead of the bike. Wouldn't I miss being able to lean into turns? Well, if the streets are covered with slippery wet leaves, I won't miss leaning. What's more, I get to drift the tires, hang off, and enjoy the tactics of controlling a hack. My point here is that there are times when riding a bike is more fun, and there are times when an outfit is more fun. You have my permission to own at least one of each.

I owned a Can Am Spyder for a couple of years, and chuckled whenever some know-it-all rider opined that it "wasn't a motorcycle."

When Bombardier introduced the Can-Am Spyder, there was a groundswell of grumbles from motorcyclists in general. *"It's not a motorcycle!"* was a typical cry. What gives me a chuckle is that today's motorcyclists often fail to realize that historically three-wheelers have been more popular than two-wheelers. Back in the 1920s and 1930s, something like 80% of motorcycles had sidecars attached.

So is the Can Am Spyder a motorcycle? Well, what defines "motorcycle?" As it happens, vehicles are defined not by the random opinions of motorcyclists, but by state laws. Yes, "motorcycle" includes three-wheelers in most states. Without belaboring the point, three-wheelers fall under the legal definition of "motorcycle."

In case you're wondering, trikes are typically easier to drive than a sidecar rig, because a trike is symmetrical. A sidecar outfit is lopsided. Left turns are different from right turns, and the power is way over on one side. Trikes are relatively stable, whether the one-front, two-rear variety such as the Gold Wing Lehman conversions, or the two-front, one-rear variety such as the Can-Am Spyder. In terms of handling, the two-front variety are much more stable in turns, and the factory exotics like the Spyder have speed-sensitive power steering, ABS, roll control, and in some models, paddle shifting.

The Ace Cycle Car is a three-wheeler powered by a Harley-Davidson motor. Seating is side-by-side, and it has a steering wheel.

For a vintage style of three-wheeler with contemporary running gear, consider the Ace Cycle Car by Liberty in Seattle. It's a modern interpretation of a 2F 1R Morgan, powered by a Harley-Davidson motor, with a sports car transmission and shaft drive. Be forewarned that it's pricey, but very high quality.

Let's dig a little deeper into why driving a hack or trike might be good for a biker. As you accumulate experience riding a two-wheeled motorcycle, you are likely to fall into habits, and once in a while it's good to question them. After a few years—or maybe 100,000 miles—you probably have lots of habits that allow you to ride almost automatically. You have muscle memory that allows your subconscious to take action without you having to think deeply about what you're doing.

Muscle memory can be a good thing, say when an oncoming car suddenly turns left across your path and your right hand squeezes the lever automatically without you needing to consciously think *"Brake!"* But muscle memory can also trip you up, as when you attempt to roll the bike farther to negotiate a decreasing-radius turn, and it won't lean any farther because your subconscious has learned maximum roll rate and lean angle. But you're probably wondering, *"But what's this got to do with driving a hack?"*

There are lots of lessons learned from driving a hack that apply to riding a bike.

Learning to control a three-wheeler requires you to think consciously about what you're doing at first. You have to rethink things such as steering, traction, roll, and tire slip. For instance, have you wondered whether it's better to keep the tires rotating during a quick stop, or just jam on the brakes and slide to a stop? Theory is one thing. Have you tested your theories? I wouldn't encourage you to experiment on a bike, because locking the front brake can quickly dump you on your padding. One California cornering school has a specially-modified bike with outriggers to allow you to experiment with over-braking, but you can also try it safely on a three-wheeler because a sliding tire won't cause the rig to fall over.

The lesson, if you're wondering, is that a tire that is still rotating has much *more* traction than a tire that is sliding. What's more, a sliding tire loses directional control. You may have read that somewhere, and agree intellectually, but thinking about it and doing it are two different animals. I'm encouraging you to experience it on a three-wheeler.

There are dozens of such lessons to be learned—lessons that apply to bikes as well as to trikes. How does rolling on the gas in curves affect tire slip angles? Is it really important to transition between brake and throttle? When you are braking, is it important how you let off the brakes?

While we're thinking about alternate motorcycles, let's not limit ourselves to tiddlers and hacks. If you really like to ride fast, the best place to do that is on a closed track. There are track schools that introduce you to racing, others that coach you on cornering control, and others that simply give you track time. It's smarter to do your fast riding on the track rather than on public roads. The track is a much safer environment, with clean pavement, few surface hazards, and perhaps an ambulance standing by in case anyone really screws up. If you choose to go fast on public roads, you need to get really good at reading the situation and changing speed quickly to match your sight distance. It's not the speed that kills you, it's the stop.

Road racing is a well-known form of motorcycle competition, but there are many other forms, including flat track, motocross and hill climb. (Photo credit: CJ Olive)

There are many forms of motorcycle competition, including vintage racing, flat track, scrambles, motocross, and hill climbs. If you think you'd be interested, find some races and go see for yourself. There are also books available, including *Driving a Sidecar Outfit*. Whatever you do, I encourage you to expand your motorcycling as part of the journey to becoming a good rider.

THE

Chapter 13: Getting Noticed in Traffic

Most of us are aware of the Hurt Report—that federally-funded motorcycle accident study that we've been referring to for the past 33 years. The official government title is so long and convoluted someone just named it after the lead researcher, Hugh Hurt. One of the big conclusions of the Hurt Report was that car drivers who crashed into motorcyclists often reported *"I didn't see the motorcycle."* Ever since, we've wondered how to get noticed in traffic, a subject we call conspicuity.

There was another federally-funded study on motorcycle conspicuity that was released in 1979. The research was done by P.L. Olson and staff at the University of Michigan. The title is also a bit lengthy. Let's just call it the "Olson Report." The intrepid researchers wanted to find out what helped drivers see motorcyclists. They developed some theories and then talked some optimistic motorcyclists into challenging real urban traffic on bikes to scientifically field test the theories.

The primary tests were to measure the "gap acceptance" of real world motorists faced with turning across traffic. The bikes and riders were equipped with various conspicuity devices such as brightly-colored fabric fairing covers and upper torso garments. The test riders not only controlled the bike, but observed how other drivers reacted, and recorded the results by pressing appropriate buttons. Amazingly, there was only one crash.

Olson Report Conclusions

I suppose you want the conclusions of the Olson Report up front. Okay:

- Wearing a brightly-colored riding jacket, especially yellow-green, is very effective.
- For daytime riding, having the headlight on seems to help, and a modulating headlight works even better.
- For nighttime riding, the combination of running lights and retro-reflective clothing seems to be important, because running lights are visible in situations when car lights aren't reflecting off your riding gear.

Unfortunately, there are no simple answers to being conspicuous because there are too many variables to provide one simple solution for all motorcyclists in all situations. For instance, with so many cars having daytime running lights these days, a motorcycle with its headlight on may not be so conspicuous. To better understand the situation, let's consider how humans see.

Foveal vs. Peripheral Vision

According to Olson, seeing is a complex process of monitoring the scene in a relatively fuzzy way with our peripheral vision, and then focusing on whatever details attract our attention. We do this so automatically that we don't realize how complex it is. The center of vision, the fovea, is the only part of the eye that sees in sharp detail. The fovea is only about one-to-two degrees outward from the center. The rest of the field of view is called peripheral. The farther out from the fovea, the less detail can be observed.

If peripheral vision notices anything of interest, then the fovea is triggered to focus on it. As you're reading this, you are focusing your fovea on the details of just one or two words and scanning the line in a sequence of quick glances. Occasionally your peripheral vision may pick up some interesting word, and divert your attention to it. Then you have to remember where you were, and go back to that.

Seeing = Focusing On the Details

Just because a motorcycle is visible to a driver doesn't mean he or she will see it. By "see" we mean comprehending the existence of some object. The bike might appear as just a fuzzy blur in a driver's peripheral vision. In order to comprehend the blurred object, the driver must focus on the bike. If a motorcycle in a driver's blurred peripheral vision doesn't trigger any interest, then it just remains a blur of no consequence.

Most of what you see is a fuzzy blur in your peripheral vision. The only area where you can see details is where you are focusing at the moment, like the license plate of that van ahead.

To make judgments about such things as speed and distance, a driver needs to take several successive glances, shared in sequence with all the other stuff being scanned by the peripheral vision. The sequence of focused glances can be very complex as the driver attempts to take in the various details and remember them.

In order to take in more of the scene, a driver focuses briefly on various details, remembering what's there, and then shifting focus in a rapid and complex sequence.

Visual Priorities

When a driver is looking for other vehicles, large objects get a higher priority than smaller objects. Let's say a driver waiting to turn left notices an oncoming truck. The truck will most likely get visual priority just because it's bigger. If a bike ahead of the truck doesn't attract attention, it can be ignored. You can understand how a driver might decide to make a quick left turn in front of the truck without seeing the bike.

Since larger vehicles get a higher attention priority, a driver might focus on various details of an oncoming truck and completely ignore a motorcycle.

Conspicuity Tactics

According to the Olson Report, one important tactic is to wear a brightly-colored upper torso garment (riding jacket), preferably in the yellowish-green spectrum. There is apparently more value in wearing a bright colored jacket than having the fairing a bright color.

More recent studies from other countries have indicated an advantage to wearing a white helmet. Bright blue and yellow are also colors that attract attention. Due to characteristics of the human eye, red and orange are less conspicuous than other colors. Black, brown, and dark blue are like camouflage in dim light situations. For riding at night, the report showed considerable benefit in having retro-reflective panels in the riding jacket.

Take a look at what road workers wear. Today's conspicuity vests typically have lots of yellow-green panels and reflective tape. You might also note that fire engines are being painted yellow-green rather than the traditional red.

The orange cones and BUMP sign might seem bright, but the hi-viz jacket is more likely to be noticed. The big red STOP sign isn't as attention-grabbing as we might assume.

Several garment manufacturers have come out with "conspicuity riding gear." For instance, Aerostich has a hi-viz garment material that is *very* bright. The piercing color carries plenty of visual punch even under incandescent and low-light conditions.

Positioning

One of the recommendations of the Hurt Report was that riders needed to develop better tactics for seeing and being seen. Creative entrepreneurs translated this to mean riders should buy products such as conspicuity vests and headlight modulators. But let's note that how you position yourself in traffic has a lot to do with whether or not other drivers notice you. For instance, if you hide behind a larger vehicle, it won't make much difference what you're wearing, or whether your lights are on. As a general rule, I suggest staying out from behind view-blocking vehicles such as trucks or busses.

This rider might have a good view of the intersection looking over the tip of the taxi, but an oncoming driver might not see the bike. In situations like this, you can understand how another driver fails to see the motorcyclist.

Do you see the motorcycle hidden behind this big truck? Neither would an oncoming driver considering a left turn. If you can't avoid following a truck or bus in traffic, drop back several seconds and move closer to the left edge of the lane.

Tacking

One tactic to make a narrow bike look larger for a moment is to "tack" from one side of the lane to the other. That displays more of the side of your bike to make it look larger, and the lateral (sideways) motion helps capture attention. Tacking away from a vehicle that could make a turn across your path also gives you more time to react to whatever the driver does.

Tacking from one side of the lane to the other makes your bike look larger and closer, and also provides some lateral motion to help capture a driver's attention.

Lights On

The Olson study seems to justify the daytime use of headlights, although they didn't test multiple headlights, nor did they have wide headlight arrays such as those on some of today's big touring and dual-sport bikes. Some riders believe in running with the headlight on high beam in the daytime, the concept being that brighter must be more conspicuous. There is no research to show that's as effective as some riders would like to believe. The Olson study did note that headlights that vary in intensity were more likely to attract attention than a light of constant intensity.

They tested headlights that dimmed and then brightened, not headlights that switched from low beam to high beam like today's modulators. The research seems to support a modulating headlight as a conspicuity advantage.

The visual priorities are larger, brighter, more contrasting, or faster approaching. But let's note that more than a few drivers have pulled out in front of big fire engines and huge railroad locomotives speeding toward them with very bright flashing lights.

Judging Speed

One reason why a headlight on high beam may not help is that in addition to "seeing" you, a driver needs to correctly judge your distance and approach speed. To do this, the driver focuses, and remembers the shape and size, then glances again and compares the new image with the one in memory. The sequence of glances and memory allow the driver's brain to subconsciously compute distance and speed. If the oncoming vehicle appears to be getting larger very quickly, the driver's brain calculates that it is approaching at a higher speed.

There are some visual problems with an oncoming motorcycle. First, most motorcycles are much narrower than the typical automobile. Second, a headlight that's only 7 inches wide isn't large enough to provide accurate speed clues, and running on high beam may only confuse the mental speed calculations. The best clues about the distance and approach speed of an oncoming motorcycle are from larger objects—say the edges of the fairing, the arms of your riding jacket, or wide-apart running lights.

Which bike do you think is closer? Here's a clue: compare the size of the riders' helmets. The smaller bike with SM wheels is actually closer to the camera. The wide headlight array and running lights on the GL help create the image that it is closer.

The Olson study mentioned that using turn signals as running lights would increase conspicuity. The Honda Gold Wing 1800 has bright running lights in the fronts of the mirrors, and this may be a very important conspicuity advantage. Adding lights or reflectors to the front of the bike, as far apart as possible, might help a driver make the snap decision that you are fast and close, and avoid pulling into your path.

If there is a practical way for you to add running lights, say to the front of your mirrors, that could be a very worthwhile way to make your machine more conspicuous. You may see some bikes equipped with two small lights on the sides of the forks, to create a triangle of lights with the headlight. That setup wasn't tested by the Olson team, but it does give an oncoming driver better clues about your distance and speed.

Is it the light pattern that gives better clues about this bike's speed and distance, or is it the wide saddlebags?

There's an important message in this for riders of smaller, narrower motorcycles, especially sport bikes, dual-sports, and scooters. The smaller size is less likely to trigger a driver to focus on you. And the narrow width makes you look farther away and slower. Those visual errors can easily cause a driver to believe there is time to pull out in front of a fast moving bike. That also might help explain why sport bikes are over-represented in crashes.

Night Riding

For riding at night, the Olson Report showed a definite advantage to using running lights in addition to the headlight and taillight. I suggest you park your motorcycle along some dark street at night and then stand back and see how it looks when illuminated by the lights of approaching cars. You might even drape your riding jacket over the saddle. If everything looks a little dim, consider adding accessory running lights or reflectors, amber on the front and red on the back, please. There is also reflective sheeting that looks black in daylight, and glows white when illuminated by a car's headlights at night. One big advantage of reflectors is that they use the other guy's electrical system rather than yours.

The Olson Report gives us some good ideas about why other drivers see us or not. It's tempting to think that some simple tactic such as adding reflectors or running with the headlight on high beam or installing loud pipes will decrease the danger. The fly in that ointment is that attempting to get other drivers to see you and get out of your way is unreliable, because even if you are excessively conspicuous, some drivers will just not see you. Statistically, about half of the other drivers on the road at any moment will not notice you, even in the best of conditions.

And since you don't know who will see you and who won't, the only reliable tactic to manage the situation is to get out of the way of any vehicles that are in a position to collide with you. That emphasizes the need to improve your situational awareness, and be both in control of the bike and the situation.

THE GOOD RIDER

Chapter 14: Managing the Risks

Photo by Ron Stone

There are lots of theories floating around about why riders are crashing, and what we might do to avoid crashing. The Centers for Disease Control and Prevention reported that between 2001 and 2008, more than 34,000 motorcyclists were killed in crashes in the U.S. Many states have come out with their own reports, but it's a statistical bowl of spaghetti. The departments responsible for motorcycle safety don't always have motorcycle experts on staff, so it's a GIGO situation: "Garbage In, Garbage Out." Police investigating motorcycle crashes are typically untrained in motorcycle dynamics, and under pressure to fill out the paperwork. A rider crashes in a corner, and the untrained officer checks "excessive speed for conditions." How can you dispute that?

In a recent motorcycle study from Oklahoma, there was a single category for "no improper action by the motorcycle operator," and that accounted for 46% of fatal crashes. But there were 13 separate categories for "unsafe speed." Guess what? Unsafe speed is listed as a contributing factor in 22% of fatal crashes.

Personally, I'm not ready to accept that state or federal bureaucrats really understand the cause of crashes. The rider who drifts wide in a corner and takes a soil sample might be assumed to be going too fast. Or maybe he just doesn't know how to get the bike turned. If he crashed during a group ride, we might blame group riding. If he had eaten French fries for lunch, someone might tie potatoes to motorcycle crashes. It's really difficult to come up with reasonable causes for crashes.

We could train riders to corner more swiftly and in better control. That's the logic of people who offer track schools. But it might not change anything. For instance, consider the poor dude who crashed in a corner. Was the cause of the crash being distracted by an uncomfortable saddle, or riding in a group, or his lack of cornering skill, or poor judgment about the situation, or having his judgment skewed by alcohol or drugs?

If a rider doesn't have adequate awareness or judgment to balance speed against skill level and the situation, then increasing cornering skill will only jack up the speed at which he crashes the next time. That's not to say that riders don't need good skills, because it's necessary to have at least threshold skills to properly control a motorcycle. So, what are the most significant reasons for serious and fatal crashes?

Four Main Causes of Crashes

The 2010 version of NHTSA Traffic Safety Facts shows the top three related factors in fatal crashes:

- Driving too fast, or in excess of speed limit
- Failure to keep in lane, or running off road
- Under the influence of alcohol, drugs, or medications

I'd like to suggest an additional category:

- Poor situational awareness

Control Skills

I'm embarrassed at the relatively low skill level of many of my fellow motorcyclists. There are lots of sports where people read up, take lessons, and practice to improve skill level. The vast majority of motorcyclists I see simply threw a leg over a bike and assumed it would all be made clear with time in the saddle. I suppose you don't know what you don't know. The license skills tests in most states are so pedantic that you'd have to be a serious klutz to not pass and get your endorsement. As a result, too many newbies get through the warm and fuzzy training without even intermediate skills. A rider who has to drag her foot skids all the way from the gas pumps to the street is demonstrating ignorance of how bikes are balanced and steered. That rider is set up to go wide in a corner and slam into something hurtful.

A big part of the business of managing the dangers of riding is having skills so well-honed that they are automatic. If someone is still struggling with such entry-level skills as balancing or shifting, their conscious attention is being squandered. The path to developing awareness of the unfolding situation is to first gain the muscle memory to control the bike subconsciously. You should no more have to think about getting the bike around a corner than you have to think about breathing or walking. Only when you have developed the right muscle memory is your brain freed to think about what's ahead. And the way you develop muscle memory is to practice, practice, practice.

The way to develop your riding skills is to practice, practice, practice. Practice whatever you find difficult.
(Photo: Scott Wilson)

Matching Speed to Conditions

The crash statistics do refer to unsafe speed as a major contributor to nasty crashes, but I'm thinking that it's not a matter of where the needle was pointed, but rather, what was happening ahead. The tendency is to ride at a more-or-less constant speed, regardless of sight distance. Our brains—developed primarily for hunting/gathering tactics—have a tough time comprehending kinetic energy. A crash report might note that the rider slammed into a truck that was blocking the road just around a blind turn. The rider was wearing his helmet, wasn't exceeding the posted limit, wasn't parked improperly, wasn't following too closely, and wasn't DUI, so he's absolved of legal blame. In the parlance of the report, there was no improper action by driver.

My thought is that if you crash into something, your actions were improper. You might have been well within the posted speed limit, but not decelerating quickly to a speed at which you could stop within the roadway you could see. The devil is a matter of kinetic energy. Most of us have a very overly-optimistic concept of how quickly we could stop the bike. As one rider put it to me recently, *"I can stop my machine on a dime."*

Most of us have seen the test reports, where a bike just like the one you ride was able to stop from 60 mph in somewhere around 120 feet. Sorry to disappoint you, but that's not going to happen for any of us in real life. The main reason is that the tests in the magazines don't include reaction time. At 60 mph, most of us old geezers over age 50 are going to squander about 100 feet just thinking, *"Oh, shoot!"* and reaching for the lever. It might take more than 250 feet to bring the bike to a stop.

Yeah, it's hard to swallow, but that's the reality. Let's simply note that the first part of being a really good rider is to develop your control skills by practicing the right tactics over and over until they become automatic.

Impairment

Historically, motorcyclists have been more willing than other vehicle operators to ride after drinking alcoholic beverages. Over the years we've gained a reputation for riding under the influence.

I suspect that the big issue with alcohol is degraded judgment. One or two beers might not seem like a big problem, but even a small amount of alcohol can affect your judgment in operating a motorcycle, choosing an appropriate speed, or becoming aware of a dangerous situation.

I wonder why reports such as that from Oklahoma don't rate alcohol very high on the list of contributing factors. If motorcyclists truly are separating alcohol and motorcycling, I'd be ecstatic. But the Oklahoma numbers don't ring true to me. According to NHTSA Traffic Safety Facts 2010, motorcyclists with blood alcohol level (BAC) of .01 or higher accounted for 36% of motorcycle fatalities. I suspect that it's a matter of accident investigations not being comprehensive enough. The accident report asks for data that's easy to obtain. Was the rider wearing a helmet? Was the rider properly endorsed? Was the rider's BAC over the legal limit? Was the rider's speed within the speed limit or excessive? I suspect that it's a matter of riders who were not legally intoxicated being listed as having no alcohol involvement.

I'm suspicious that state accident investigations are overlooking low (but legal) BACs or drugs that affect judgment. If you're impaired, you won't be able to fully access your control skills, or really comprehend what's happening around you.

In any case, I urge you not to ride with any alcohol in your system, and if you are on a group ride where someone consumes alcohol, separate yourself from that group.

Situational Awareness

To avoid riding into a crash, it's essential to use the conscious part of your brain to think about what's going to happen in time to take appropriate action without a lot of drama. Situational awareness doesn't come automatically. You may need to learn how to look, and what danger looks like. It's important to scan the situation ahead and all around to comprehend what's happening, and then predict what's going to happen. You can decide to adjust your cornering line or speed, and forward that thought to your subconscious. For example, if that corner ahead appears to be off-camber or a decreasing radius, you can just command your subconscious muscle memory to slow the bike to a speed appropriate for a tight turn, without a lot of wasted brainpower.

Developing your awareness of the unfolding situation may take some effort. You may need to practice scanning techniques, memorize common crash scenarios, and perhaps do some commentary riding. The rule of thumb is to continuously scrutinize the situation within the next 12 seconds—the roadway you'll be covering within 12 seconds at your present speed. Think of casting your attention out 12 seconds, then reeling it back toward you—like a fisherman casting a fly line. Of course, your attention must also include what's happening on side streets and behind you.

It's also helpful to learn and remember those constantly repeating scenarios that typically lead to collisions. For example, you notice a car on your right that could suddenly pull out into your path. Or, you observe the raised pavement edge created by the highway crew grinding away the old paving. You enter an elk zone, and see the warning lights start flashing. You notice the vehicle ahead slowing for no apparent reason. Once you are aware of the situation, you can take action to get out of the way. You can brake lightly approaching a possible intruder to shorten your stopping distance, or position the bike to cross the edge trap without sliding out.

Since developing your awareness of the situation is largely a mental activity, it helps to study the subject off the bike as well as while riding. Books, lectures, magazine articles, and Internet forums can provide valuable lessons.

If you can work on the above four crash factors, you will go a long way toward managing your risks. And if you would like to dive into the statistics, I suggest those from NHTSA as the most comprehensive and accurate. Do an Internet search for "NHTSA traffic safety facts" and access the latest year.

Suggestions for Managing Danger

- If you're just thinking about getting into motorcycling, or you are mentoring a new rider, be realistic about the potential dangers. Come to grips with the risks, your own willingness to accept the risks, and your attitude about managing the risks. If you or your protégé don't want to become a highly proficient rider, or if the dangers are just unacceptable, or if motorcycling just makes you nervous, hang it up.
- Absolutely separate drugs and riding. The average sober motorcyclist may be 30 times more likely to die in a motorcycle crash than the average passenger car occupant. But a rider under the influence of alcohol or drugs jacks the risks up way higher. It's not just alcohol, but medications that degrade vision, judgment, muscle control, and reaction time. If you're over 65, recognize that prescription drugs can be a big factor in increasing the danger.
- Develop your situational awareness to a high level. Train yourself to scrutinize the situation as far ahead as you can see

details. Learn what trouble looks like, what to do about it, and take control of the situation. My book *"Proficient Motorcycling: The Ultimate Guide to Riding Well"* is a good source of information about reoccurring traffic, road, and surface hazards.

- Practice the correct control skills to gain the muscle memory to control your machine accurately without having to think about it consciously. Proficiency doesn't come easily. You need to learn the correct habits. Then it takes thousands of repetitions to make skills automatic. Training courses are available to help you reinforce the correct skills and unlearn bad habits.

If you want to dig a little deeper into the statistics, or see how one state compares to another, go to *http://www.nmcti.org* and click on "data." You can also search online for "NHTSA traffic safety facts" for the latest year. If there has been a big increase in the motorcyclist fatality rate in any state, that's a clue that the state's rider training and licensing programs are focused on something other than saving lives.

THE GOOD RIDER

Chapter 15: Foreign Travel

I've been writing about riding skills for several decades. When I say "riding skills" you might think I'm talking about physical control skills such as counter-steering and braking. Mental skills are even more important, because avoiding crashes is a matter of being aware of what's happening in time to do something about it.

I don't know of any better way to hone your mental skills than to take a motorcycle trip to a foreign country. For the American rider, Canada or Mexico would qualify, but I'm thinking more of places like Ireland or the European Alps, or South Africa, which offer experiences much different than what we encounter in North America. Of course, any motorcyclist who has heard about riding in the Alps will probably start salivating at the idea of tackling those twisty roads over spectacularly scenic mountain passes.

But riding in spectacular surroundings is really just the icing on the cake. The most important payback from foreign travel is jacking up your situational awareness skills. Traveling in a foreign country exposes you to different driving styles, different geography, different money, different food, and different languages. It's a continuous process of figuring out what's happening and dealing with an ever-changing situation.

One huge benefit of foreign travel is gaining insight into how others solve the same problems. That's not just a matter of how citizens of other countries treat the laws and customs, but also how you relate to motorcycling. For instance, a big 1200 cc machine might seem ideal for riding across Montana or Texas, but it would be more of a liability when negotiating switchbacks climbing over a mountain pass, or splitting traffic near a big city. The European attitude about motorcycles is to choose the right bike for the task, not necessarily the biggest and fastest machine.

The attitude about motorcycles is typically different than in the U.S. In many countries, other drivers assume that a motorcyclist will pass them. It's not that they are relinquishing the road, they simply know from experience that bikes have the performance to pull off a high speed pass on a twisty road. That's not to say that European drivers are less than aggressive. I can remember one occasion in the French Alps where I had to swerve the bike up against a rock cliff to miss an oncoming Mini in a four-wheel drift around a blind turn. That's an example of maintaining your situational awareness—or risking a fatal collision.

There are many roads in Europe where traffic can be scarce away from the big cities. But you can't let your guard down. On a corner just like this I had to tuck up against the rocks to avoid an oncoming Mini in a four wheel drift.

You can't help but ride and think more aggressively in Europe. Let's say you are headed from Northern Italy into Switzerland, and you've planned to ride three passes on your way to Interlaken, the Simplon, the Furka, and the Grimsel. You might start out at a sedate speed climbing over the Simplon, but by the time you get to the Furka, you start to realize that if you keep toddling along, you're not going to get to Interlaken before dark. So, you ease on a bit more throttle, lean over a bit more, pass a few cars, and by the time you get to the Grimsel you're braking hard for switchbacks and dragging the outside of your boot soles on the pavement. It's not a matter of absolute speed, but getting used to more aggressive riding.

The mountain passes in the Alps are typically well paved, but warning signs are sparse. It's up to you to control the situation, not for the road department to tell you how to ride. Other drivers generally assume that a motorcyclist will pass them.

The most important lesson I learned from Europe is that controlling my motorcycle is primarily my job and I'm responsible for whatever happens, and translate that philosophy into riding in traffic. If a car driver is about to make a sudden left turn across my path, it's my responsibility to see it coming and get out of the way. If someone cuts around the back of a tour bus and crashes into me, it's a costly lesson about staying out from behind big view-blocking vehicles. I'm not going to absolve some careless driver of the legal responsibility, but in a crash it's me who is going to get hurt. So, in terms of my own risks, the responsible party is whoever is holding onto the grips.

I would suggest that an American rider's first foreign trip be to an English-speaking country. There will be plenty of puzzles to solve without having to translate your questions into a different language. The Isle of Man makes an ideal motorcyclist destination for a variety of reasons. Man is located centrally in the Irish Sea between Ireland, Wales, England, and Scotland. There are lots of twisty roads. It's a very scenic place, with green pastures overlooking the sea, and curiosities such as four-horned Manx Loaghtan sheep, stone castles, giant waterwheels, and operating steam trains. And of course it's the venue for some genuine motorcycle road racing. For more information about the Island, visit *http://www.iomguide.com.*

The Isle of Man is picturesque and worthwhile visiting at any time.

What's really spectacular about road racing on the IOM is that the 37.73-mile course isn't on a track, but on a circuit of public roads. Average lap speeds for professional racers are 120 mph or faster. (Photo, Courtney J. Olive)

The biggest draw for motorcyclists is the Tourist Trophy (TT) which includes a fortnight of road racing contests around a circuit of public roads. It's not a racetrack. Spectators can ride the same 37.73- mile mountain circuit between races, along with local traffic.

The downside of the TT is that it's overwhelmed by European spectators. It's a bit of a multicultural madhouse, which requires you to jack up your situational awareness. Lodging, ferry reservations, etc., must be booked months in advance. Typically, practice week is the last week of May, followed by racing the first week of June. Personally, I prefer going to the Island during Grand Prix (GP) week in August. A new Isle of Man

Festival of Motorcycling started in 2013, which includes the Manx GP. For 2013, the festival schedule is the last two weeks of August.

Man is a magnet for motorbikes, and the Brits like to ride their old machines to the GP. "Reliability runs" are contests to see how close a rider can come to a perfect time for a loop ridden in traffic on vintage and antique bikes. Machines are separated into different age categories.

During GP week you'll see lots of machines like this. It's not out of the question that this gent bought this bike new, or at least inherited it from his father. You'll see rows of Vincents, Velocettes, Nortons, and other British marques parked in front of hotels on the streets of Douglas.

The main reason why I prefer the GP is that it's a bit more laid back than the TT. There are all the trappings of a race week, but fewer race-crazed spectators from the continent. You probably won't need advance reservations for everything. I particularly enjoy the very close/nose-to-tail 500 Classic racing, the vintage "reliability runs," and the variety of machines parked right on the street like a huge outdoor museum.

Man is a beautiful island to visit anytime, but for a motorcyclist it's a lot more entertaining during the TT or GP. Just to whet your appetite, go to *http://www.iomtt.com*. You'll find everything you need to know, including history, maps, schedules, tickets, lodging, and ferry schedules. I'm encouraging you to get yourself to Man ASAP, because every year there is an effort to stop the racing.

If the Isle of Man doesn't infect you with the foreign travel disease, let me suggest some other possibilities. Consider one of the guided tours in Southeast Europe, the Alps, and the Adriatic by Adriatic Mototours. They are far enough removed from the central European motorcycle scene to be more realistically priced. For more information, go to *http://www.smtours.com*. Of course there are hundreds of different tour companies. An Internet search for "Motorcycle Tours Worldwide" should produce plenty of resources.

An organized tour is a good way to get introduced to foreign motorcycle travel. It's more expensive than traveling independently, but you'll have a tour agent pick you up at the airport, answer questions, and do translations as needed. Motorcycle rental, tour guides, lodging, and meals will be arranged for you. And they will transport your luggage from hotel to hotel in a van, which means you don't have to carry all your gear with you on the bike.

The typical motorcycle tour is around 14 days, which is about right for a first visit to a completely new environment. Since you have to go to a great deal of trouble to get yourself to some other part of the world and arrange for a motorcycle to ride, anything less than two weeks seems like a waste. Three weeks may be as much as you can tolerate before the barrage of input gives you mental indigestion.

Europe is bursting with history, and there are so many old castles that your tour guide might just buzz right on by without stopping. That's one of the drawbacks of an organized tour.

Organized tours pack in as much as possible in the minimum time to give you the most bang for your buck. I've participated in many organized tours over the years, both in the U.S. and in foreign countries, and enjoyed them all. But they are almost all whirlwinds. The schedule may call for you to hit the bricks earlier than you would prefer, or to cover more kilometers than you would have liked, or to buzz right on by some interesting castle because there isn't time to stop to take pictures. And unless you make other arrangements, when the tour is over they snatch the keys back, and off you go to the airport to catch your long flight back home.

Some tour operators provide self-guided tours, where they rent you a bike, outline the route, and perhaps book lodging at nice hotels. Often you can rent a GPS with appropriate regional maps. The self-guided approach helps keep costs down, but still gives you a predictable experience, with some flexibility to stop where and when you want.

Many passes in the Alps have cafes where you can stop for coffee and a snack. On a sunny day the customers will be mostly motorcyclists.

The most adventurous plan (and potentially the least costly) is to just rent a bike and head out on your own. When you're riding by yourself you don't need to book rooms in advance at expensive hotels. You can just follow your nose and start looking for a small hotel, *gasthouse*, or bed & breakfast in the late afternoon. Guide books are available to help you locate lodging, which is plentiful in Europe.

On a visit to southern Germany, we discovered that the little café just below the entrance to the Neuschwanstein castle had rooms ("zimmers") available. After the castle closed its doors for the day and the hordes of tourists suddenly evaporated, we were able to ride up the bus road for a great shot of the side most tourists never see.

The first time you see an interesting residence like this, you'll probably stop for a photo. But soon you realize that all the buildings look like this, so you just capture the scene in your memory.

Okay, I appreciate that the idea of heading off to Brazil or Switzerland or South Africa to ride a motorcycle might be a bit much to wrap your brain around at the moment. But if you want to become a better rider, I suggest that foreign travel is an important step. Just let the idea simmer, and see if something starts to boil next year—or five years down the road. Meanwhile, do some low cost research to satisfy your curiosity.

One excellent text that focuses on some great motorcycling roads is *"Motorcycle Journeys Through the Alps & Beyond"* (4th edition) by John Hermann. John outlines routes, towns, and lodging that he knows to be interesting and often outstanding. He also offers some common sense suggestions for people who need a primer on European customs. Another helpful book is Toby Ballantine's *"Motorcycle Journeys Through*

Western Europe." Both books are available from Whitehorse Press at *http://www.whitehorsegear.com.*

My suggestion remains to do some traveling in foreign countries by motorcycle. It's essential to your continued education. And if you live outside of North America, well, come on over to this part of the world!

There are different levels of lodging in Europe, with significantly different prices. A hotel will have lodging plus a restaurant and other amenities. A gasthaus is like a small hotel that might have a restaurant attached. A B&B ("zimmer" in Germany and Austria) is a private residence that rents out their spare bedrooms, and provides a simple breakfast in the morning.

THE GOOD RIDER

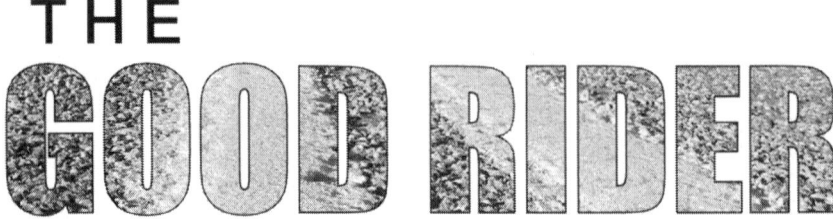

Chapter 16: Riding Unpaved Roads

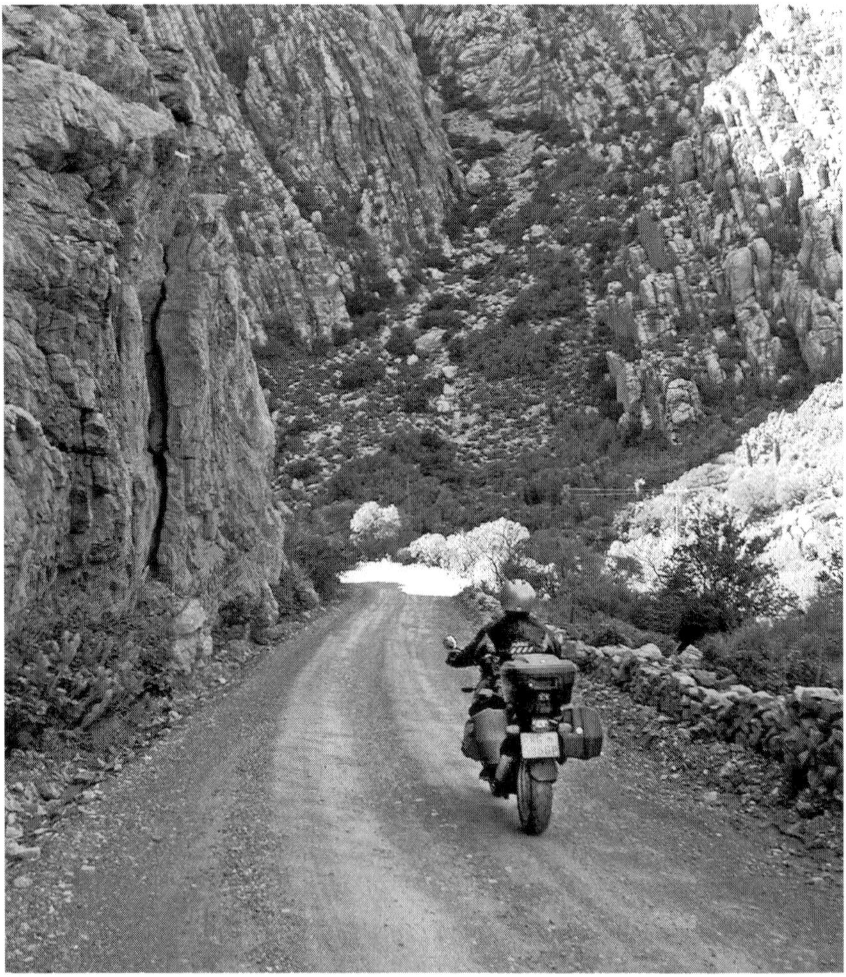

For those of us who ride paved roads most of the time, riding off pavement can be a nervous affair. As we ride paved roads, we get into the habit of depending upon reasonable traction to balance, steer, and brake. When we find ourselves on an unpaved road, it's immediately obvious that the bike doesn't respond the way we expect.

For instance, steering and balancing aren't as easy, because the reduced traction of the front tire means that pushing on the grips doesn't result in the bike quickly responding. If you attempt to control direction by pushing on the grips, the front wheel may turn, but it may not cause the bike to lean, at least not as quickly as you expect. Even a very experienced street rider can be unnerved by this steering vagueness.

Of course, tensing up on the grips doesn't help. I can remember riding on a gravel road for the first time. The bike started drifting wide toward the berm of sand and gravel at the outside of the turn. When I attempted to correct by counter-steering, it felt as if the front tire were going to slide out, and I didn't want *that* to happen. So, I allowed the bike to keep easing over closer and closer to the deep stuff, while I panicked. Fortunately for me, the corner straightened out before I hooked the front tire in the berm and washed out.

After a few excursions on the dirt, I began to figure out what was going on. Riding on street tires is a big part of the problem. Street tires just don't have enough grooves and knobs to get a grip on a loose surface. The first lesson for me was that the throttle is just as helpful at controlling direction as steering the handlebars. Other lessons followed, and I eventually learned to negotiate a dirt road without a lot of drama. That's not to say I *like* dirt, but rather that I can do dirt when needed. I've ridden Forest Service roads in the Northwest, desert roads in Southern

California, farm roads in southern Brazil, and unpaved mountain passes in Southern Africa.

During a trip to South Africa, I decided to ride the rented street bike over the Swartberg pass. Even on street tires, I was able to manage the steep gravel road by taking it slowly and choosing the most tractable surfaces.

In September 2008, I was on my way to join Fred Rau for one of his organized Southwest tours. I had a spare day, and decided to head southeast on Soda Lake Road, a somewhat remote road in a valley about halfway between Atascadero and Bakersfield. I was on a BMW R1150

GS dual-sport machine appropriate for such a situation—except that the bike had tires that were more street oriented. The bike was fully loaded with all my gear for a three week trip, and I was alone.

The northwest end of Soda Lake Road is nicely paved, and I enjoyed being off by my own far away from the craziness of California traffic. I knew the southeast half of the road was unpaved, and I was relieved to discover that it was well graded and mostly free of deep gravel or soft sand. But just a mile or two short of the southwest end, I hooked the front tire in a soft sand berm and crashed. It took me two days to get back on the road, and the experience permanently colored my thoughts about what we call adventure travel.

I was relieved to find the unpaved half of Soda Lake Road was hard packed and reasonably smooth, but I failed to predict that there would be a soft sand berm created by the desert wind that would allow my front tire to hook and spit the bike off into the sagebrush.

I awoke gasping for breath after the crash, and snapped this photo. With a cracked rib and a sprained shoulder I couldn't get the bike upright even after unloading all the gear. It was an expensive lesson about not traveling alone on remote roads.

Let's acknowledge that dirt riders—even very good dirt riders—crash once in a while. Dirt riders know that crashing goes with the territory. That's why they wear super-heavy offroad boots, knee braces, spine protectors, armored gloves, and so forth. I chuckle at those BMW ads showing a monster 1200 cc GS launching off a sand dune and flying through the air, because even the professional riders involved in such photo shoots may crash the bike a few times. Of course during a photo shoot, there will be lots of muscle handy to help get the bike upright, and perhaps even someone with medical knowledge to tape up the rider's sprains.

Speaking for myself, I'm not about to go leaping off sand dunes on a $20,000 machine. For me, those adventure travel ads are sales hype—and they are working. The BMW GS models are hot sellers, and there are several companies producing every possible accessory anyone would need to build a durable adventure travel bike. There are lots of adventure riders around who love to tackle the back roads, and I know some of the serious riders who have ridden around the world, crossing such remote areas as Siberia and the Atacama Desert. I admire the perseverance and skill of serious adventure riders, but I'm not one of them.

I used to own a Suzuki DR350, a lightweight single-cylinder machine with knobby dirt tires. I had plans to take the DR out on local logging roads in the mountains, and perhaps take it on some organized dual-sport adventures. But there were always other priorities that got in the way. So, when I did take the DR for a spin, it was more often on paved roads, running errands such as picking up some plumbing fittings or checking the mail. I also had a BMW R100/Ural sidecar rig, with off-road wheels and serious knobby tires. I'm willing to do things on a sidecar outfit that I just don't have the nerve to do on a two-wheeler.

Here's my point: if I'd been riding the knobby-equipped DR or the airhead sidecar rig on Soda Lake Road, I probably wouldn't have crashed. But of course, neither the DR nor the airhead rig would have fun for the long superslab transits from Washington to California, or through Nevada to Utah. Theoretically, the big 1150GS could do it all. I say theoretically because there are some real life concerns that enter the picture. For example, what do you do when you crash or break down or run out of fuel on some remote road?

A dual-sport machine such as this IMZ-Ural is great fun on unpaved roads, but it would be best to transport it rather than attempt to drive it cross country on the superslab.

Over in Escalante, Utah, I met two BMW dirt riders on 650 cc machines. They had just ridden through from Glen Canyon on a desert track I would love to have ridden myself, but not on a fully loaded GS with a combined weight of maybe 1,000 pounds. The riders were smart on several counts: they were on machines more appropriate for dirt roads, they were riding together, and they were equipped for desert travel with food, water, GPS, and emergency supplies. The lesson for us all is that adventure travel on dirt back roads demands a well-equipped machine, desert supplies, and a traveling companion to help pick up the pieces if things don't go as planned.

I often travel by myself, and would be tempted to head off on remote roads from time to time if I were riding an adventure travel machine like the BMW GS. But after that Soda Lake Road crash, I decided to change my style, and sold that bike the next spring. There's no point in riding a big dual-sport machine if it's not appropriate to head off by yourself on some remote dirt road. I'm at the point in life where I don't have the energy to do what I used to do, and I can't afford the results of little adventures such as crashing, either in terms of physical injuries, or in terms of doctor and towing bills.

That's not to say that I would stop the bike because of a dirt detour on the highway, or some wet grass at a rally site. I think we should all know how to negotiate a few yards—or perhaps a few miles—of ground that's not hard-surfaced.

My first suggestion for those who are still paranoid about taking a street bike on dirt is that practice makes perfect. The only way to come to grips with riding on dirt is to ride some dirt. You could take your current street machine out on some unpaved roads, but it makes more sense to borrow a proper dirt bike with knobby tires—something light enough that you can easily pick it up from a spill.

If you do decide to head out on some dirt road, make arrangements with a fellow rider to go along with you. Not only does that add a social component to the deal, but if there is a problem there are some extra muscles and brain cells to help solve it.

I highly recommend taking a formal off-pavement class. You'll have the guidance of instructors who have the training to help you absorb the necessary knowledge and skills.

Many of the organized schools also provide motorcycles and riding gear. For a list of off-road training schools in the U.S., go to *http://www.amadirectlink.com/roadride/riderresc/schools.asp*

If you just want to ease into a bit of dirt riding on your road machine, here are some pointers:

Get your weight off the saddle and supported on the foot pegs. If your machine is a cruiser style with forward-mounted pegs or boards, standing on the pegs isn't easy or practical. But if your machine allows standing on the pegs, get used to that style of balancing. With your weight supported on the foot pegs, you can more easily lean the bike independently of your body. You'll notice that dirt riders spend most of their time on the pegs, not sitting on the saddle.

You can practice standing on the pegs while on pavement. I suggest finding some vacant parking lot where you can practice away from traffic. Get the bike in a straight line at 20 mph or less, and just stand up. Tuck your knees against the tank to hold your position. Keep practicing, and ride slower and slower. When you master riding the bike slowly in a straight line while standing on the pegs, try making a slow circle. And when you get that down, practice a figure 8 while standing on the pegs.

After you've practiced standing on the pegs, try the same maneuvers while counter-leaning. That is, when making a left circle, place your weight mostly on the right foot peg. Then ride straight ahead with your weight on the right peg, then with your weight on the left foot peg.

When you've mastered counter-leaning, try hanging off on the other side. Place your weight on the left peg and make a left circle. Weight the right peg and make a right circle. This is preparation for shifting your body weight around to keep the bike perpendicular with the surface, as for making a turn on loose gravel.

Remember that humans tend to steer our motorcycles in the direction we are looking. So, when you're making a tight left circle, pivot your head around to the left and look toward the other side of the circle. Avoid looking down at the ground in front of your front tire—unless that's where you want to land.

After you've practiced the slow-speed-standing-on-the-pegs maneuvers, take the bike out to an unpaved road. Ride it standing on the pegs, weighting the pegs to keep the bike vertical. Try easing on short bursts of throttle to help get the bike turned. Easing on a bit more power helps the rear tire to drift sideways, pointing the bike in the opposite direction. That is, if the bike is leaned over slightly to the left, a little throttle will cause the rear end to drift right—which points the bike left. That's what we mean by "steering with the throttle."

I suggest not attempting to use your boots as skis to keep a bike upright on slick or loose surfaces. First, the bike will be less stable with your feet off the pegs. Second, if you happen to drag your foot under the foot peg you can sprain or even fracture your ankle. A bike is balanced by counter-steering, shifting your weight on the pegs, and by throttle control when turning. If your tires don't have enough traction to keep the bike upright, it's not likely your boots will do any better.

THE GOOD RIDER

Chapter 17: Are You Fit for Duty?

Most experienced riders know the importance of keeping the motorcycle maintained. Even with today's very reliable machines, you can't expect them to perform well without routine maintenance. But what about you, the rider? Do you evaluate yourself before every ride, and decide whether or not you are fit for duty today? And do you do routine maintenance on your body?

Vision

Until we experience vision problems, it's hard to comprehend how much we rely on our eyes. But even normal eyes have some quirks that effect our motorcycling. For example, all eyes have small blind spots. The blind spot of the left eye will be off to the left. The blind spot of the right eye will be off to the right. The blind spots aren't obvious, because with two good eyes, both eyes together will give you the whole picture. What's more, the brain fills in any missing information. The brain will even fill in a blind spot with the expected background.

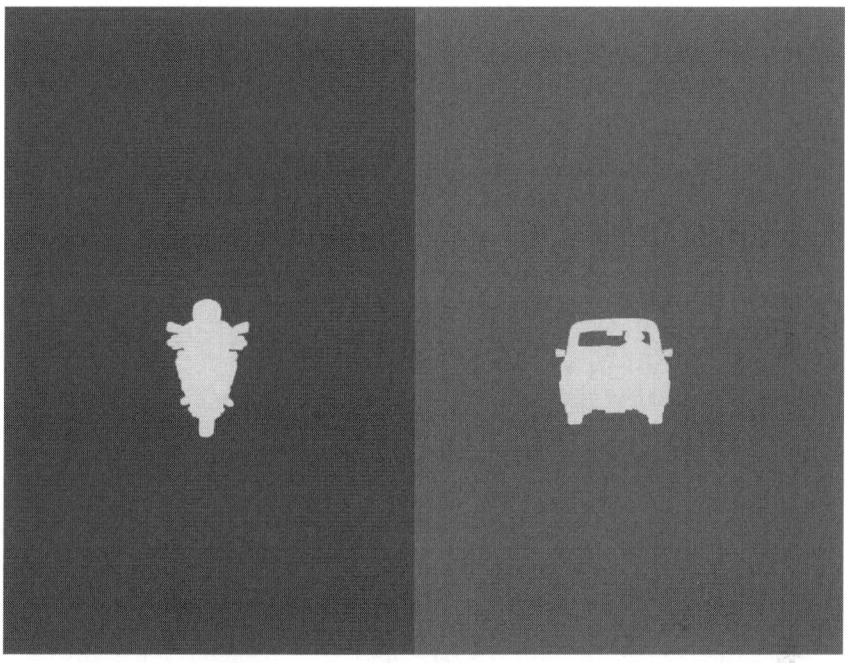

*This image needs to be at least 6 inches wide to work and you need the color version which you can download at http://www.soundrider.com/resources/blind_spot.jpg.
Hold your hand over your left eye, focus your right eye on the motorcycle, and pull the image closer. The car will disappear, and the brain will automatically fill in the area of the car with the surrounding background color. Hold your hand over your right eye, focus your left eye on the car, and pull the image closer. The bike will disappear and the brain will fill in the background color.*

The point of this is that it's your brain that creates the images you see. Not only is it normal to miss things that are in view, you may see things that aren't there. Riding in traffic, you could have a blind spot in the same position as that left-turning car, or that pothole in the pavement. Or, you might not expect to see a car about to pull out of an alley, so your brain fills in the space as vacant. If you'd like more information about this, search the internet for "blind spot test."

Even in healthy eyes, your vision may be slightly nearsighted or farsighted; or portions of what you see can be distorted or blurred. Such problems can usually be solved with corrective lenses, either glasses or contact lenses.

The bad news is that the lens in the eye starts to harden by about age 40, reducing your ability to focus close up. So, as you age past 40 or 45, you'll typically have more trouble adjusting your focus. For example, it may take longer to focus from the road ahead down to the instruments, and then back to the situation. At night, older eyes typically have more trouble with the glare of oncoming headlights, and it takes longer to adjust from light to dark, or dark to light, which makes night riding more of a liability. If you can handle some additional bad news, smoking, diabetes, high blood pressure, hypertension, and fatty diets all have a negative affect on vision.

Because I am diabetic, I have my eyes examined every year by an ophthalmologist. Those are physicians specializing in the eyes. Sure, you can visit an optician and get prescription lenses, but it's important to have an ophthalmologist check for developing eye problems such as glaucoma (blurred vision) cataracts (clouded vision) or macular degeneration (distorted images or blind spots in central vision).

Hearing

Lots of us have some hearing loss. My motorcycling career has spanned 46 years, and for the first 30 it wasn't common knowledge that wind noise was a big problem. When I first heard about hearing protection I wasn't interested. My attitude was, *"Real motorcyclists don't need earplugs."*

The turning point for me was a discussion with an audiologist. I explained that I'd been riding motorcycles for many years and hadn't noticed any hearing loss. The audiologist responded that he loved tough bikers like me, because we generated a lot of business for him fitting hearing aids. These days I wear earplugs on every ride, and I'd like to convince you to do the same.

Like most parts of the human body, the ear is a bit more complex than it looks from the flabby side. Those big exterior funnels focus sound waves into the ear canal, down to the ear drum. The ear drum jiggles a set of tiny bones in the middle ear that amplify the movement and transfer the vibrations to a snail-shaped organ (the cochlea) that generates electrical nerve impulses to the brain. The cochlea is lined with tiny hairs that respond to different frequencies. But when the sound vibrations are too great, the hairs get yanked back and forth so violently that some get broken off. As more hairs break away, you lose hearing in that frequency.

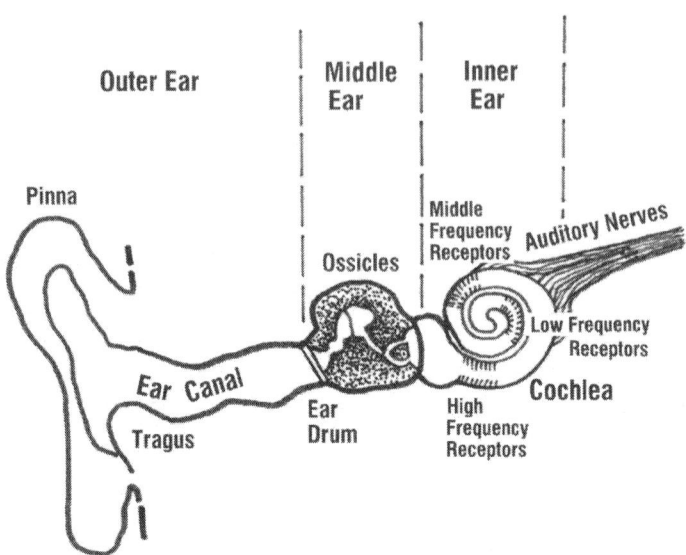

Sound is detected by tiny receptor hairs lining the snail-shaped cochlea. Very loud noises can snap off a receptor hair, degrading the ability to hear sounds in that frequency.

Noise is usually measured in decibels (dB) and weighted on various scales. "A" refers to the human hearing scale. So, for measuring noise in human terms, the loudness scale is dB(A). 100dB(A) is about ten times louder than 90 dB(A) because the dB scale is logarithmic. Every 3dB *doubles* the level. Really noisy power tools such as planers and routers generate about 100dB(A). At 80 mph, wind noise is around 10dB louder than a router cutting through a board.

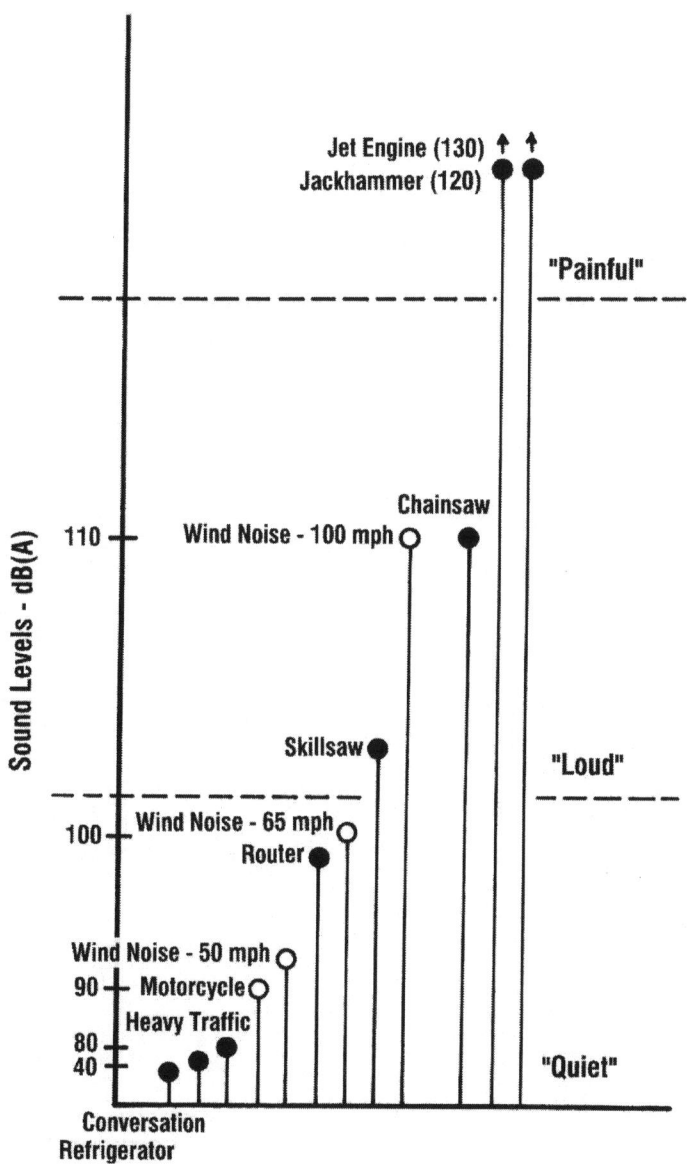

Wind noise at 65 mph is slightly louder than a router cutting through a board. Note that the dB scale is logarithmic, not linear. Every 3dB doubles the level.

Chapter 17: Are You Fit for Duty?

Sounds can also be measured by frequency, usually measured in cycles per second, called "Hertz" (Hz). Researchers have found that wind noise is mostly in the low frequencies below about 300 Hz. Wind noise drops off rapidly above 1,000 Hz.

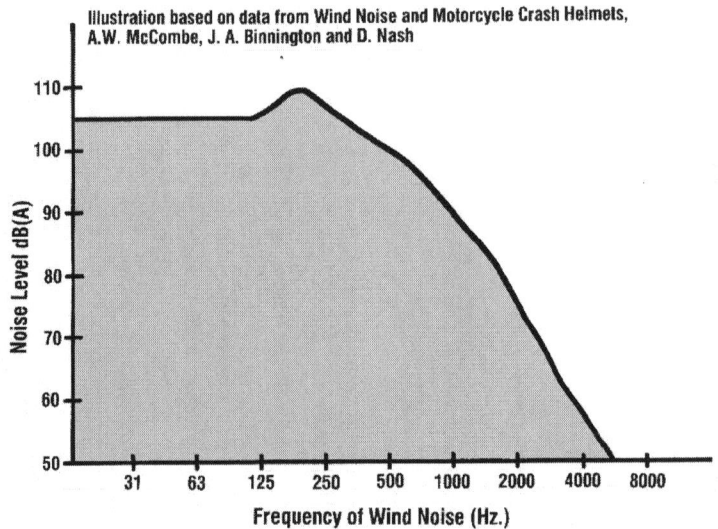

Wind noise is mostly at low frequencies, more like a rumble. For some reason our brains don't register low frequency rumbles as being loud.

Yeah, but doesn't a helmet reduce the noise?

Some helmet manufacturers advertise a helmet as being quieter, mostly as a result of shapes that reduce buffeting. Some helmets also reduce noise, and can strangle a whopping 25dB at frequencies above 4,000 Hz. But remember, wind noise is loudest down in the low-frequency range, under 1,000 Hz. That means a helmet might reduce the scream of a loud sport bike or a diesel turbo, yet do little to reduce wind noise.

Hearing protection doesn't need to be expensive. There are cheap "throwaway" foam ear plugs that can reduce noise by about 30dB in the wind noise frequencies. In real-world terms, that means you and I can reduce noise levels in our ears to safe levels.

When I first started researching wind noise, I thought it was simply a matter of preventing hearing loss. But then I went on an aggressive ride through gusting cross winds without earplugs, and realized halfway through the ride that I was really fatigued. It wasn't just fighting the crosswind, I was also fatigued from the noise. And I know that fatigue lengthens reaction time. I made sure I inserted the plugs for the flip-flop.

Occasionally, I forget to insert my earplugs, and then realize the mistake as I get the bike up to speed. The temptation is to tolerate the noise until the next rest stop, but that adds to the cumulative noise damage and fatigue. So if I take off and then realize I've forgotten my plugs, I'll pull over at the next safe spot to remove my helmet and insert the plugs.

It's important to get the earplugs inserted correctly. The trick for getting plugs stuffed into your ear canals is to roll the plug between your fingers to get it squeezed into a smaller diameter, then quickly insert it while pulling up on the ear with the other hand. If the plug doesn't want to stay in, it might not be inserted far enough, or your ear canals are an odd shape. Some people have "corkscrew" ear canals. If you just can't seem to get plugs to go into your ear canals, you may need custom molded plugs.

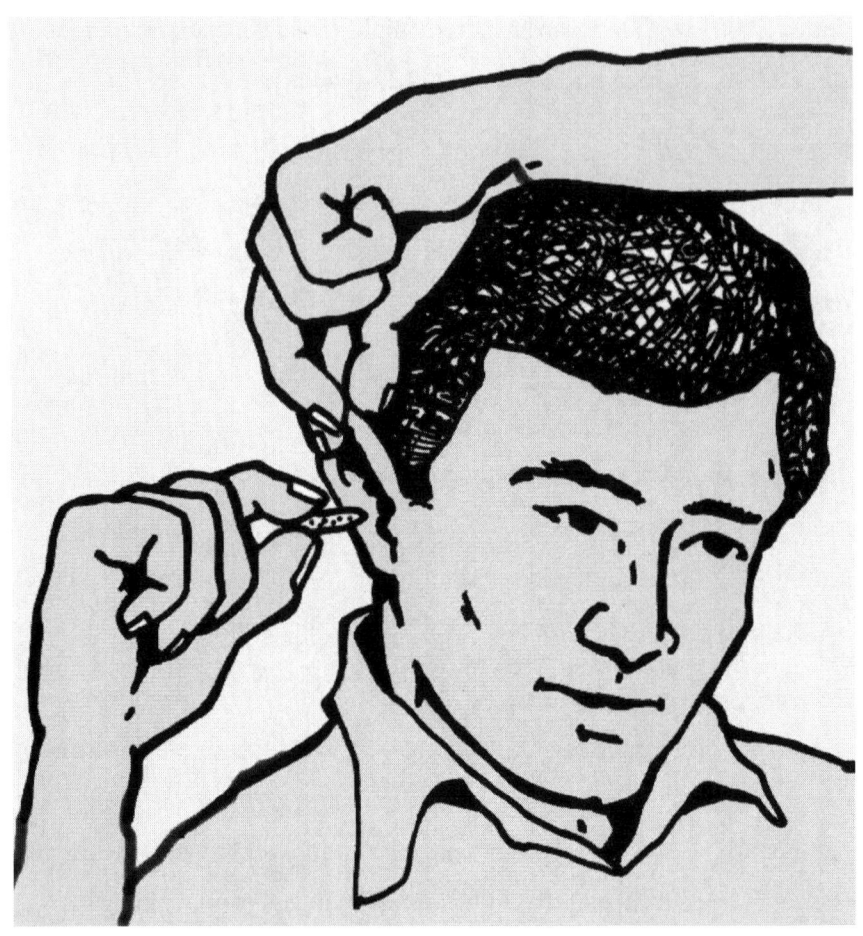

The trick to inserting a foam earplug is to roll it between your fingers to get it squeezed smoothly into a smaller diameter, then insert it while pulling up on the outer ear with your other hand.

Familiarity with the Machine

A big part of your fitness to ride is being familiar with the machine you'll be riding. Some of us have more than one bike, or we may occasionally swap bikes with another rider. You might be very capable of handling the unfamiliar machine in normal circumstances, but if a hazard suddenly appears, your muscle memory might be wrong for the machine you're riding. I managed to crash a borrowed sport bike myself in 2010, attempting to avoid a collision with a junk truck. I squeezed a bit too hard on the brake and flipped the bike end over end, splatting myself onto the pavement. It was a painful reminder that skills need to match the bike I'm riding.

Whenever you will be riding a machine that's unfamiliar to you, it would be wise to do some practice maneuvers on it early in the ride. The same goes for a brand new motorcycle.

Average Age: 49 and Increasing

Age definitely affects our fitness to ride a motorcycle. All the results of aging make it harder to control the bike and the situation, including physical strength, balance, eyesight, hearing, and mental processing speed. The situation is that the average age of motorcyclists is going up. Motorcyclists are growing older, while fewer young people are getting into motorcycling. Back in 1990, the average age of a motorcyclist in the U.S. was 26.9. By 2010 the average age was 49, increasing about 6.5 years every ten.

It's not uncommon to find riders at motorcycle events who are in their 60s or 70s. David Hough (left) and Clement Salvadori (right) might appear to be "old bikers" but neither of us would qualify for oldest rider at a typical motorcycle rally.

Most people are at their physical peak at about age 22. Typically, by about age 60, most of us notice our vision has gotten fuzzier, our hearing is less acute, our balance is wobblier, our joints are less flexible, and our reflexes slower. After about age 70, it's common to experience health issues that call for a change in diet, medications, or invasive surgery. If we manage to hang in there past age 80, health issues will likely take precedence over motorcycling.

Remember that medications affect your thinking and vision as well as your physical systems. So if you've been taking prescription medications, especially pain meds, be suspicious of any self-judgment that *"I can do this."* It might just be the pills talking.

One big problem for older motorcyclists is that the aging body is less able to recover from injuries. The older rider who arrives at the ER typically faces a longer stay and more complications because of medical baggage such as cardiac problems, diabetes, arthritis, or emphysema.

It's appropriate to consider your fitness for the ride when you're younger, but as you age it's much more important. Slamming into the pavement at age 70-something really hurts, and the injuries tend to linger on. Whatever your age, it's important that you maintain your body and mind, evaluate your fitness for the ride before you fire up the motorcycle, and be very aware of the symptoms of any medical issues.

THE GOOD RIDER

Chapter 18: Riding Gear

A few years ago during a cross-country transit, I stopped at a little cowboy town in eastern Montana. As I was finishing my dinner at the local restaurant, a motorcycling couple came in. To be polite, I stopped to socialize on my way out. After some preliminary chatter, they explained that they had been riding west for several days. I couldn't help but notice that the male rider's face, neck, and arms were severely sunburned. I mentioned that he could use more sunscreen before the next ride. His companion quickly replied, *"Oh, he always looks like that."*

That comment motivated me to look them over a little more carefully. They were wearing the standard biker costume of jeans and T-shirts, and they hadn't draped any jackets, gloves, or helmets on the chairs as they sat down. Outside, as I walked by their big American cruiser, I didn't see any riding gear hanging off the machine. Apparently these riders just get on the bike and ride. If it's daytime, they get sunburned. If it rains, they get wet. They didn't seem to comprehend that the human body doesn't take well to sun, wind, rain, hostile temperatures, flying gravel, or yellow jackets.

To me, they appeared like aliens, unaware of how the earth's environment can kill you slowly— or quickly. It's not just a matter of protecting your skin from abrasions. There are other equally serious issues such as skin cancer. It just seems obvious to protect my body from hostile environmental conditions. I'm mostly associated with BMW riders, and almost all BMW riders wear *All the Gear All the Time* (ATGATT). So, I've come to believe that wearing riding gear and protecting yourself from environmental hazards is what serious motorcyclists do. That's why it's such a shock for me to see riders without gear.

I really have trouble understanding why some people ride without any protection. Is it a cultural issue? Does peer pressure keep someone from wearing gear? I have to suspect that if a rider isn't too sharp about obvious stuff like sunburn and dehydration, they probably aren't too clever about riding skills. I'm not especially concerned about adults suffering pain as a result of their folly, unless I have to help pay for it. I guess I'm more concerned about the big picture—the increasing numbers of nasty and fatal crashes in the U.S. that are driving up medical bills and attracting government attention.

In a typical year there are more than 100,000 motorcyclists injured nationwide. We're not talking just sunburn here. 29,000 of those injuries are "incapacitating"—meaning that some riders needed to be screwed, glued, and stapled back together, and some are spending the rest of their lives in wheelchairs.

I'm not suggesting that proper riding gear could have done much to prevent someone from being killed. But I know that riding gear plays an important role in *preventing* crashes. And if you prevent the crash, you also prevent crash injuries.

For instance, controlling a bike at speed is a lot harder with grit or sawdust blown into my eye, or a yellow jacket splatting into my cheek, so I favor a wraparound face shield on my helmet. I know that noise fatigue, mental distraction, temperature, and age each add reaction time. So as I grow older I ride less under strenuous or unfavorable conditions, and I take steps to control noise, fatigue, and dehydration.

Before the ride, I smear my face and neck with sunscreen. It's not just that I don't want to discover a nasty cancerous patch on my face five years down the road, but that I don't want to be distracted by a sunburned neck rubbing on my jacket collar later in the day. Likewise, I wear earplugs, not just to protect my hearing from wind noise damage, but also to reduce fatigue and keep reaction time shorter. I use evaporative cooling in hot conditions, because I've seen riders who have gotten overheated and spent the next week crawling between bed and toilet trying to get their fluids under control. I don't want to have to delay my trip for preventable medical reasons.

Body Armor

I don't think I'm paranoid about road rash, but I feel more comfortable wearing gear. It's not just a matter of crash padding, but protecting myself from sun, wind, rain, flying debris, and insects. Back when I first started riding, there wasn't much in the way of motorcycling gear other than leather jackets and boots. My first riding jacket was an overstocked police jacket, and my helmet was a three-quarters Buco with a flat competition face shield. It took a few years for suppliers to start manufacturing better gear, and for me to figure out why good gear is worth what it costs.

I still have the Langlitz leather jacket and pants that were custom made for me in 1981, and I wear them on day trips in good weather. Competition-weight leather is still the most abrasion-resistant material for riding gear, but leather has its disadvantages for long-distance motorcycle travel, including the difficulty of making it waterproof, and the buildup of odor. Some leathers are supposed to be waterproof, but in my experience the only reliable way to waterproof leather is to cover it up with raingear. However, leather is very comfortable, and good quality leather does last for years and years.

Leathers are very abrasion resistant, reasonably comfortable, and long lasting. These Langlitz leathers were custom made for me in 1981, and are still very functional. Over the years I've had one panel replaced. One of the practical features of a Langlitz jacket is the front zipper running up the right side of the neck.

If I wear my leathers, I carry raingear such as this hi-viz two-piece PVC suit. I've cut away the hood and left just a tall collar to keep water out of my neck. The leather boots are insulated Red Wing "Field and Stream" Wellingtons.

For all-around adventure travel, I've been wearing an Aerostich Darien jacket and pants. My Nolan helmet and elkskin gloves are back on the bike.

These days, I most often reach for my Aerostich "Darien" jacket and separate pants. The Darien has removable impact pads at the shoulders, elbows, and knees, and I've added a back protector pad as well. The

"TF3" impact pads are made from dense foam that stiffens itself during a sudden impact. That means it's relatively soft and comfortable, but provides excellent impact protection in the event of a crash.

I find the separates are less likely to leak than a one-piece suit with long zipper closures. The Darien is not advertised as waterproof but my experience is that it's waterproof enough for even a continuous downpour—except for the front pocket zippers. I don't try to waterproof the pocket zippers, I just keep my maps and wallet in plastic bags inside the pockets. I don't carry separate raingear anymore, except when I'm wearing my leathers.

I also carry a self-stowing insulating Darien liner. Aerostich gives you a choice of several liners, with and without sleeves; with or without electric heating elements, and in various weights. The liner is reversible, and is handy for wearing as a light jacket when off the bike.

Lots of BMW riders wear Aerostich, but not everyone prefers it. My advice is to drop in at a big rally and talk to riders about their experiences with different riding gear. I suggest a BMW rally because a high percentage of BMW riders wear good riding gear.

Let me also suggest that price is not as important as fit and quality. You might find some gear at bargain prices, and later discover that it is so uncomfortable you never wear it. You might choke on the price of good, custom-fitted gear, but every time you wear it, you'll know it was worth every penny.

Chaps are very popular with a lot of cruiser riders, but I'm not a fan. First, when the weather turns cold or wet, chaps don't offer much in the way of waterproofing or insulation. And if you find yourself sliding down the road, there is no butt or knee protection. They sure *look* cool, though, walking the streets of Sturgis.

An electric vest helps keep the body core warm, so more warm blood gets pumped to the extremities.

For cold weather, I carry an electric vest. I prefer a sleeveless vest to keep the bulk down. Besides, keeping my body core warm keeps warm blood flowing to my arms and legs. My favorite vest is from BMW, but I know other riders who prefer Tour Master, Firstgear, or Gerbing's. I have a coil cord with a lighted switch to connect my vest to one of the 12V outlets. I've tried heat controllers, but the wiring and controls are bulky and often troublesome. If my vest gets too hot, I just turn it off or unplug it for a while. On my traveling machines, I have multiple 12V outlets with paired Molex and SAE connectors, hot-wired to the battery. That allows a choice of connections for electric vest, battery charger, GPS, tire pump, or whatever.

The Helmet

You don't need a *crash* helmet if you're clever enough to avoid crashes. What's more, even the best helmet can't protect the brain from direct impacts at speeds higher than about 20 mph. But from my perspective, a good helmet does more than offer impact protection for my brain. My helmet provides insulation, waterproofing, and wind deflection; it keeps out most of the flying grit and insects; and it provides a handy mount for a face shield.

I mostly wear a flip-front helmet these days, because I want a helmet that covers my jaw, but I find it almost impossible to put on my glasses through the face opening in a one-piece full coverage helmet—even if I can squeeze my head in without peeling my ears off. A flip-front allows me to put the helmet on without removing my glasses, and then close the front. A flip-front is also handy for situations such as fueling, paying tolls, or taking a drink of water.

The helmets I usually reach for these days are a Nolan N-100 or N-103. I'm more of a "round-head" and Nolan seems to be more of a round-head shape than Shoei or Arai. I like that Nolan helmets have metal latches, not plastic; and that the retention strap has a ratcheting type buckle rather than D-rings. Be aware that helmet manufacturers may change their sizes slightly from year to year. My older Nolan N-100 was a "large." My newer N-103 is a "medium. That's a hint of the importance of trying on a helmet for fit before buying it. I highly recommend buying your helmet from a dealer where you can try on various brands and sizes.

I've heard some riders grouse about a flip front helmet not providing reliable jaw protection. I suspect that's a matter of the latches. I've personally crash tested a couple of Nolan helmets, and the fronts stayed put.

The Nolan flip-front helmets seem to fit my roundish head well. Different models have different features, such as retractable sun visors. I have confidence in the metal latches on the flip front.

I've read advice from helmet manufacturers and others in the industry that a helmet should be replaced every three to five years. That seems a bit conservative to me. I've had some discussions with technical reps at helmet manufacturers, as well as with experts at the Head Protection Research Laboratory. HPRL has tested helmets as old as 20 years, and found most of them still pass the DOT tests. The experts seem to agree that a helmet is still good if the EPS liner is in good condition. So I pay less attention to the age of a helmet, but I do periodically peel back the comfort fabric in my helmets and inspect the EPS liners. If the foam plastic has turned yellow or is starting to disintegrate, that's the end of its useful life. Likewise, if you crash and hit your head, it's time for a new lid.

When looking for a new helmet, I cruise the aisles at the winter bike shows, where there will be a variety of different brands, lots of customer assistance, and perhaps even a show discount. I look for a helmet that feels almost uncomfortably snug, with full head contact with the liner. After a few thousand miles, it will loosen up. When trying on a helmet, I prefer sitting on a bike like mine to see how it fits in my normal riding position, and whether I can see ahead without discomfort.

Neck Protection

I usually wear some sort of neck cover to bridge the gap between helmet and jacket. My favorite is the Aerostich "Wind Triangle," a waterproof, windproof fabric piece that fastens around my neck with hook and loop patches. The bottom point goes inside my jacket. Those of us with thick necks can order the XL size.

I wear an Aerostich "Wind Triangle" to seal the gap between jacket and helmet. The lower point goes inside my jacket. It's windproof and waterproof.

I don't change my gear much for hot weather. Lots of riders believe that taking off insulation cools you down, but whenever air temperature is above body temperature you want to keep your insulation on. When it's really hot you can use evaporative cooling.

For temperatures above 80° F, I add a cooling vest under the jacket, with the air vents unzipped.

If it looks like it's going to be a hot day, I soak the vest and neck cooler in water in a waterproof stuff bag in the morning, so they are saturated and ready to put on later. My evaporative vest is from *http://www.soundrider.com*. I wear a neck cooler that Aerostich calls an Evap-O-Danna ("evaporative bandanna"). It's made of a water absorbent fabric that cools through evaporation. The big advantage of a neck cooler is that it keeps the big arteries to the head from overheating.

The evaporative vest looks like an electric vest, but it's full of crystals that soak up about a gallon of water. As the water evaporates it cools the chest and body core. It works well inside a breathable jacket such as this open weave DIFI, or inside any jacket with the vents open. I keep my riding pants on to help insulate my legs from engine heat.

Gloves and Boots

I prefer leather gloves and boots. The toughest and softest leather is probably goat skin, but it's harder to come by in the U.S. My glove of choice for all-around conditions is natural elkskin with gauntlets. Elkskin isn't waterproof, but it has a natural insulating quality, and it doesn't stretch much when wet. Since leather dye tends to bleed when wet, I prefer the undyed "natural" color, rather than black. For summertime trips, I just let the gloves get wet and then dry out in the wind stream as I ride. For wintertime or serious cold wet conditions, I add a waterproof cover.

There are lots of great motorcycle boots on the market, but I have wide feet, so I have to pass by the (D width) motorcycle boots on dealer shelves, and go to a boot store. My boots of choice for many years have been Red Wing "Field and Stream" in a pull-on Wellington style with a stepped composition sole. "Field and Stream" means the boots are waterproof and insulated. Yes, I wear insulated boots winter and summer, rain or shine. When it's hot, the insulation helps keep my feet from being cooked by the hot pavement and exhaust pipes.

Practicality

Since I wear my riding jacket during every ride, I carry a lot of stuff in the jacket pockets. I realize that carrying hard objects such as a knife or multi tool in the pockets of riding gear could result in injuries during a crash. However, I'm much less concerned with the contents of my pockets than I am with the shape of the fuel tank. In a crash, a lumpy fuel tank with a steep rear end can cause serious damage to the rider's pelvis. If you're thinking about riding a sport bike, I would suggest choosing a machine that doesn't have a steep rise in the fuel tank in front of the saddle.

I use small pouches to better organize what's in my jacket pockets. There's a pouch for skin, lip, and eye protection in the upper left pocket. The right sleeve pocket holds a pouch with tire gauge, penlight, ball point pen, and a thumb drive with medical information. The right chest pocket is big enough for maps plus temporary storage of items such as a camera or sandwich. The left chest pocket is smaller, so I use it for a smaller wallet with just a credit card and some ready cash. That makes it easier to fuel up without having to dig down to my inside rear pants pocket. I've learned the hard way to avoid carrying my full wallet in my outer jacket pocket. If it's raining, I make a point of stowing my travel wallet inside a heavy waterproof plastic bag. That makes it easier to fuel up without having to dig down to my inside rear pants pocket. If it's raining, I make a point of stowing my travel wallet in a heavy waterproof plastic bag.

I've learned the hard way to avoid carrying my main wallet in my outer jacket pocket. If you inadvertently leave your main wallet somewhere-- say lying on top of a gas pump--you could lose everything, including your license. So, I keep my full wallet in an inside pocket, secure and out of sight.

I carry small pouches in various jacket pockets to make it easier to find things.

THE

Chapter 19: Dealing with the Environment

Back at the beginning, I suggested a number of skills that a rider should possess to be considered a good rider, including being skilled at managing different environmental conditions, including hot, cold, wet, dry, windy, and high or low altitude.

Several of us had an opportunity to test our wet weather skills in October 2012, during our 250X250 ride: 250 miles on 250 cc bikes. We had planned a nice little ride from Sequim to Cape Flattery and back, with an overnight stop at Sol Duc Resort. September had been beautifully warm and dry. We had optimistically picked the second weekend of October, hoping the gorgeous weather would last.

It was a bit of a shock when the weatherman forecasted the first major storm of the season blowing in from the west the day of our little ride. It didn't seem like a big deal as we headed west, since it was only drizzling. The reality was that the storm was just winding up to hit us at midday. As we rode farther west on Highway 112 we ran smack dab into a serious gale.

The road surface was coated with leaves and needles. Tree limbs were snapping off and flying through the air to shatter on the pavement. Small lakes appeared in the low spots. Sudden crosswind gusts pushed the bikes around. Our face shields fogged up. The elk that dashed across the road inches ahead of me wasn't part of the weather, but it seemed as normal as dodging falling tree branches.

We made it as far as Clallam Bay before I lobbied to forget Cape Flattery, turn south, and head directly for the hot springs. I know that storms can get really nasty out near the Cape, and it's not unusual for huge trees to come down, blocking the road. Sometimes a big section of the saturated cliffs slides away into the water, taking the road along with it. I didn't want to get the group stranded on the wrong side of a closure for several days.

In retrospect, I wasn't really prepared for the storm. I hadn't brought along my serious wet weather gear. My leather gloves had soaked up a quart of water. My boots were soggy. And more than a little rain had penetrated into my jacket sleeves and collar. Truth be told, hypothermia was not far away.

We all survived, and the decision to not ride the additional miles into the teeth of a gale was probably wise. Part of riding in severe weather is knowing when to fold 'em. But speaking for myself, I should have been more pessimistic about the weather. The KLX 250 ran fine, conservative riding helped me to avoid sliding out on the slippery leaves, and my dry bag did its job. I kept my camera dry in a plastic bag, and never pulled it out. Maybe I should have brought the underwater camera.

Lots of us get lulled into a false sense of optimism when riding into worsening conditions. But bad weather can seriously affect your life and limb. That includes not only wet conditions, but hot, cold, and windy. Yes, we can often cheat the weather by cutting the trip short or taking frequent breaks. But to be a serious traveler, we need to be fully prepared for whatever comes along.

Rain riding can be more serious than it appears, because wet clothing chills down as you ride along. Evaporative cooling is good news for hot weather, and in fact the primary way to survive. But chilled clothing at even 40°F can pull your body core temperature down more quickly than you might suspect. And even if you take a dry break somewhere, wet gloves will still be soggy when you continue the ride. Let's review some thermodynamics to help prepare for the next stormy ride.

When hands, feet, or head get chilled, body core pumps more warm blood to the extremities to help heat them up. But if the core can't keep up with the heat demand, it starts squeezing off the blood supply. If the core starts to cool down (hypothermia) blood flow to the brain is constricted. The effect is similar to being drunk, and it's common for a hypothermic rider to make silly mistakes and bad decisions.

If the wet weather is combined with cold, say rain turning to slush, the problem gets worse, because if my face or hands get coated with ice, the skin can freeze.

If my only choice is to tough it out and continue the ride, it's important to add insulation, and add heat if that's an option. An electric vest can add heat to the body core, tricking it into continuing to pump warm blood to the extremities. One of the other riders was smart enough to wear his electric vest. Why didn't I think to bring my electric vest? Why hadn't I brought along my waterproof boot and glove covers, and maybe a more serious neck protector? Why didn't I remember the veteran trick of buying a newspaper and stuffing it inside my jacket to add insulation? Apparently I need to remind myself of the appropriate survival techniques that I've learned but forgotten.

The big advantage of an electric vest is that it keeps the body core warmer, which keeps warm blood flowing to the extremities, including the brain.

Hot Weather

Hot weather is just as much of a problem as cold weather. Your body core can't stand losing or gaining much heat. When your central organs start to warm up (hyperthermia), it opens up the taps to the extremities, pumping more warm blood out there which hopefully will return cooler. The trouble is, when the ambient air temperature is warmer than body temperature, your skin will just soak up heat from the air. The result can be heat cramps, then heat exhaustion, and eventually life-threatening heat stroke. Taking off your jacket or opening up your jacket vents will only make it worse. More air just means more heat pumped back to the core.

There are two practical solutions for hot weather riding. One is to add insulation to slow down heat transfer from the air to your skin. It may feel hot inside your insulated jacket, but it's not as hot as the desert air. The other practical solution is to use evaporative cooling. A neck cooler is good because it can absorb heat from the big carotid arteries that are exposed to the air between jacket and helmet.

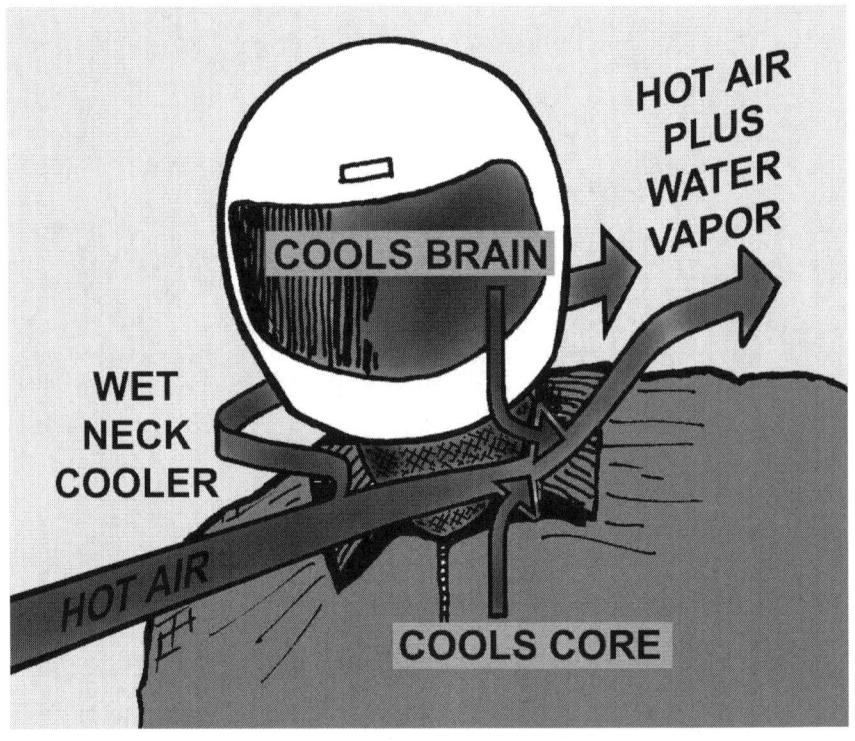

Hot air helps evaporate the water from a wet neck cooler, cooling down both the brain and the core.

An evaporative vest is also good, because it can carry lots of water, and it surrounds the body core. Of course it's important to keep the evaporative coolers wet, which means keeping a water bottle handy. If all the water evaporates, the cooling ceases.

I always get a chuckle out of riders who buy a mesh jacket for an August trip through Death Valley. Yes, the mesh will allow more air though. Hot air, we must note. And more hot air contacting your skin will merely heat it up faster. So, if it's 117°F, a dry mesh jacket will help heat up your skin to 117°F. Unless you're producing lots of sweat, the only way a mesh jacket will help cool you down is to wear an evaporative cooling vest underneath.

Another useful trick for cooling down (if you're riding through civilization) is to load your jacket pockets with ice. On a really hot day, after I've fueled up I buy a bag of crushed ice, and pack it into my jacket pockets. The ice will suck heat away from my skin as it melts, and the ice water will evaporate, helping to cool me down.

Dang Winds

Gusting cross winds are another weather challenge. Riding westbound through the Columbia River Gorge can be a real workout as the gusts push the bike around. Less experienced riders may find gusting cross winds to be confusing and scary, but air does flow predictably. The challenge is to figure out what the wind is going to do, based on the shape of the landscape and other vehicles.

For example, if the wind is blowing over the top of a cut on your right, you can expect it to curl over the edge like the surf crashing onto a beach. Even with a strong wind from your right, it should be no surprise to encounter a curling gust rolling over the edge and bouncing back toward the hill.

When the wind is from your right, it will curl over the top of a cut like a wave crashing on the beach, and it may swirl back toward the hill.

When the wind is from your left, it will curl over and around an oncoming truck, and you should be prepared for sudden turbulence.

Winds through the Columbia River Gorge are almost always west to east, so if you're riding west you can expect headwinds. But you will also encounter cross winds where the wind reflects off of headlands. As you round a cliff on your right, you will encounter a sudden blast of wind from your right.

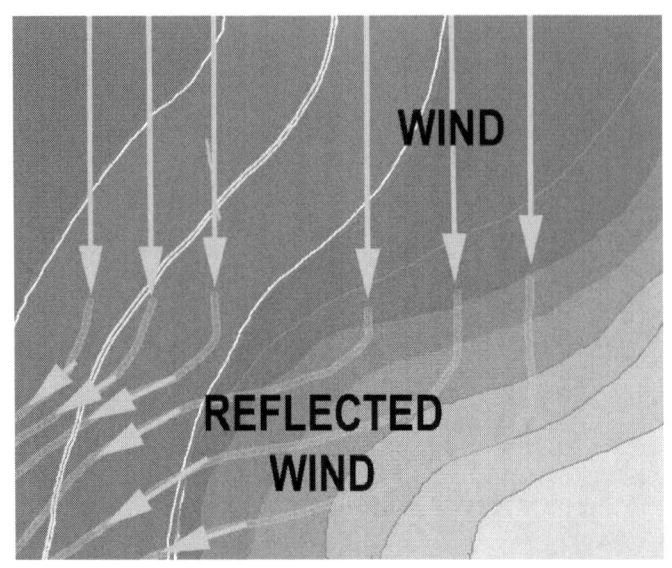

Be aware that wind will reflect off of headlands.

When you are riding into the wind, you should expect a sudden gust from your right as you round the headland.

So even though you mostly can't see the air moving, you can learn to predict what's happening based on the shape of the land, and the positions of other vehicles, bridges, billboards, and trees. The air moves in predictable patterns. What would you expect riding upwind through a tunnel? There might be a steady headwind in the tunnel, until you reach the other end, where there is likely to be a gust blowing from your right due to the shape of the cliff.

When you are riding into the wind, you should expect a steady breeze blowing through the tunnel, and then a sudden cross wind from your right as you exit the other end, where the wind is reflecting off the cliff face.

Once you have an idea of what the wind is going to do, you can prepare to counteract it. What's needed to counteract a strong gust from one side is to immediately roll the bike into the gust. That is, if you round a bluff and encounter a sudden blast from your right, you must immediately press the grips to the right to get the bike leaned over to the right. And when the gust abates, you need to quickly press the grips the other way to get the bike rolled back toward vertical. You're not trying to turn the bike, just roll (lean) it upwind to prevent being blown out of your lane.

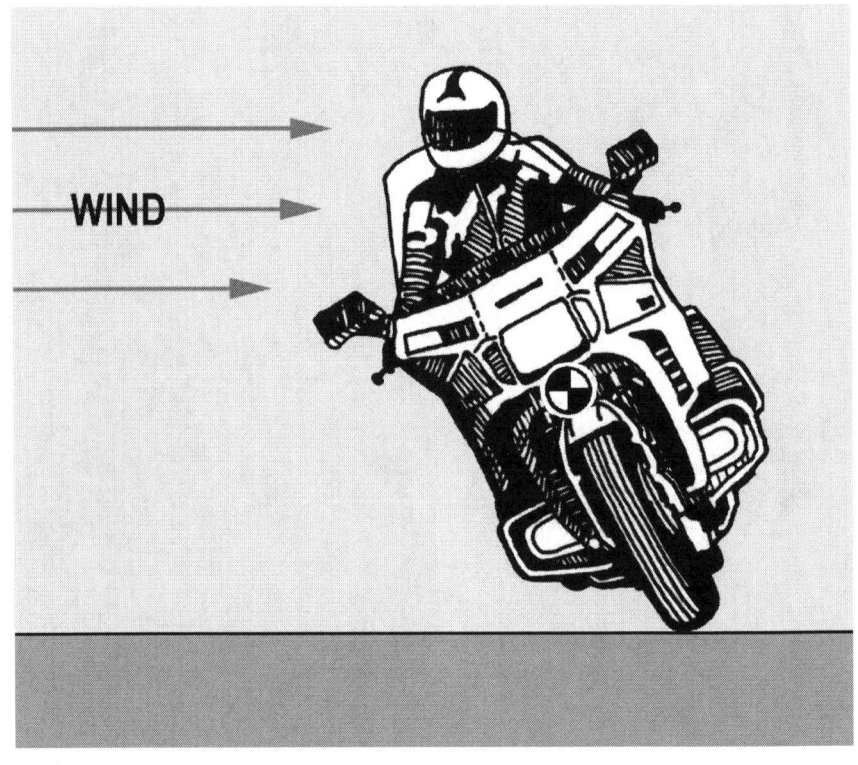

When you are hit by a sudden cross wind, you must immediately press the grips toward the wind to get the bike leaned over. The bike won't necessarily be turning, just leaning into the wind.

Higher Altitudes

Riding at higher altitudes also involves some challenges. First, the air gets thinner with increased altitude. You and your motor will get less oxygen for every breath. Imagine riding up Pike's Peak. On the way up, you may feel a little light-headed. As you climb off the bike at 14,110 feet, you'll probably be gasping for air, and maybe feel like you're about to pass out. It's the scarcity of oxygen at the higher altitude. You may also have noticed that your engine seems sluggish and down on power. That's also because of the reduction in oxygen.

As you gain altitude there are other issues that can work for or against you. Temperature drops with altitude. You might start out at the bottom of the pass at 50° F, and find the temperature at the top is down to 28° F. You can use that to your advantage on a hot day. Choose a road that gains altitude. For example, if you are riding north from Sacramento, and its 115° F temperature, turn off toward Yuba City and head uphill through Lassen Park. Up there, it might be 60° F or even cooler.

Of course, if the temperature is only 40° F down in the valley, you might want to avoid any mountain passes, because there could be a blizzard blowing up on top. Even if it's not snowing on top, the Rocky Mountains are famous for afternoon thunderstorms, lightning strikes, and baseball-sized hail, even during the summertime. Once you understand that thunderstorms usually peak in mid-afternoon, you can plan your July transit of Monarch Pass in Colorado in the morning rather than in the afternoon. By the way, hail and lightning are good reasons to hunker down somewhere. Your rubber tires aren't going to insulate you from a lightning strike.

When you encounter blowing dust, sand, or sleet, it's a good time to get off the road.

When you encounter blowing dust, sand, or sleet, it's a smart idea to get off the road and take a break, especially if you're heading up a mountain pass.

Years ago I was riding through the hills in northeast Oregon heading for La Grande; coming down into a valley there was something really strange going on. It looked like the air was full of tinsel waving horizontally. I couldn't figure it out until about halfway across the valley where I was slammed by the leading edge of a sleet squall. The gust knocked the bike downwind across the centerline, and I just kept it turning, then powered back to a pile of gravel I had just passed. I dropped the bike on its side in the lee of the gravel pile and hunkered down beside it as the wind blasted sleet over us. The memory lingers on to remind me that there are times when you need to get off the bike and hunker down.

And it's not just that your bike might be blown off the road. An oncoming vehicle might be blown into your path. In one situation reported to me, two riders were engulfed in a blinding dust storm with near-zero visibility. They slowed but continued to forge ahead. What the riders couldn't see was an oncoming car being blown across the centerline. One bike missed it, the other hit it.

If you're being blown around and the view is obstructed by a dust storm, you have to assume that other drivers will be wandering over the centerline.

Let's keep that thought in mind about knowing when to fold 'em.

THE

GOOD RIDER

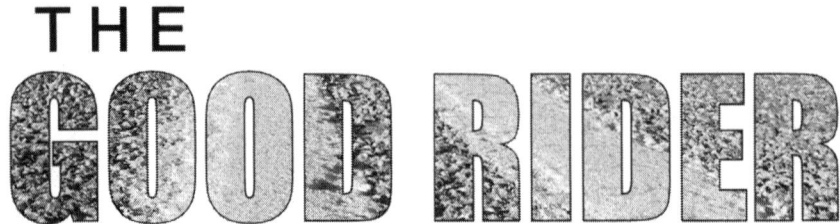

Chapter 20: Riding in Cold Weather

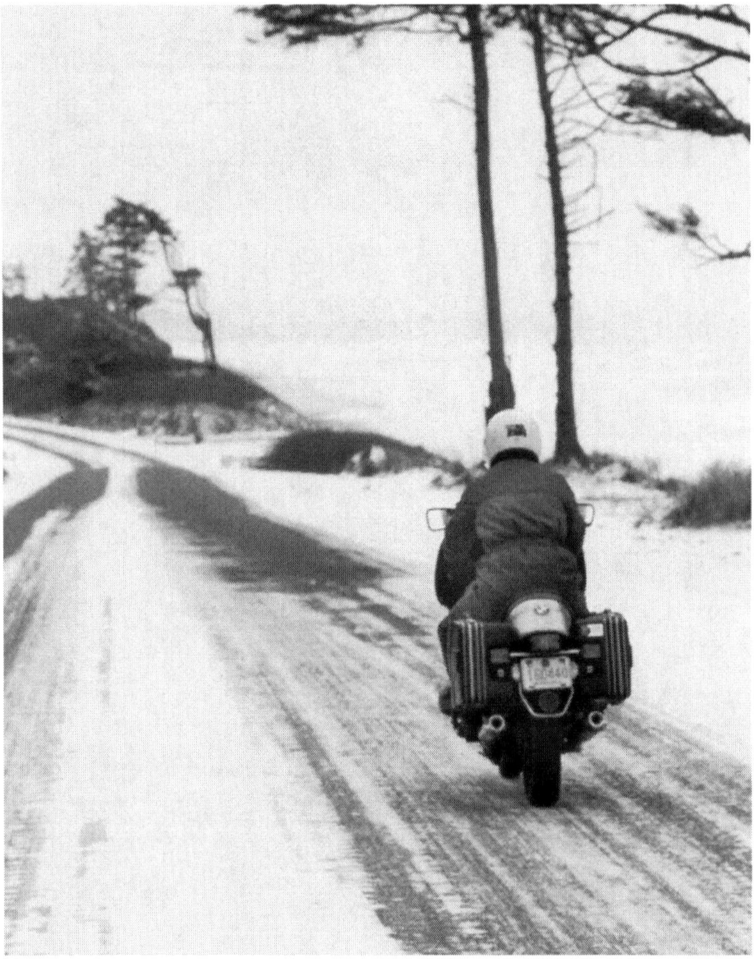

Sometimes you're out for a ride when you get caught by freezing weather. Or maybe you're moving to Vermont, and aren't satisfied with limiting your riding to the short summer season. Let's think through a few suggestions for surviving a cold ride that you didn't predict. Then we'll deal a little more seriously with heading out on a cold ride on purpose.

Turning Back, or Not

There is a lot of wisdom in knowing when to turn around. One year I was ascending the Angeles Crest highway in California the day after Thanksgiving, and was passed at warp speeds by a rider carving corners on a Ducati. But at the first sign of frost in the shadows, the Ducati rider wisely turned around and zoomed back downhill. There's no point in blazing ahead into worsening conditions if you're just out for a fun ride.

But if you're on a cross-country trip and get caught in a storm, it's a different situation. The only sensible option may be to continue ahead. Say you're making a transit across Montana, and get overrun by a cold front blowing down from Saskatchewan. The next warm restaurant is 60 miles away in Lewistown, and the last one was ninety miles back in Circle. That front is going to run over you whether you stop, retreat, or continue, so the only reasonable option is to keep moving toward Lewistown.

Now, when you find yourself in this situation, I want you to remember this: pull over and assess the situation. Okay, its cold, the wind is howling, and sleet is starting to stick to your face shield. But take my word for this: pull over, huddle down in the lee of the bike, warm your fingers on the engine, get out the map, and consider your options. Is it wise to keep going into worsening conditions, or should you beat a retreat? Are there any farms nearby where you could seek shelter? If the only reasonable option is to keep going, what can you do to prolong the onset of hypothermia? What extra insulation can you add under (or over) your riding gear?

When the weather is closing in, it's a good idea to stop and evaluate your options. If your only choice is to keep pressing ahead into a cold front, what can you do to avoid hypothermia?

Staving off Hypothermia

Hypothermia refers to the central body core (heart, lungs, liver, etc.) starting to cool down. The core will do whatever it can to survive, including sacrificing extremities. So, when your core cools down—even a degree—the system squeezes off blood flow to the feet, hands, and head. That will conserve core heat, but also means less oxygen to the brain. As you become hypothermic, your woozy brain loses track of what's happening. At first, maybe it's just stopping the bike without putting a foot down, or cruising off the road into a snow bank, then laughing giddily at the result. It should be obvious that in a hypothermic state, a rider can make serious or even fatal control errors. That's why it's so important to evaluate the situation and take action while you're still able to think clearly.

Insulate the Neck

One of the most important defenses against hypothermia is insulation of the head and neck. Normally the brain gets a major flow of warm blood, which also means it can radiate a lot of heat. The crushable EPS liner in a helmet is similar to a foam ice chest, so that helps insulate the head, even if the blood flow is being slowed. But it's important to close off that gap between collar and helmet. My preference is for a windproof, waterproof covering such as the Aerostich Wind Triangle. For really cold conditions, I may add a balaclava or a neoprene breath guard to double the insulation and redirect my breath away from the face shield. Whatever your choice of neck protection, it's something you need to remember before leaving home.

The head and neck can lose up to 50 % of body heat. That's why it is so important to insulate your neck from the windblast. Even if it's not raining, a rain suit adds an additional layer of insulation.

Survival Tactics

If you have an electric vest with you, get it out and put it on, even if you have to remove your jacket for a moment. The electric vest should be worn over a shirt but under your jacket liner. Got some dirty socks in the saddlebag? Slip 'em on over your gloves. Wrap a spare T-shirt around your neck. If you don't have an electric vest, put on an additional shirt or two, even if they are dirty. If you pass a newspaper rack, buy a paper and stuff it into your pants legs. Got raingear? Put it on for a little added insulation. The point is, take steps to add insulation while your brain is still functioning.

When you recognize the symptoms of hypothermia in yourself or in others, take action. A hypothermic rider may not comprehend that fingers or toes are being frozen. Don't be bashful about flagging down a passing vehicle, and asking for help. Yes, we know we're supposed to be tough and independent out there, but when you're hypothermic, it's too late to tough it out. Got a CB radio? Get on the horn and explain the situation. You may find truckers more sympathetic to your plight than other drivers. If you're still miles from shelter when you realize you're in trouble, get out your cell phone and call 911. Yes, it's a life-threatening emergency.

Rehydrating

Remember that the body gives off water vapor through breathing, so you need to replenish your fluids even if you've just ridden through a slushy downpour. If it's sub-freezing, you may need to warm up your water bottle on the engine or mufflers. Coffee or tea are acceptable but go through the body faster than plain water. If you find a café open, order some hot soup to provide both nourishment and rehydration. Definitely avoid alcoholic beverages, which cause dehydration as well as degraded judgment.

If you're fortunate enough to find a warm building where you can take a break, remove or unzip enough outer insulation to allow your body to soak up room heat, and move around to get blood circulating to the extremities again. Spend long enough inside to get warmed, refueled, rehydrated, and your body core cranking out heat again. If your feet are tingling, remove your boots and check your toes for frostbite. If you're shivering, that's a sign the core is bordering on the cold side, and you need some additional warm-up time before continuing.

Cold Weather Riding On Purpose

Riders who live in northern climates may start thinking about getting the bike out in the winter, even when there is snow and ice on the ground. It's possible to ride in winter conditions, but it takes both preparation and skill.

For riding in snow, it's essential to have tires with good traction. Dirt bike knobbies work acceptably in fresh snow, but may not work well on ice. Studs are available that screw into the tire blocks for serious wintertime traction.

Getting Prepared

A fellow moto-journalist described his electric jacket liner as a quantum leap in cold weather riding gear. One reason an electric vest is so useful is that keeping the chest and core organs warm keeps more blood flowing to the extremities. However, I consider electric heating to be a supplement to insulation, not a replacement, especially for trips into more remote areas where there will be few warm restaurants to duck into when a critical wire breaks.

While we're thinking about gear, let's note that impact pads can really help cushion your fall onto a frozen surface. The better impact pads are made of a foam that suddenly increases resistance upon impact, like the Aerostich "TF" series. I can tell you from personal experience that frozen ground is very hard.

It's also important to find some system that will keep your face shield clear. You can scrape off sleet and snow from the outside with a gloved finger, but it's difficult to scrape off frozen breath from the inside. One solution is an inside anti-fog visor that locks onto pins. It also helps to have some sort of breath guard that directs your breath down rather than onto the face shield.

Keeping your hands and feet warm is another issue. Some machines have electrically-heated grips. Or you can install heating elements under your grips. You can get electrically-heated gloves and socks, but the wiring can quickly get complex and frustrating. And before you wire up too much extra heating, be sure to evaluate your charging system.

Even with electric heat, your hands will welcome some sort of wind protection in front of the controls. Back in the good old days we had

"Hippo Hands," big insulated covers that enclosed the hand controls. Another approach is to wear snowmobile gloves with thick felt liners. It also helps to have wind deflectors in front of the controls. You may be able to adapt dirt bike hand protectors, or fabricate your own wind deflectors from heavy plastic.

Note the custom wind deflectors mounted in front of the grips, to divert the wind blast around the hands. An adjustable lip on the upper edge of the windscreen does the same for the rider's neck.

Some bike preparation is necessary to get the bike ready for the cold. Water vapor can condense and form puddles in the fuel system, and when it freezes it shuts off fuel flow. There are fuel additives to help flush the water through, but it's best to drain some fuel from the bottom of the tank (and carburetor bowls) before a cold ride, to remove any collected water from the system. You may want to change the engine oil to a lower viscosity appropriate for the temperature, and check the coolant if you have a radiator. See your owner's manual for specifications.

Keeping the Shiny Side Up

All right, let's assume you understand all about body protection, and you've got the gear and the tactics to avoid hypothermia and stay hydrated. The next question is: how do you keep the shiny side up? On slick surfaces, you know it's a thin line between a little slip-slide and an instant slam-dunk. One of the advantages of a bike is that you can put your tires over the most tractable surface. If the car wheel tracks are polished ice or confusing ruts, traction might be better out on the shoulder, or between the wheel tracks.

If you are determined to ride a two-wheeler on snow and ice, look for the best traction and fewest ruts, such as that crunchy snow over at the edge of the road.

Ride as smoothly as possible, avoiding any sudden steering, throttle, or braking changes. Follow cornering lines that maximize the turn radius and minimize lean angle. For really slippery turns, slow down to an appropriate speed for the radius of curve and angle of camber, and weight the bike to keep your wheels perpendicular to the surface.

If you keep the wheels perpendicular to the surface, the bike can slide sideways a bit rather than immediately falling down.

You can lessen the risk of falling on slippery surfaces by placing more of your weight on the foot pegs rather than on the saddle. With your weight supported on the foot pegs, it's easier to lean the bike independently of your body. You may be tempted to put your feet down to help stabilize the bike, but if your tires don't have enough traction to hold the bike upright, your boot soles probably won't do any better. And when you do fall, it will be less painful if your ankles aren't bent back under the foot pegs or trapped under a hot exhaust pipe.

Be aware that bridges will freeze sooner, and stay frozen longer, than adjacent pavement. Riding uphill, approach a little faster at the bottom, then ease off the gas and let forward energy carry the machine up. Approaching a downhill section, slow to a crawl at the top, stay in a lower gear, and use both brakes lightly to hold back speed. If the tires start to slip, ease off the brakes.

Be aware that an icy surface will be more slippery when the ice is just starting to melt, say where an area of frozen pavement is being thawed by the sun.

An icy street will be most slippery where it's just starting to thaw, like that area ahead in the sun.

Notice that downhill section ahead. You'll want to slow to a crawl before you get there. Use both brakes together, but very lightly.

You can also increase traction by letting some air out of the tires, dropping pressure down to 18-20 psi. Soft tires are less likely to skid. Just remember to pump them up to normal pressures again when you get back on clean pavement.

The Third Wheel

If you get motorcycle withdrawal symptoms from not riding during the cold winter months, maybe it's time to consider a sidecar rig. A sidecar outfit can slip and slide without falling down. With a single drive wheel, you can position the rear wheel over the most tractable surface. And if that's not enough, you can lever on serious knobby tires, and maybe screw in some studs. A sidecar rig is a seriously practical vehicle for wintertime use.

One big advantage of a rig is staying upright on slippery surfaces, whether it's snow or mud. This IMZ-Ural comes from Russia, where they know a thing or two about icy roads.

But before you start thinking seriously about bolting up a sidecar, be aware that a rigid motorcycle/sidecar combination is not just a two-wheeled motorcycle with a big *thing* on one side, but an entirely different three-wheeled vehicle with different handling characteristics.

Learning to drive a three-wheeler requires time and effort. If you're not really that serious about winter motorcycling, a sidecar might be more than you're willing to tackle. But if you've got the right stuff, driving a rig will give your winter riding some new perspective, and very likely a few new grins.

If you do decide to learn to drive a hack, the S/TEP (Sidecar/Trike Education Program) is offered by many state rider training programs. Visit *http://www.evergeenmotorcycletraining.org* for more information. There is also a good do-it-yourself book on the subject: "*Driving a Sidecar Outfit*," available from Printwerk Graphics.

THE GOOD RIDER

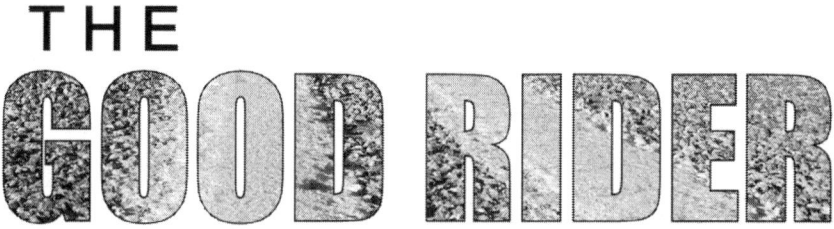

Chapter 21: Surface Hazards

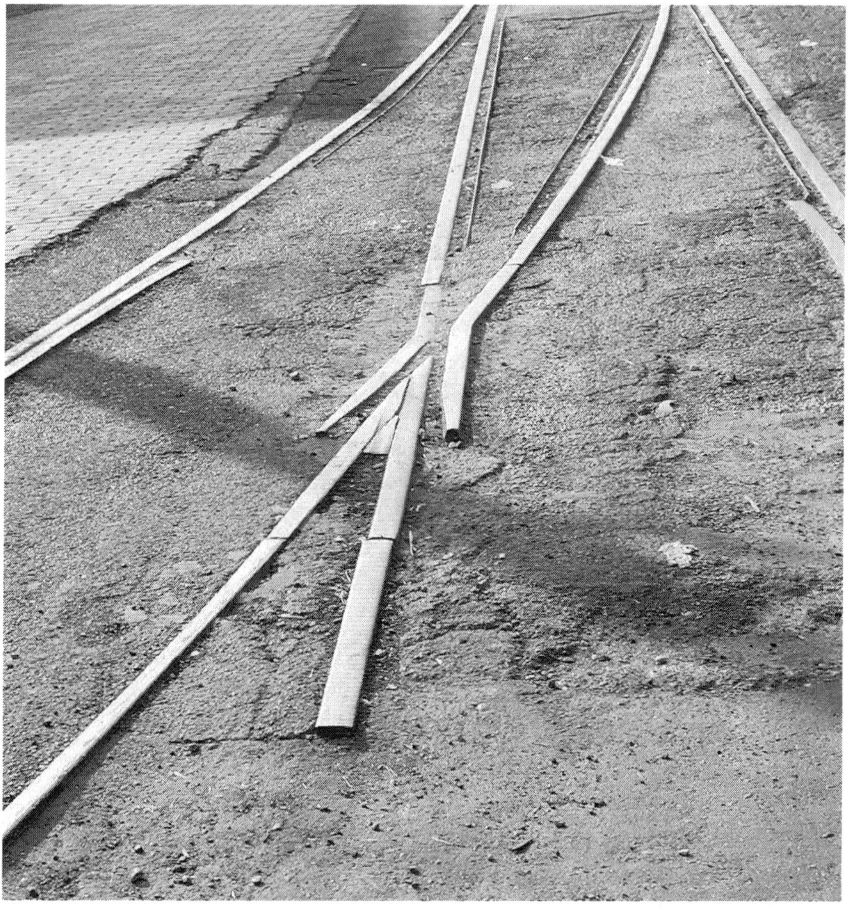

Back at the beginning I suggested that a good rider would be able to negotiate whatever surface hazards came along. Surface hazards are the main difference between how you drive a car and how you ride a bike. A car (or a motorcycle/sidecar combination) can slide a tire on a slick spot or groove, and not lose balance. When you're riding a bike, you need to maintain your awareness of the road surface to avoid being drawn into some booby trap that causes you to lose control.

Bikes are more susceptible to surface hazards because we must keep them balanced in addition to accelerating, braking, and cornering. In a nutshell, balance depends on front tire traction. Let's run through a few surface hazards.

Rails

Railroad and streetcar rails have caused a lot of motorcycle crashes. The rails may not stick up above the surrounding pavement, but the shiny steel can allow the tire to slip rather than roll across. What's more, some rails have slots and grooves large enough to capture a motorcycle tire. The most dangerous situation is where the traffic lane is parallel to the tracks, or crosses the rails at a narrow angle. And, in addition to the rails, there are often steel covers over switching mechanisms. Any steel in the street gets polished smooth by passing traffic. Where the road curves across the rails, the bike will normally be leaned over, which encourages a slide-out on either the shiny rails or the aprons next to the rails. Both wood and plastic aprons can be very slippery when wet.

The traffic lane directs you to cross these streetcar tracks over a connecting switch with deep slots. If you simply ease across the rails, it is very possible your front tire could be captured by the slot, causing you to lose balance. See if you can figure out how to get across without falling.

Here, you're making a right turn over three sets of tracks. Fortunately, the aprons alongside the main rails are concrete, which has much better traction than wood or plastic. In this situation, you might delay your turn so you can get the bike turned to cross all the rails with the bike vertical.

You'd be crossing these tracks with the bike vertical, so the only problem would be if you needed to stop. The trick would be to brake on the pavement, then release the brakes when crossing these slippery plastic aprons.

Edge Traps

"Edge trap" is the name I've given to a raised pavement edge running parallel to your direction of travel. Think of a raised edge as a curb. I call them "traps" because if you allow your front tire to snuggle up to a raised edge, the wheel typically gets trapped by the edge, and steers along the edge rather than bumping up and over. A car can bounce over a raised edge with less of a problem, because there are always other tires to help maintain stability.

The raised pavement on either side of this lane may not look like a serious hazard, but situations like this have caused more than a few motorcycle crashes.

Edge traps are common in construction zones, most obviously where the asphalt surface has been milled away in preparation for repaving. Construction contractors typically have little awareness of motorcycle dynamics, but they realize something is going on when a number of motorcyclists crash in a work zone. Since they often don't understand why the crashes are occurring, the response is merely to erect a warning sign such as "Motorcycles Use Extreme Caution." Actually that's poor advice, because the way to cross a raised edge is to steer wider and then attack the edge at maximum angle to bounce the front tire up and over. It's an aggressive, not cautious maneuver.

You might be thinking about passing those slow movers ahead, but think again. There's a steep edge at the center created by the new layer of pavement in the right lane.

To get the front wheel to jump up and over a raised edge like this curb, you need to attack at a minimum of 45 degrees, and roll on a bit of throttle. It's the same technique for crossing edge traps in the street.

If all edge traps were as obvious as a curb, we would be less surprised by them. But there are raised edges that don't look very dangerous, yet can affect balance and steering. You should be on high alert in construction zones, especially where the traffic lane is diverted over different types of pavement. Actually, the change in surface color or texture is your best clue about a possible surface hazard.

Here's a temporary detour where traffic is being diverted to the other side of the center divider. You should be cautious about the area where the temporary surface joins the concrete. That's a typical scenario for an edge trap. You'd want to stay to the right a little longer, then steer left and attack the concrete edge at a wider angle.

Steel Plates

Where a maintenance crew needs to dig a hole to access utilities, they just remove a section of concrete and dig a deep trench. To allow traffic to cross over the trench, they will lay down huge sheets of thick steel. The steel can be slick when wet, even if it's not polished smooth and shiny by passing traffic, but there are some other special motorcycle hazards involving steel plates. The edges of a steel plate form edge traps.

So, when you're crossing a steel plate, stay away from the edges. And if you must cross an angled plate, treat the raised edges as potential edge traps. Don't be surprised if the plate bounces up and down, or if part of the trench is exposed at one side.

When you must cross a steel construction plate, stay in the center and avoid the edges.

Slick Pavement

Pavement can be slick because of contaminants. Various lubricants get dribbled on the surface, including oil, fuel, and antifreeze. Commercial trucks and buses are notorious for oil leaks. It's not that the drivers want to spill anything, but the cost of repairing leaking seals and gaskets is so high that the owners tend to put off maintenance until it's really bad. I overheard two truckers talking about their rigs. One driver laughed that he had burned 12 quarts of oil between Ellensburg and Seattle—a distance of about 130 miles. And that's just one truck.

When you're riding a highway with heavy truck traffic, remind yourself of the likelihood of lubricating oil and diesel fuel being dribbled on the surface. Mostly, the contaminants will dribble in the center of the lane, but they will also ooze downhill. Knowing that, you might want to favor a lane other than the one used by heavy trucks, and when you must use the same lane, choose one of the wheel tracks rather than the center.

Not all trucks dribble contaminants. It's more likely with older equipment. You might also observe the cargo being transported, and stay far away from any vehicles hauling live animals. Trucks are also notorious for spilling diesel fuel from their saddle tanks. That's most likely in the first tight curve after a fuel stop. The fuel tank caps need to breathe, and when a tank is topped up, centrifugal force in a corner can cause the fuel to spurt out. Because of that, you should use extra care on corners and especially on-ramps near truck stops.

It's more likely that an older, well-used truck will be leaking oil. And you should also stay far away from any vehicles carrying live animals, since they may be leaking something other than oil.

Chapter 21: Surface Hazards

If this is the first curve after a truck stop, you should expect diesel fuel dribbles in that lane. Diesel fuel can be extremely slippery, even in dry weather.

Tar Snakes

When the pavement forms cracks, it's important to seal them to prevent freezing water from doing further damage over the next winter. Road crews typically fill the cracks with a liquid asphalt sealer. But the most economical sealers have much less friction than the more expensive goo. If the road crew squirts the cracks full and don't add some sort of abrasive, the resulting "tar snakes" can be very slippery, especially when wet. Since you don't know what sort of sealer was used, it's best to keep your tires away from the tar snakes when possible.

The crack sealer used by many road maintenance crews is much more slippery than the old pavement. It's a good idea to keep your tires off the tar snakes when possible. Can you imagine a cornering line here that will allow you to avoid most of the slick tar?

Slippery Pavement Blends

Some pavement is made with additives that make it slick. Highway engineers around the world continue to experiment with pavement blends that are flexible enough to resist cracking, and durable enough to resist wear. But some blends with the desirable qualities have a lower coefficient of friction than regular asphalt pavement. Theoretically, vehicle tires will eventually scrub in the slicker surface, but meanwhile a passing motorcyclist may lose traction on what appears to be excellent pavement. Your best bet is to talk to local motorcyclists when you are traveling in unfamiliar environments, and to ride conservatively where they mention special hazards such as low-friction pavement.

Some highways, including Utah 95 between Hanksville and Blanding, are reputed to be test areas for different pavement blends. You might want to ride conservatively and enjoy the view.

Grated Bridge Decks

In the interests of saving weight, engineers often design bridges with grated decks. A grated deck is made of thin strips of steel on edge, separated by corrugated spacers. It's seldom possible to get the decking lined up perfectly, so vehicle tires tend to jerk from side to side when crossing a grated deck. The wandering and noise is not a hazard for a car or truck driver, although crossing a bridge with a grated deck can be unnerving for a driver who doesn't understand what's happening. For a motorcyclist, a grated deck can be a serious hazard, and certainly the instability will get your attention. It's a matter of the tires jumping from one side of a decking strip to the other as the bike tries to rebalance itself.

How badly your bike wanders and lurches depends on its tire profiles. A narrow front tire will jump around more than a wide profile tire. There's not much you can do to reduce the wandering or increase traction. It's best to avoid grasping the bars with a death grip. Counter-steer normally to control the front wheel, and let the rear tire come along for the ride.

If grated decks make you nervous, you can do a little research to plan your river crossings on bridges with solid decks. For example, in the Columbia River Gorge, the bridge at Hood River is grated, and comparatively long. The bridge on Highway 97 at Biggs has a solid paved surface. Take your pick.

The bridge across the Columbia River at Hood River has a grated deck. The bridge across the Columbia on Highway 97 at Biggs has solid pavement. Which one would you prefer?

THE GOOD RIDER

Chapter 22: Dazzled by Farkles

Motorcyclists have always been enthusiastic about customizing their machines. Various brands and models have bred specialty aftermarket suppliers. For owners of some brands, customizing is mostly a matter of special paint and upholstery, added chrome, and extra lights. But in addition to the selections of customizing parts, today we also have arrays of electronics, including radar detectors, GPS, helmet-to-helmet radio, trip computers, selectable instrument displays, position locator beacons, and voice-controlled super phones with Java, streaming video, motion detection, and geographic positioning.

The use of electronic devices is getting more popular, perhaps because it is common today for people to use wireless gadgets full time, and that extends to motor vehicles. As the years have gone by, I've noticed more and more electronic farkles being added to automobiles and motorcycles. In addition to the usual cockpit features such as cruise control, there are now onboard computers with monitors that can manage a variety of functions from trip information to entertainment. And automakers generally see electronic farkles as a sales advantage, ot a safety hazard.

Today's cars are stuffed full of electronics, including a touch screen in the dash.

I'll admit to being a bit of a curmudgeon, and resisting the latest gadgets. I suspect it started with a trip to New Mexico, in the dark ages prior to cell phones or GPS. The best we had for mobile use were tape decks for entertainment, and CB radios for short distance communication. Some riders were also "hams" and carried portable radios with a bit longer range. Mostly, we used paper maps for navigating, and phone booths for communicating with home.

One day I was climbing up over one of those high Colorado passes, blue sky above, steep drop-offs below, and quaking Aspen trees fluttering in the breeze. I had managed to stuff an automobile radio/cassette tape deck and a full-sized CB radio beneath the windscreen on the Guzzi's bulbous English fairing, and at that moment I was listening to the Blue Danube

Waltz from Space Odyssey, through my home-brewed stereo helmet speakers. But then something started to come unglued. The bike started wandering all over the road. I suddenly realized the curves in the road were out of sync with the rhythm of the music.

I immediately switched off the tape deck, and thought it all over. I decided my main purpose in riding was to enjoy the throb of the engine, the interesting curves, and the ambience. I wasn't there for electronic entertainment. What's more, I really enjoyed the traveling, and didn't want to waste any time communicating with anyone. Since then I've avoided adding any more electronic gadgets than absolutely necessary.

Distracted Driving

The increased use of electronics in vehicles is causing a significant change in the cause of fatal crashes. Prior to 1982, the majority of fatal vehicle crashes involved alcohol. Today, the majority of fatal crashes involve distracted drivers. Distracted driving is becoming a serious hazard for motorcyclists because more distracted drivers are likely to be wandering into your path.

According to a University of Utah study, a driver on a cell phone is more impaired than a driver with a BAC of 0.08 percent. And no, it doesn't help to use wireless or hands-free devices, because the distraction is the conversation, not the device. Transport Canada did some research on where drivers looked when using a hands-free cell phone. On the phone, drivers not only ignored more of what was happening ahead, but narrowed their field of view.

A driver who is focusing on the road rather than on a conversation has a field of view something like this.

A driver distracted by a phone conversation, whether hand-held or hands-free, tends to focus on a much smaller and closer field of view.

In a survey by Nationwide Mutual Insurance, more than 80% of drivers admitted to hazardous behavior while driving, including changing clothes, steering with a foot, painting nails, or shaving.

In tests by the Center for Cognitive Brain Imaging at Carnegie Mellon University, brain power allocated to operating a vehicle decreases by 40% when the driver is listening to music or a conversation. That's not just theory, they did fMRI scans of drivers' brains while driving a simulator. It's not just a matter of attention wandering, but that the part of the brain that processes movement also processes language (spoken or written), so they compete for attention. Something has to give, and it's the attention allocated to driving.

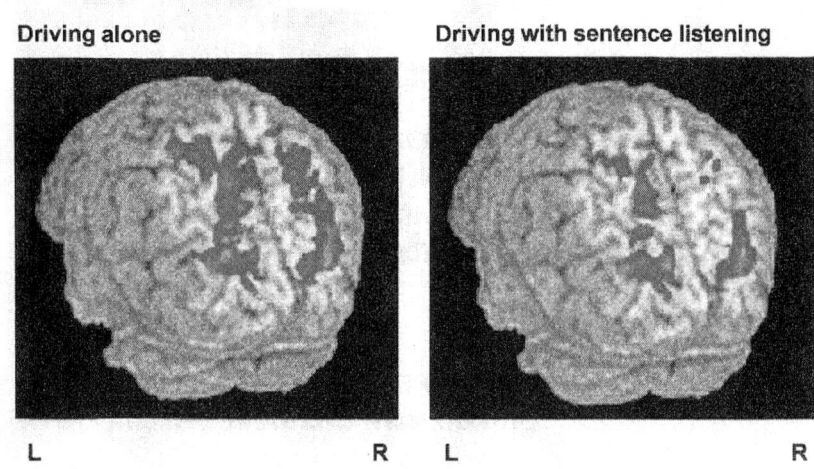

Functional magnetic resonance imaging images.
Source: Carnegie Mellon University

The National Safety Council estimates that 11% of drivers in the U.S. at any time of day are talking on cell phones, but it's not just cell phones that precipitate crashes. A survey by the AAA Foundation for Traffic Safety reports that 41% of drivers admitted they had fallen asleep or nodded off while driving, at least once. Four percent said they had fallen asleep behind the wheel in the previous month. And a CDC Report indicated that drowsy driving causes an estimated 1,550 deaths per year.

The Myth of Multitasking

For many years we've heard (and maybe believed) the myth that people can somehow deal with multiple tasks at the same time. Lots of people apparently believe they can multitask, say driving a car, carrying on a conversation with passengers, listening to music, and having a texting interchange—all at the same time. Of course, military pilots are asked to do multiple complex tasks.

But the majority of humans can't do multiple tasks simultaneously. Apparently, we deal with tasks sequentially. That is, a driver looks ahead and steers the car, then switches mental focus to the in-car conversation, then switches to hearing some of the music, then switches to reading the text message, and so on. What appears to be multitasking is really rapid switching between tasks. Whether one task is really distracting depends upon how much conscious thought it consumes. Tasks such carrying on a conversation, deciphering to the words of a song, multiplying numbers, or taking evasive action to avoid another vehicle are all cognitively demanding. Chewing gum, humming a tune, walking, or breathing aren't very cognitively demanding.

The important point here is that when you are focused on one cognitively demanding task, you must temporarily ignore the others. Another point is that the more you make a task automatic, the less cognitively demanding it is. That may explain how someone can steer a car while talking on the phone.

Although we might be quick to criticize the motorist who doesn't see any problem with texting or painting fingernails while driving, we might note that lots of motorcycles are equipped with cognitively demanding farkles such as GPS, navigation computers, music systems, and helmet cameras. So, let's consider how adding gadgets affects the danger.

Reaction Time

What does an alert rider do when a hazard suddenly appears? Brake? Swerve? Accelerate? The correct answer is "none of the above." The rider must mentally process what's happening before deciding to take action. Reaction time may occur in an instant, but always adds some delay to any evasive action.

First it takes a moment to receive the sound or image, then another moment to perceive that something out there needs attention, a few more microseconds to interpret what it means, and another handful of microseconds to figure out what to do. There is no universal number for reaction time, although accident reconstructionists often use 1.5 seconds. Some sharp young riders can probably react within 0.75 second.

Let's pause here to note that while a rider is reacting to the situation, the bike is continuing along at the same speed. Once the rider has processed the information, the brain can command the muscles to take action (movement time) and then it takes some time to accomplish the action (device response time). The decision might be conscious and therefore slower for a novice, but subconscious (and quicker) for an experienced rider.

Let's imagine a motorcycle approaching a side road. The rider observes a vehicle about to emerge, and sends the image up to the brain, where it is compared to memories of other such situations. The rider consciously decides to slow the bike and move left to avoid a possible collision. A novice might have to spend additional time remembering how to steer or brake. The veteran rider's hands operate the controls subconsciously, resulting in a very quick 0.75 second reaction.

A veteran rider might shortcut the process by accessing memories of similar situations and by taking evasive action automatically (subconsciously). A novice rider might take longer to process the information and take action.

Let's assume the bike is approaching the situation at 40 mph. Three-quarters of a second to react is about as quick as we could expect, but during that time the bike will travel 44 feet. Assuming excellent traction and very proficient braking, stopping distance might be as short as 58 feet. Add it up: 44 +58 =102 feet.

The Distracted Brain

But what if the rider is distracted, say glancing down at the speedometer, or listening to the GPS's spoken route instructions? The rider has to switch from the task of controlling the bike to the device, and then switch back to the situation, and each mental switch requires a bit of time. Every time the brain switches tasks, it takes a moment to focus on the action, remember the rules for that type of action, and dredge up any related memories. There are no hard and fast rules for task switching time, but we'd be safe saying that each switch takes at least 0.2 sec.

Of course, a rider who suddenly perceives a threat such as that emerging SUV can ignore all the other distractions and switch attention back to the SUV, but it won't be instantaneous. The big danger is that a distracted rider may be so interested in something in the cockpit that he delays focusing on a life-threatening hazard ahead. That's exactly why a pedestrian talking on the phone might step off the sidewalk into the path of a bus, or why a driver painting her nails might slam into a bike waiting at a stop sign.

Imagine a rider approaching a confusing intersection. He glances up at the light, then catches a couple of seconds of familiar music, then glances ahead at a car, then back to the speedometer. Suddenly the GPS voice distracts him for a couple of seconds. He may be looking at the situation, but not really focused on what's unfolding while his brain is trying to decipher the spoken messages, and decide whether or not the GPS direction is appropriate.

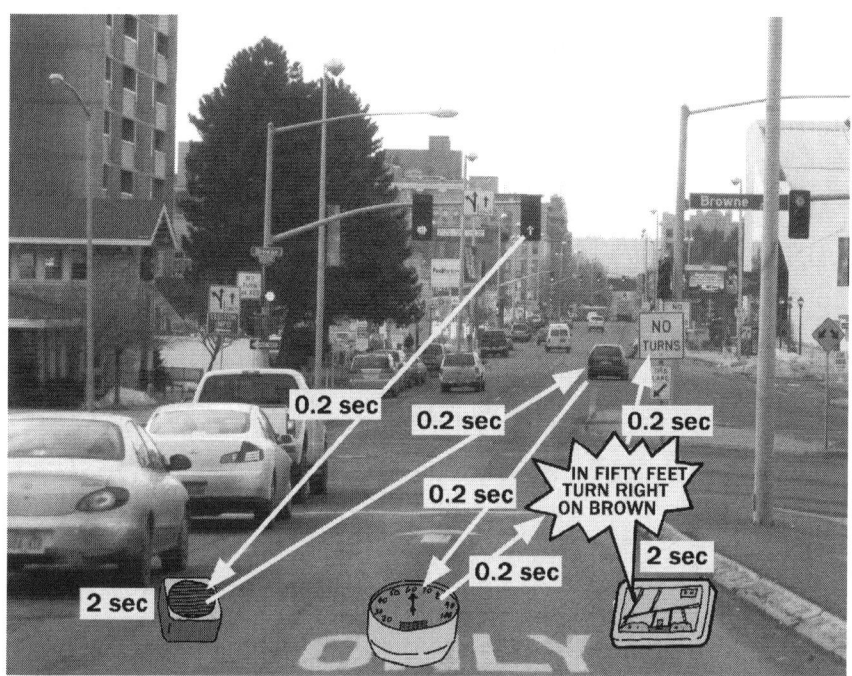

The rider's attention might be focused for four seconds on the music and the GPS, but there might be an additional second of switching time.

Consider that it's not just the four seconds spent on the music and GPS voices, but also the switching time, which in this example adds up to another full second. The point is that time spent attending to a distracting device or switching between tasks is time the rider's brain is not attending to the unfolding situation. If the rider manages to limit the distractions and switching time to just 5 seconds, the bike will travel almost 300 feet at 40 mph.

There's some additional bad news for those who have busily been getting older for the past 50 or 60 years. The top of the curve for reaction time was at about age 22. For every ten years over age 22 you can tack on another quarter of a second to your reaction time. If you're over 60, your reaction time might be 2.5 seconds—about 150 feet at 40 mph, and more than 200 feet at 55 mph. That's a lot of distance in which something nasty could happen.

Suggestions

Continue to develop your muscle memory so that your subconscious can respond automatically to threats without as much cognitive processing. The subconscious can't think ahead, but it can respond to traffic problems while they are occurring. The more you can control the bike automatically, the less competition there will be for cognitive attention.

Develop habits for your stops, to avoid unnecessary distractions. On one trip in New Zealand, I couldn't find my wallet when we stopped for gas. I found my outside jacket pocket unzipped and empty, and concluded that my wallet must have fallen out on the last leg. Three of us backtracked 15 or 20 kilometers in a futile search for my "missing" wallet, and you can bet your bippie I was distracted by thoughts of dealing with no cash or credit cards in a foreign country. Finally I pulled the bike over and did a more thorough pat down, locating a lump in the jacket liner pocket, where I'd temporarily stowed my wallet while buying lunch. I would have saved a lot of dangerous distraction and embarrassment by immediately returning my wallet to the outside jacket pocket after a purchase. Decide where you are going to put important stuff and always put it there immediately, no exceptions.

Distracted driving is now the leading cause of serious automobile crashes in the U.S. According to State Farm Insurance, distracted driving is the number one killer of American teens (which should be a clue about who to watch for). It's very important to both reduce your own distractions and to be prepared to get out of the way of other motorists who are too distracted to realize you are there. When you see a driver who doesn't seem to be paying attention to the situation, focus on moving away from that vehicle.

If you must focus brainpower on multiple tasks while riding, reduce speed. Slower speed means the bike will cover less distance while you're distracted or switching between tasks. If you find that you subconsciously roll off the throttle when the situation gets complex, that's because your brain wants more time to process the information.

Consider taking a break for mentally demanding tasks such as entering a route on the GPS or locating a fuel stop. Language processing draws cognitive resources away from riding. Any device that requires you to pay close attention to spoken or written words is a potentially serious distraction. When the bike is in motion, turn off anything that's not needed.

Chapter 23: Breakdowns

A few years ago my primary bike had a serious engine failure three hours from home. The engine had occasionally been misfiring, and I thought it might be a bad spark plug cap. But before I could replace the cap, the engine suddenly lost power with a loud clatter, and I coasted to a stop by the side of a busy arterial. Pulling the spark plug allowed me to see bits and pieces of shrapnel inside the cylinder. The exhaust valve had broken, punching a hole through the piston. The "low speed miss" had actually been a symptom of the valve head breaking off.

Such incidents are a rarity these days, because today's motorcycles are so much more reliable than they used to be. You may never experience a roadside breakdown. You may even wonder why some of us "old codger" bikers are so concerned about the contents of a new bike's tool kit, or whether it has a center stand, or how much trouble it is to get to the battery terminals. Many contemporary machines are so complex that owners are discouraged from trying to do any maintenance.

But with a bike problem, help can be hard to come by. You shouldn't expect that other motorists will stop to help you alongside today's roads. It can be way too much money and effort hauling the bike to a dealer if the problem is easy to fix. And sometimes you're just too far from help to transport the bike. So there is good reason to learn how to manage the occasional breakdown yourself. I advise gaining some basic knowledge of your machine, and having a plan of action to recall when you become stranded.

How People Handle Breakdowns

The problem with breakdowns isn't so much getting the bike fixed; it's the difficulty in controlling the panic when the bike fails. A panicked rider might try something stupid or dangerous—say, pushing a dead bike across four lanes of traffic—which a calmer rider would instantly recognize as very poor judgment. Let's think through the process of handling a roadside breakdown, to help you prepare for whatever problems you might happen to encounter in your travels.

Biker Bob

Bob was on his way to a motorcycle rally when he hit a chunk of concrete, cracking his front wheel rim open, and instantly deflating the tire. He managed to wobble over to the side of the road without crashing.

Traveling Ted

Ted was on an organized tour from England to Spain. At a small fishing village on the south coast of Spain he attempted to restart the engine, and there was a sudden pop and a gusher of motor oil out the right side. Ted didn't know what else to do, so he hired a local van to haul the bike back to the hotel.

Paul the Wrench

Paul and his wife were on a month-long trip from Texas to the Pacific Northwest. In a small town in Montana, Paul's wife noted that her odometer had stopped working. Paul checked the speedometer drive in the rear hub, and to his amazement found the axle had failed, allowing the wheel to wobble around.

Different Strokes

These three riders had vastly different problems, and they solved them in different ways. Bob knew immediately what the problem was. And he also knew that his bike wouldn't go another yard without a different front wheel. Bob remembered his BMW member directory (BMW Owners Anonymous) from the owners' association, and called a club member not too far away, who offered to bring out a loaner wheel complete with a useable tire. The helpful club members even switched the wheel for Bob, and he was soon on his way.

Ted panicked, because he isn't mechanically inclined, and there didn't appear to be any motorcycle shops in the remote area. But there were other riders on the tour who were mechanically inclined, and they dived in to help solve Ted's predicament. The oil was drained and saved, and the holed clutch cover was carefully removed. Apparently, when Ted had pressed the starter button, the bolt holding a gear on the end of the crankshaft had spun out, punching a hole through the clutch cover. The loose bolt was snugged up with a dribble of thread sealer one rider was carrying. Someone had some high strength epoxy glue; someone else had some cleaner, someone else had some gasket cement. A small disc was cut out of a beer can and epoxied into the hole in the cover. The next morning the repaired cover was reinstalled, and the oil poured back in. The patch held all the way back to England.

Paul is a veteran mechanic, but he needed some new parts. He called the parts man at his local dealership, who shipped a new axle and bearing overnight. The next day Paul installed the new axle, but was momentarily stumped because tightening the belt sprocket nut required a large metric wrench. Paul checked around town. No one had a metric socket large enough, but he found a huge metric box wrench at the local auto parts store and bought it. They were soon back on the road.

Paul solved the axle problem by installing parts overnighted from his dealer. But he had to buy a huge metric wrench to snug up the drive belt pulley.

Different Reactions

Bob's situation proved the value of belonging to an association of fellow riders. Ted's predicament showed the value of traveling with others, who not only had the needed mechanical skills, but also the emergency supplies necessary to complete the job. Paul needed a tool to complete the repairs, and scouted the nearby auto parts stores to find a wrench that would work.

When the Bike Goes Bonk

There's a common thread in these stories: handling emergencies depends upon keeping a level head after the bike leaves you stranded. Before the problem, you were focusing on the route, maintaining your schedule, and enjoying the scenery. Suddenly, all that changes, and it's easy to panic.

To help avoid the panic, take a deep breath, calm down, and temporarily switch off your travel plans. For the moment, ignore getting home in time for dinner, or getting to the motel where you have a reservation, or getting back to work tomorrow morning. Those are all lower priorities now.

The first priority is getting yourself off the road and into a safe zone where you won't get run over. If at all possible, coast over to the shoulder while the bike is still moving. Then push the machine away from the traffic lanes, preferably behind a tree or building where the air is calmer and quieter. If you absolutely can't move the bike away from the side of the road, at least push it to the outside edge of the shoulder. And while you're working on it, keep an eye peeled for cars zooming toward you. It's more common than you might think for drivers to gawk at vehicles stopped on the shoulder and smash into them.

The next priority, once you've got the bike in a safe zone, is to focus on the problem. If the failure is obvious, say a flat tire or a broken drive chain, you won't need to do any diagnosis. But if the problem is not obvious—say, the engine refuses to start at a rest area—you'll need to do a little sleuthing to figure out what's wrong. Maybe it's just out of gas. Maybe the ignition switch failed. Dig out your owner's manual, and see if it has a troubleshooting guide. Or, remember the saying, "The King is a FINK".

The King is a FINK

F: Fuel

Extinguish any lit cigarettes, open the fuel filler cap, and rock the bike from side to side to be sure there really is fuel sloshing around in there, and that it smells like gasoline, not diesel oil. If the fuel valve is opened by a vacuum line, check that the hose is still connected. If the engine still won't start, don't just keep cranking, save your battery. If your bike has carburetors, turn the fuel valve to prime or reserve, and open a drain screw in the bottom of a carburetor. You want to see clean fuel dribbling out, not dirty black water. If your bike has a fuel pump, turn on the key and listen to hear if the pump seems to be working. If you don't hear the pump, check the electrical connector to make sure it's connected, and look carefully at the fuse for that circuit.

I: Ignition

Turn on the main switch, and check that the headlight is shining brightly. If you can't get any lights, turn off the switch, and make sure both battery terminals are clean and tight. Be sure that the big black ground wire from the battery terminal to the frame is secure at the engine end as well as the battery terminal. If a connector looks rusty or corroded, remove the fastener, scrape the contact areas clean with a knife or flat screwdriver, and reconnect. When you disconnect the battery cables, always remove the ground (black) cable first, and reconnect the ground cable last, to avoid a short circuit.

If the battery and connectors are good, check for a spark. Remove a spark plug, reconnect the wire to the plug, hold the threaded part of the spark plug to bare metal on the engine, and crank the starter for a second or two. You want to see a series of blue sparks zapping between the electrodes on the plug.

N: Neutral

Shift the transmission to neutral, retract the side stand, squeeze the clutch lever, and try to start the engine. Interlock switches at the transmission, clutch, or side stand may be interrupting the ignition. It's possible that a blob of asphalt or a stone has lodged in the side stand switch, or that a connection to the neutral switch has unplugged itself. Some machines are wired so that the starter will crank the engine without firing the ignition if the side stand isn't retracted.

K: Kill Switch

Check that the kill switch (engine shutoff switch) is in the RUN position. It's a good habit to always use the kill switch to shut off the motor. But you'd be amazed how many bikes are hauled in to repair shops simply because the kill switch was nudged out of the RUN position. Check your kill switch and save the embarrassment. In the event the switch seems intermittent, cycle it between off and run several times.

What's the problem, anyway?

The point of all this detail stuff is to figure out what has failed. What is the problem, anyway? Don't get too complex here; just try to identify the basic problem. Did you run out of gas, or did the engine make a nasty noise and grind to a stop? Did the battery actually fail, or did a cable come loose? If the engine runs but won't pull the bike, does the clutch cable have some slack when the lever is released? Is the drive chain still there? Is the rear wheel still bolted to the drive?

Such questions might sound silly here, but a panicked rider may overlook an obvious problem. Panicked riders have been known to keep blipping the throttle trying to make the bike move, without realizing the drive chain fell off a half mile back. If emergencies absolutely panic you, it's important to be as calm and logical as possible. Get out a pencil and paper and write down your thoughts. Record what you have checked and how.

If you can figure out the basic problem, you're well on the way to solving it. There's no point in transporting the bike if all you need is fuel, or a battery terminal snugged up. Don't overlook that owner's manual under the seat—it may have suggestions for troubleshooting. If you're still stumped, try calling your dealer and talking to the service department. It will be helpful to run through the list of things you have checked.

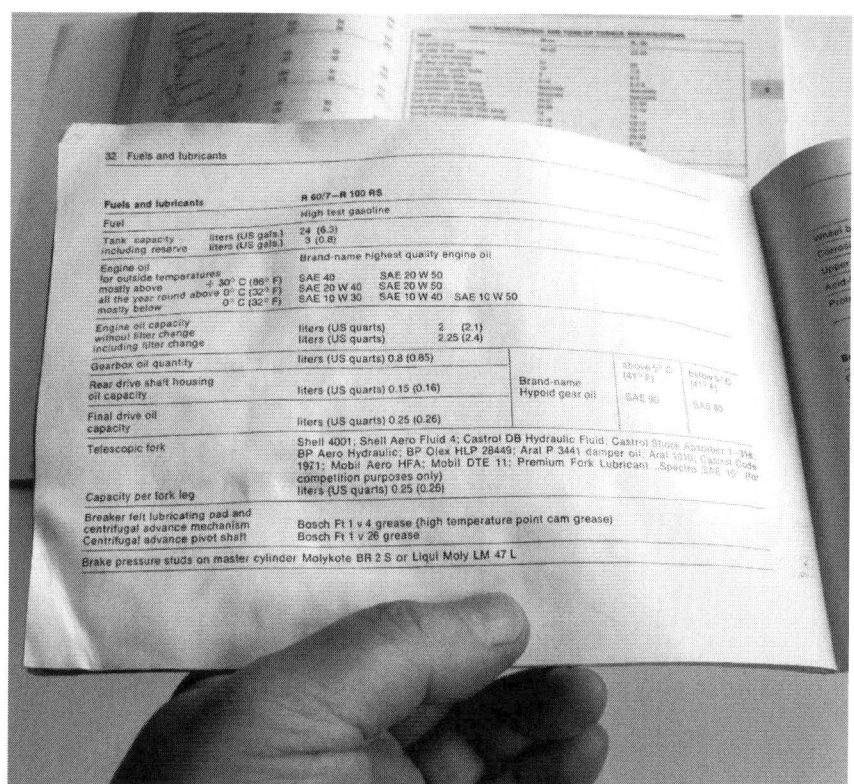

The owner's manual, which you should be carrying on the bike, has specifications and often some troubleshooting advice.

When you do experience a breakdown, here are some suggestions for reducing the hassles:

Pick a Comfortable Place to Work

If your machine starts bucking, clanking, or wheezing, pick a comfortable place to check it out. Don't leave civilization hoping it will cure itself. Find a shady spot out of the wind and away from traffic. Consider stopping by a motorcycle shop, or parking near a motel while you fiddle with the problem. If you do need to make some repairs or get a part shipped to you, it's a lot less frustrating with help, communications, transportation, food, and shelter nearby.

Remember Where You Left It

If you must abandon your machine to go for help, write down where you left it (mile markers, crossroads, business signs, etc.). It's a lot easier to lose track of where you left it than you might think. Out on a strange highway, it can be even more confusing. Was that mile 215 on I-15, or exit 15 on I-215? Did you hide it behind a yellow billboard or behind a big yellow building? Use your map, T-shirt, or forearm, but write down the specifics before you leave the scene.

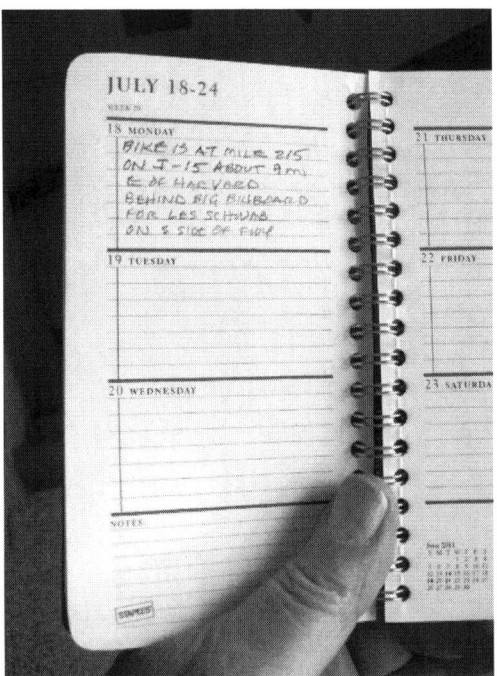

It's a lot easier than you might think to lose track of where you left your motorcycle. Take a moment to write down the location before you take off.

Now what?

Okay, your bike sputtered to a stop. You've pushed it away from traffic, controlled your panic, and figured out what the problem is. Now you have several options:

Push It

If you're within sight of a nearby gas station or dealership, you might be able to push the bike in. Just remember that pushing a heavyweight machine is exhausting. You might not want to abandon your shiny bike by the side of the road, but a motorcycle isn't worth the risk of heat exhaustion, a heart attack, or a collision. If the problem is fuel, it's a lot easier to walk or thumb a ride, buy a fuel can, and bring fuel back to the bike.

Fix it Yourself

Assuming you have the necessary know-how, parts, and tools, you may be able to do a little shade-tree mechanical work, and fix the problem yourself. Maybe all you need to do is replace a blown fuse, or clean a battery connection, or pry a stone out of the side stand switch.

Stay with the bike and get help to come to you. Assuming you can get a phone signal, call for help. If you have friends or family not too far away, they might be your first call. If you belong to a club that has a volunteer emergency network, you can try calling local riders for help.

Call for a Tow

The big advantage of towing is that you won't have to abandon the bike. If you have towing coverage, call the appropriate emergency number. Bear in mind that towing is seldom quick, easy, or cheap. The insurance dispatcher will contact the nearest towing companies to find one that will honor their coverage, and then call you back to confirm who is coming and when. It's important to request a tow truck with a flatbed suitable for carrying a motorcycle. You'll also need to explain where you want the bike to be delivered. Typically, it's necessary for you to accompany the bike in the tow truck. If the tow is farther than your insurance coverage allows, you'll need to pay the overage to the driver at the end of the tow, although you'll get the discounted rate per your insurance contract.

The big advantage of towing is that you won't have to abandon the bike. But inquire about your coverage to avoid a lengthy tow that's way beyond what your insurance will pay.

Abandon the Bike and Go for Help

If the bike has a serious problem that requires a repair shop, call the nearest motorcycle shop and see if they have a truck or trailer. If not, ask them if there is a nearby car rental office. If you'll be transporting a dead bike all by yourself, it's hard enough getting it pushed up onto a low trailer. It's just about impossible for one person to push a dead bike up a steep ramp into a truck.

Being Prepared

The clever rider takes a few extra precautions prior to leaving home, especially for a long trip.

Do Your Maintenance

Get your bike serviced before heading out on a long trip. The technician can check for potential problems as well as changing oil and handling other periodic maintenance. Even if you have the bike serviced at a dealership, check it over yourself, snugging up any loose connectors, feeling wheel bearings, inspecting cables, lubing the drive chain, etc.

Check Your Tool Kit

Check your tool kit while you're still close to the hardware store. See if the wrenches in the kit are adequate to reach the spark plugs, axle pinch bolts, handlebar clamps, and other obvious fasteners. The side of the road fifty miles from civilization is a poor place to find out that you don't have a patch kit or air pump, or a wrench to fit the axle nut.

Check your tool kit while you're still close to the hardware store. In addition to hand tools, I usually carry a tire plug kit and 12V air pump.

Consider carrying a few common spares tucked away in the fairing, or taped inside a saddlebag lid. Spare fuses, light bulbs, and small fasteners can be wrapped in foam. A small 12V test light is handy for checking electrical continuity, and it can also serve as a work light. A few crimp-on electrical splices (and pliers) can be lifesavers in reconnecting broken wires.

Have a Spare Key

I've had more than one occasion where my ignition key mysteriously disappeared while I was loading the bike. Did those teenage boys watching me have something to do with it? I have no proof. But I now carry a spare key hidden on the machine. I suggest you do likewise.

Read Your Manuals

Read your manuals while you are still close to your refrigerator. You might want to take a few notes, say tire inflation pressures, suspension settings, and oil specifications. I like to write the tire pressure on the rim next to the valve stem.

Even if you're only half-serious about maintenance, I suggest getting a shop manual for your machine. Most shop manuals include general information about tools, fasteners, torque values, lubricants, and sealers, as well as detailed instructions for tasks such as setting valve clearances, with lots of illustrations and photos. The shop manual is too big to carry along with you, but you can study it during the wintertime to gain more familiarity with your machine.

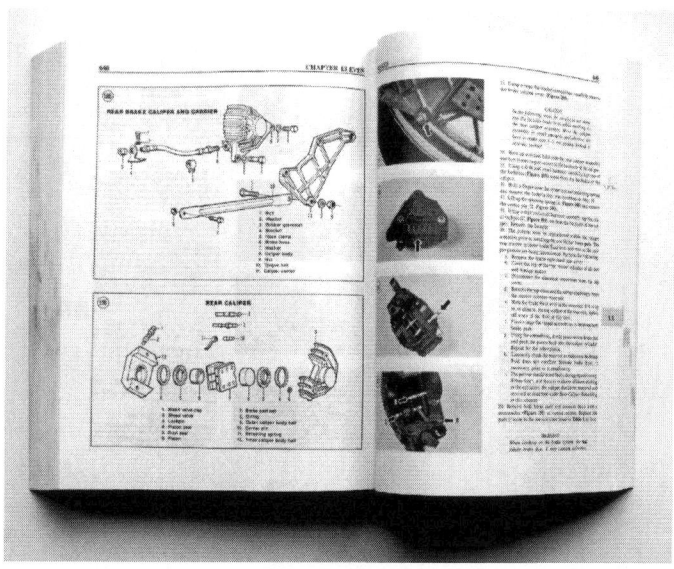

Get a shop manual for your bike, even if you don't intend to do any maintenance. The more familiar you are with the workings of your machine, the less panic you'll have when trouble occurs.

Carry Your Insurance Information

In a panic, some riders forget all about their emergency towing coverage, or can't remember the phone number, or their membership number. Its fine to have a card in your wallet, but it's much better to put the numbers out in the open where you won't forget them. I suggest writing the contact numbers on a label, protected with clear packaging tape, and attached where you can't miss it five years from now.

Anonymous Directories

Various motorcycle clubs and associations have emergency directories. For instance, the BMW Motorcycle Owners of America (*http://www.bmwmoa.org*) has an anonymous directory that lists phone numbers of volunteers by geographic area. Members receive a pocket-sized directory at no additional expense. You may be eligible to join an owner's club even if you don't own that brand.

Some motorcycle enthusiast organizations produce a directory of volunteers willing to help other members. The Anonymous Book is produced every year by the BMW Motorcycle Owners of America, and provided free to members.

While volunteers generally bend over backwards to help stranded club members, you can't assume they will be available 24/7. On the other hand, you might find an enthusiast just down the road with a trailer handy, working tools in the garage, and spare parts on the shelf. The potential for assistance makes it worthwhile to carry a club contact list.

Emergency Roadside Service

For the most comprehensive assistance, you can purchase emergency roadside service from commercial companies. The obvious advantage of commercial plans is 24/7 roadside help, but extra benefits may include trip routing, maps, emergency messages, cell phone rental, and discounts on car rentals and lodging. Since the services change from year to year, check with your dealer's finance rep, or with the membership representatives of your club, to see if you and your machine qualify for a roadside assistance policy, and the cost. In the event of a bike failure, you'll typically be transported by tow truck to the nearest dealer for your brand. Be sure the towing includes realistic mileage limits.

Medical Emergencies

Although you might be most concerned about the bike breaking down, there is also the chance you might become incapacitated or injured. If you have compound fractures or gaping wounds, you'll obviously need emergency medical help coming to rescue you. But what if you just start feeling funny, or wake up in the morning with pain in your chest? Are you having a heart attack, or just reacting to last night's pizza? We motorcyclists are a tough breed, and we're tempted to drag ourselves out to the bike and continue the trip. But it's a lot smarter to seek medical advice while you're still in town. My point in mentioning medical emergencies is that if you haven't yet had to interrupt a trip because of your health, it's very likely you will as you grow older.

As with motorcycle breakdowns, it's good to think through medical emergencies in advance. When you arrive at the hospital, they will need to know details: What's your blood type? Who is your medical insurance company? What's your policy number? Who is your doctor, and what's his phone number? It's best to have such details written down.

I carry a simple paper list of my medical and personal information in a jacket pocket, and an expanded version on an encrypted thumb drive that can be plugged into any computer when additional details are needed. I include other personal information on the thumb drive, including credit card and insurance policy numbers and contacts, motorcycle license and vehicle ID numbers, and images of my driver's license, insurance cards, and passport.

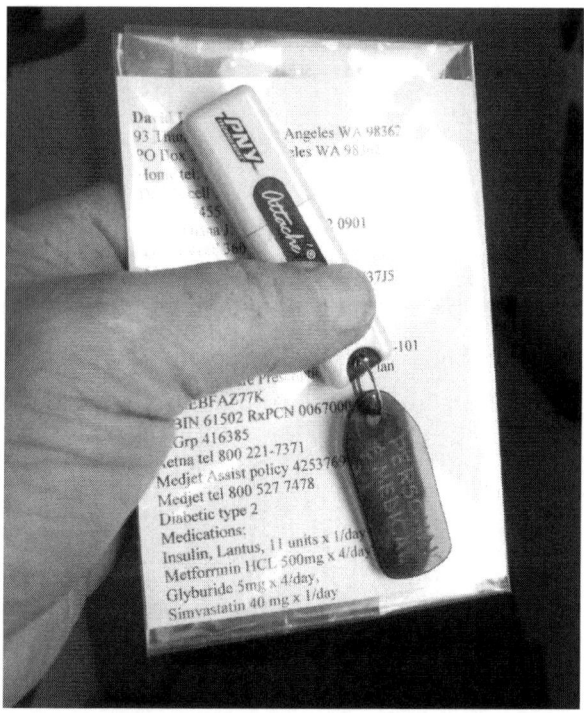

I print out a small paper copy of my basic medical information, seal it in a waterproof plastic cover, and carry it in a jacket pocket. I also carry an expanded version with other personal data on an encrypted thumb drive.

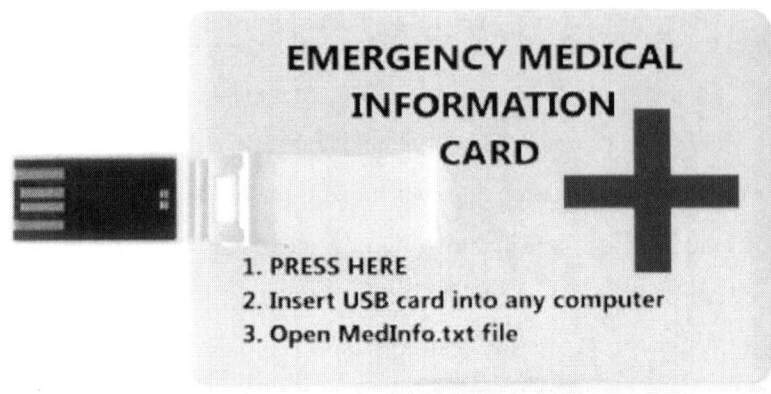

Once I left my thumb drive in the hotel room on a day I needed it most. This inspired Tom over at soundrider.com to come up with a credit card USB drive riders can carry in their wallet.

In the event you do crash or become incapacitated, it would be helpful to have some immediate medical information handy for the first responders. The Medical Information Carrier available from Whitehorse Gear is a tiny waterproof envelope that attaches to the outside of your helmet, including blood type and other emergency details. Aerostich has a similar Rescue Facts Emergency Pack that attaches to your helmet or jacket sleeve. You insert your information and it's available for the EMTs whether you're conscious or not.

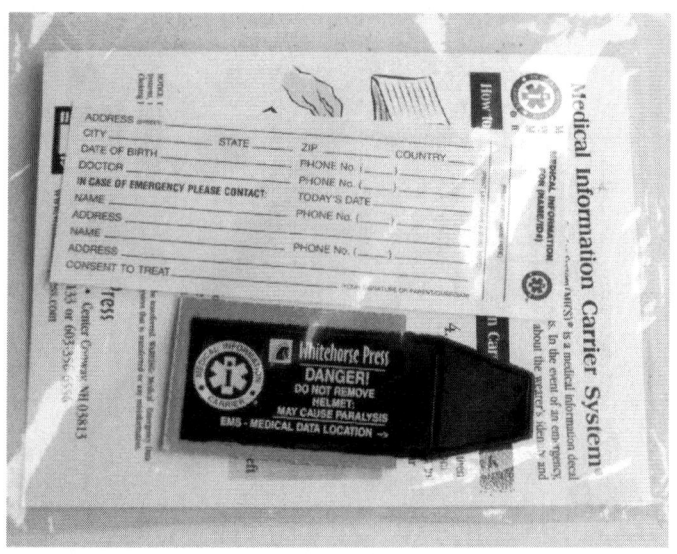

A medical information carrier can be secured to the outside of your helmet, for easy access by emergency responders. It comes as a kit with a form to fill out. The carrier has an adhesive back.

If you're confused, hurting, or pumped full of morphine, you and the ER doctors will appreciate having the information readily available. I encourage you to make a paper list now, while you're thinking about it. You might also think about your emergency policies, including both towing and medical evacuation (and travel medical coverage). Travel medical coverage can pay for transportation, physician services, hospital care, and medicines. Some policies will cover transportation of your motorcycle to your home. Check the coverage before leaving on a trip, and purchase special coverage as needed, say for a European trip.

Whether it's a bike breakdown or a medical problem, don't think it's the end of the world. After you've survived and recovered, it will become the highlight of your trip, the tale getting taller at each telling. It's all part of the great motorcycle adventure, but it's a lot less stressful if you're prepared in advance.

THE GOOD RIDER

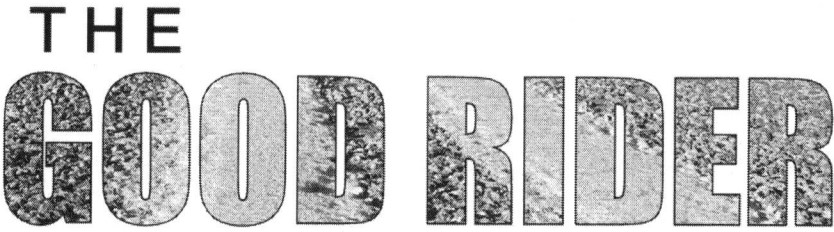

Chapter 24: Mechanical Skills

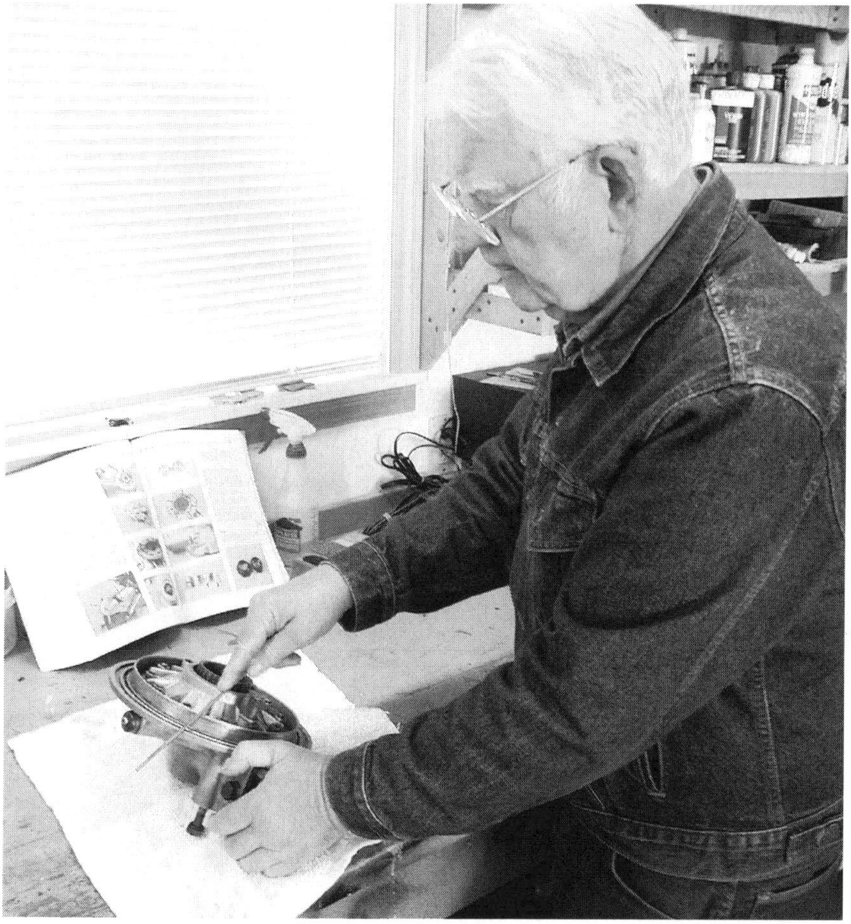

I've suggested that one part of being a good rider is having some mechanical skills, both to maintain your own motorcycle when needed,

and to diagnose and make simple field repairs on the road. It's not that I'm interested in taking business away from dealers, but a motorcyclist needs to be more independent than a car driver. Unlike automobile repair shops, motorcycle shops are fewer and farther between.

If you are mechanically inclined already, it's just a matter of studying the manuals and figuring out what's special about your machine. Even if you intend to have all the servicing done by a dealer, it helps to have a good idea of the service intervals and what's involved. There are also some tasks that you must be responsible for, including keeping the tires inflated, the fuel fresh, and the battery charged.

If you've managed to avoid getting your hands greasy until now, doing maintenance is part of becoming a good rider. Not a mechanic? It's time to start your education. Machines do have different quirks that make them confusing, but most bike systems follow predictable paths, and the detailed information is available. Manufacturers provide an owner's manual to help you learn the controls, systems, and service intervals.

If you haven't read your owner's manual recently, get it out and read it. Yes, every page. I suggest carrying the owner's manual on the bike, protected in a waterproof plastic sleeve. The manual has simple-but-important details such as lubrication schedules and tire pressures. Some manuals include troubleshooting procedures.

Manufacturers also produce a service manual (aka "shop" or "maintenance" manual) for each model or series. The service manual goes into detail about specific maintenance and repair techniques, usually with detailed step-by-step illustrations. I encourage you obtain the service manual for your machine, and study it. The book is too large to carry with you on the road, but you should study it in the wintertime, and consult it for specific tasks. I can't possibly explain how to maintain your bike here, but I can explain a bit about using the service manual.

The manual must be the correct one for your specific machine. Often, a manual will cover several similar motorcycles. Service manuals typically have a general information section up front that describes tools, lubricants, sealers, inspection, and measuring of parts. It's a wealth of information for the beginning mechanic.

KLX250S
KLX250SF

Motorcycle Service Manual

Be sure the manual is specific to your machine and year of manufacture.

MODEL APPLICATION

Year	Model	Beginning Frame No.
2009	KLX250T9F	JKALXMT1☐9DA00032 LX250T-A00032 PNKLX250TTMC00032
2009	KLX250W9F	JKALXMW1☐9DA00001 PNKLX250WWMC00001
2010	KLX250TAF	JKALXMT1☐ADA08022
2010	KLX250WAF	JKALXMW1☐ADA02826
2011	KLX250TBF	JKALXMT1☐BDA09821

☐:This digit in the frame number changes from one machine to another.

The service manual will usually have a chart showing which machines the manual applies to.

Quick Reference Guide

General Information	1
Periodic Maintenance	2
Fuel System	3
Cooling System	4
Engine Top End	5
Clutch	6
Engine Lubrication System	7
Engine Removal/Installation	8
Crankshaft/Transmission	9
Wheels/Tires	10
Final Drive	11
Brakes	12
Suspension	13
Steering	14
Frame	15
Electrical System	16
Appendix	17

Service manuals are typically divided into sections dealing with each system, say engine in one section, and suspension in a different section. This is for a Kawasaki machine. Other brands may be slightly different

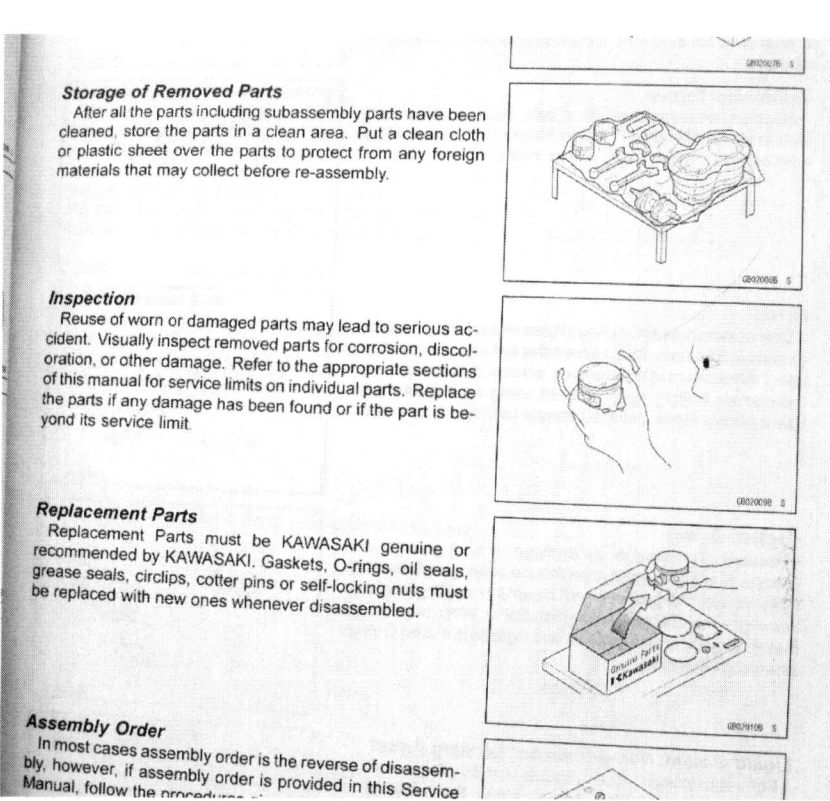

Storage of Removed Parts
After all the parts including subassembly parts have been cleaned, store the parts in a clean area. Put a clean cloth or plastic sheet over the parts to protect from any foreign materials that may collect before re-assembly.

Inspection
Reuse of worn or damaged parts may lead to serious accident. Visually inspect removed parts for corrosion, discoloration, or other damage. Refer to the appropriate sections of this manual for service limits on individual parts. Replace the parts if any damage has been found or if the part is beyond its service limit.

Replacement Parts
Replacement Parts must be KAWASAKI genuine or recommended by KAWASAKI. Gaskets, O-rings, oil seals, grease seals, circlips, cotter pins or self-locking nuts must be replaced with new ones whenever disassembled.

Assembly Order
In most cases assembly order is the reverse of disassembly, however, if assembly order is provided in this Service Manual, follow the procedures...

Often there is a general information section up front that provides an introduction to tools, bearing and seal installation, fastener torques, thread lockers, gaskets, lubricants, etc. That's a good place for the newbie mechanic to start.

When you're ready to tackle some job, find the appropriate section in the service manual. For example, let's say you need to change the output chain sprocket. You'll find that in the Final Drive section, and you can study the pictures and illustrations to figure out what's involved. The exploded view shows every single part, and can be useful when reassembling.

11-2 FINAL DRIVE
Exploded View

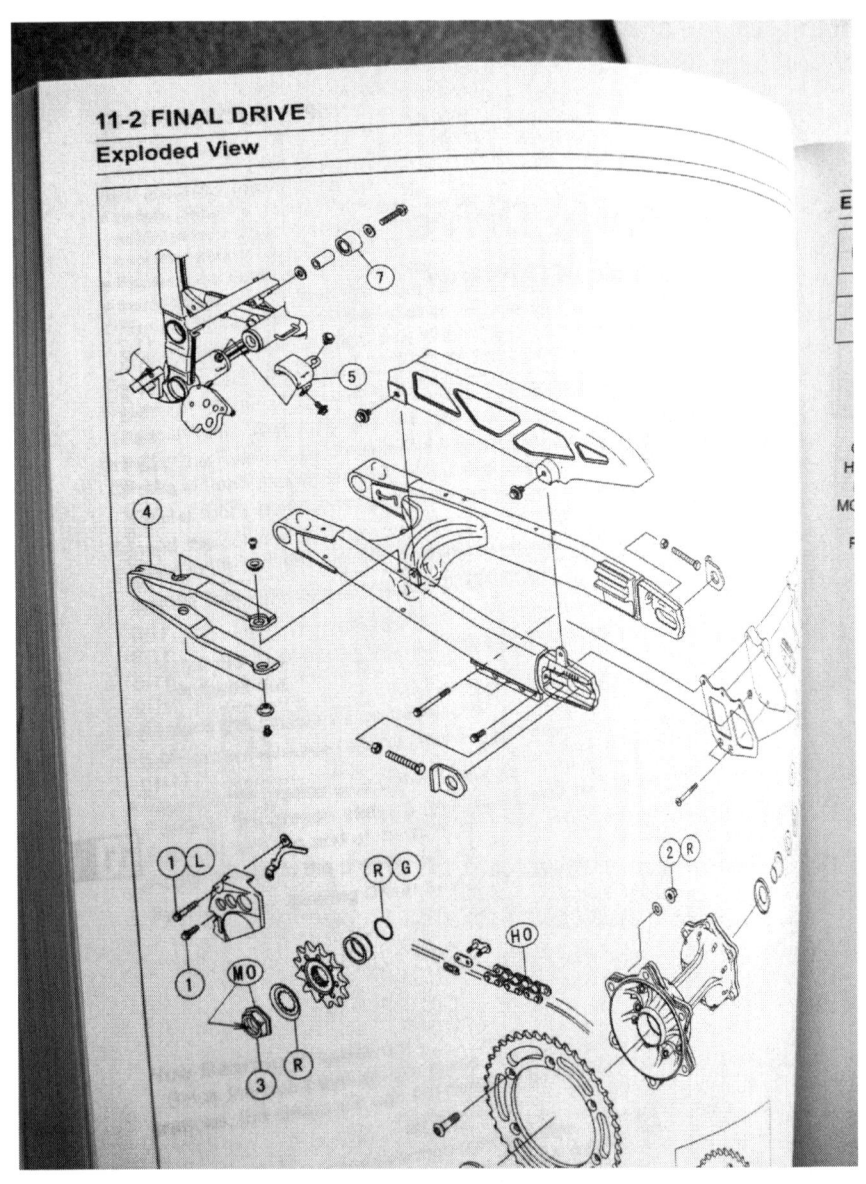

The exploded view shows all the parts in the assembly.

Finally, you can get to the detailed instructions, in this example a step-by-step explanation for removing and installing the sprocket. There will be notes, cautions, and warnings to give you further instructions, and the appropriate tools will be shown in use.

11-8 FINAL DRIVE
Sprocket

Engine Sprocket Removal
- Remove:
  Engine Sprocket Cover Bolts [A]
  Engine Sprocket Cover [B]
  Chain Guide [C]

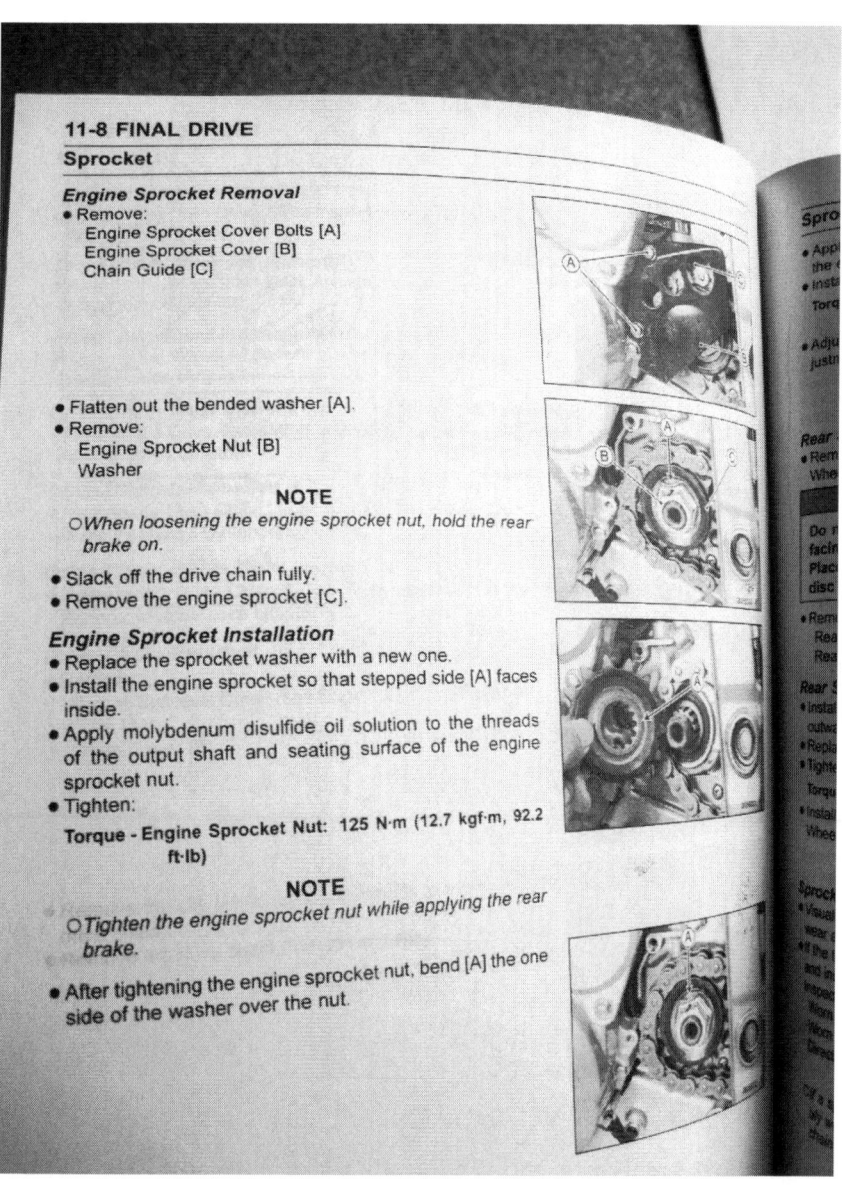

- Flatten out the bended washer [A].
- Remove:
  Engine Sprocket Nut [B]
  Washer

NOTE
○When loosening the engine sprocket nut, hold the rear brake on.

- Slack off the drive chain fully.
- Remove the engine sprocket [C].

Engine Sprocket Installation
- Replace the sprocket washer with a new one.
- Install the engine sprocket so that stepped side [A] faces inside.
- Apply molybdenum disulfide oil solution to the threads of the output shaft and seating surface of the engine sprocket nut.
- Tighten:
  Torque - Engine Sprocket Nut: 125 N·m (12.7 kgf·m, 92.2 ft·lb)

NOTE
○Tighten the engine sprocket nut while applying the rear brake.

- After tightening the engine sprocket nut, bend [A] the one side of the washer over the nut.

The step-by-step detailed instructions walk you through the steps for removal, inspection, and replacement of all the parts in the assembly, with photos or illustrations.

Chapter 24: Mechanical Skills

Tools

Don't despair if you don't have any working tools. Whatever the job, the tools to do it will typically be less expensive than the labor cost of having the work done by someone else, and once you buy a tool you'll have it to use next time. Steel tool cabinets with multiple roller drawers are handy. When you fill your first one with tools, you can buy a bigger roll-around tool chest and stack the smaller one on top.

You don't have to buy the most expensive tools around, but it's less frustrating to work with decent tools than with cheap tools. Professional mechanics often buy high quality tools from vendors who come around to different shops with a tool van. Generally, tools at auto parts stores will be acceptable, and lots of mechanics use Craftsman (Sears) tools. It's best to avoid the cheap tool sets at your local hardware store. You'll have enough to think about without having to figure out how to keep a cheap socket from rounding off the nut or falling out of the ratchet handle. My advice is to buy whatever tools you need for the current task. If money is short, you don't need to buy a complete 176-piece metric socket set; you can buy just the 17mm socket and ratchet handle you need today. Eventually you'll amass a good collection.

The Workspace

You will appreciate an enclosed workspace. It's a lot easier with comfortable temperature and good lighting. I've done valve adjustments and final drive swaps in campgrounds and in parking lots, but when you're tackling a challenging maintenance task, it's better to have some enclosed work area where removed parts won't get lost in the grass and your service manual won't get mangled by the wind.

Eventually, you should become knowledgeable enough to be able to diagnose problems on the road, and if possible, get the bike going again. A "shade tree" mechanic learns tricks such as spreading a towel or T shirt under the bike to catch small parts.

If you're really concerned about starting your wrenching career on your big buck road bike, consider picking up a cheap used machine, say a 250cc Honda or Kawasaki. Get the service manual for that machine, preferably the official one from the dealer. Then tackle one job at a time.

Will you make mistakes? Of course! Will you strip threads, lose parts, and forget how it goes back together? Probably. That's why I suggest getting a simple, "expendable" machine to learn on—not the bike you need next Saturday for the club ride. I also suggest making a search for a mentor.

The Mentor

It's really helpful to have someone who can coach you through mechanical problems, loan you a special tool, and explain what to do to fix something that broke or jammed. I recently changed the front drive sprocket on my used KLX 250. It should have been a simple half-hour task, except someone had glued the nut onto the threaded shaft with high strength thread locker. In the shop manual it mentions using Loctite on the small screws that hold the plastic cover in place. My guess is that the previous owner had spotted the Loctite reference without reading carefully enough, and used it on the big nut. In any case the nut was glued on solid.

I jammed a wood block over the rear brake pedal to lock it on, ran a tie-down strap around the tire to hold the wheel, and tried again. It wouldn't budge. I heated the nut with a torch and added a length of pipe over the end of a breaker bar. It still wouldn't loosen. After an hour or two of trying I gave up and drilled into the nut to cut it off in two pieces without ruining the threads on the shaft. A newbie mechanic would have been stymied by this simple task, because it wasn't coming apart like the service manual says it should, and the manual doesn't go into cutting off parts to remove them. That's where a mentor would come in handy, explaining the options and perhaps demonstrating non-normal techniques that aren't in the books.

It's possible but unlikely that you will find your mentor at a motorcycle dealer. Time is money, and they just can't afford to have a technician squandering time explaining things rather than doing the job. You might find an independent repair shop where the mechanic can occasionally take the time to explain the correct techniques, but you should expect to pay for the extra time.

There are people around who love working on machines, and some might be in a position to help you. There are retired shop owners or mechanics with considerable knowledge who are willing to share their skills just to avoid boredom. There are also brand-oriented clubs that have periodic workshop days where you can take on various maintenance tasks under the watchful eye of veterans. In any case, find yourself a mentor.

Practical Advice

The inexperienced mechanic may think the first task is to take things apart. Whoa! The first task is to read the manual. Most of what you need to know is in there. Technicians are often amazed at the dumb questions riders ask, questions that are fully explained in the owner's manual. There's a socially impolite acronym used between technicians and service reps after a series of dumb questions: *RTFM*, where R stands for read, and M stands for manual.

Not only is it disrespectful to waste someone's time with dumb questions, it's proof that you really aren't very sharp. So, get in the habit of reading the manuals, first the owner's manual, then the service manual.

The second task is to remove all the spooge, grease, and goo so you can see what's going on. That's one area where elbow grease by the owner is well spent. Lay down several layers of newspaper under the machine, put on some nitrile gloves, and scrub the goo away with a stiff brush and a solvent such as kerosene or clutch and brake cleaner. Not only can you afford to take the time needed to dissolve and scrub away the goo, you'll get to study every detail. Then, once the parts are spotless, take pictures before you take something apart. You can refer to the images later when it's time to put it back together.

Let's note that even if you take your machine to a professional shop for work, it's worthwhile to meticulously clean it before taking it in. It's not merely an insult to expect a technician to scrub through the goo to get down to the mechanism, you'll probably get less attention to detail. Maybe there's a frayed wire that really should be replaced, but it hasn't failed, so it gets ignored. The guy (or gal) doing the work is likely to think, *"If he doesn't care about his machine enough to clean it, why should I care about little details that aren't part of the job at hand?"*

Tires

Even if you scrub and polish your bike before taking it in for service, there are some tasks that are totally your responsibility. You must maintain your tire pressures. It's not enough to have your tires inflated by the dealer at the start of the season. You need to get down there and check tire condition and pressure, preferably before every ride. It's handy to have a compact 12V compressor such as the Cycle Pump, both for use in the shop and on the road. Eventually you will want to learn more about tires. You'll also find a lot of useful information in your owner's manual.

There are lots of small pumps on the market, but the Best Rest is compact, reliable, and enclosed in a very durable aluminum housing that keeps it operational for years. This is the pump used by many motorcycle tour companies. The optional gauge works in-line, making it easy to read inflation in real time (Photo courtesy of Best Rest Products LLC)

Tire pressure should be checked cold, which is to say before the bike has been ridden for the day. The tire pressures listed in your owner's manual are a good place to start. If you change tires to a different brand you can call the tire representatives and ask for specific pressures based on the weights you will be carrying. The important part of tire maintenance is to never run the bike at highway speeds when they are not at appropriate pressures.

There is also a great DVD on tire servicing available from Best Rest Products, *"Tire Changes and Repairs,"* that is especially helpful for dual-sport riders. Visit *http://www.bestrestproducts.com* to learn more.

Fuel

Another owner responsibility is fuel, but beyond octane, you probably won't find much about fuel in the manuals. What you really need to know is that today's gasoline blends are unstable. They turn sour within a month or two unless treated. Why won't your bike start after sitting all winter? That four-month-old gas could be so stale it won't ignite. And if it's six months old, it may have gummed up the small orifices in the fuel system.

Yes, there are detailed instructions in the service manual for taking the fuel system apart and reconditioning it. But it's a lot less trouble and expense to just add fuel stabilizer (such as STABIL) when you intend to park the bike for two or three months. I prefer to use a stabilizer rather than emptying the tank. A full tank of fuel will help prevent water condensation. If you prefer to drain the gas from the tank for winter storage, it will burn in the car when mixed with fresher fuel.

Periodically the fuel filters and screens need to be cleaned or changed. If your bike has a carburetor, the residue in the bottom of the float bowls should be cleaned out at least once a season, whether you do it or the dealer's technician does it. There are other periodic tasks that need attention, all spelled out in your owner's manual.

Battery

You should also keep your battery clean and charged. Motorcycle electrical systems are much less powerful than auto systems, and bike batteries are smaller. Won't running your bike occasionally keep the battery charged? Even if your charging system is fine, a battery won't stay charged for months on end. All batteries discharge, but bike batteries tend to go flat quicker because of their relative size.

There can also be "parasitic" loads on your battery, say from a clock, or "leakage" from imperfect diodes in the charging system, or from corrosion near the terminals. The result can be that your "fully charged" battery that has been resting for two months is now almost flat. It's not just a matter of not having enough voltage to crank the starter, but that a discharged battery loses much of its future life. The solution is to plug the battery into a reliable automatic charger whenever the bike is going to be parked for a week or more. You don't have to remove the battery to charge it.

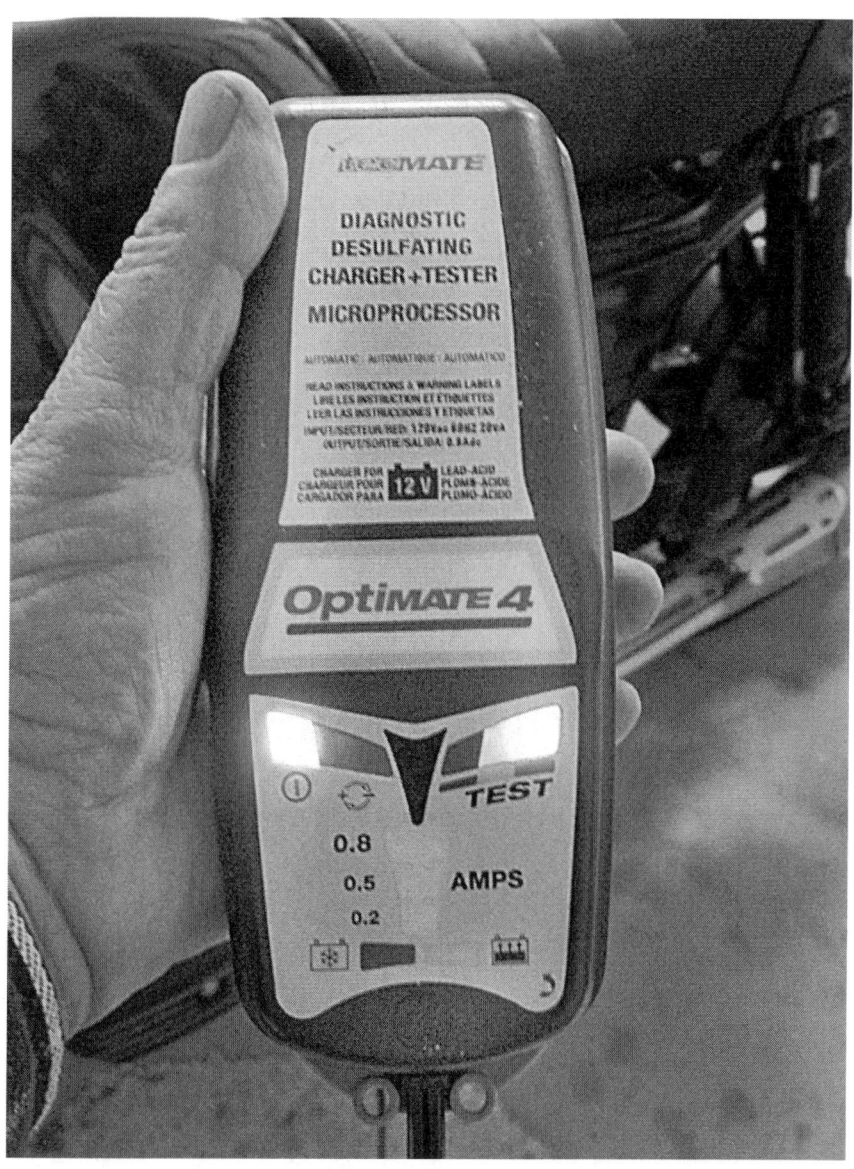

A high quality automatic battery charger will not only keep your battery charged for next month's ride, it will lengthen the life of the battery. An automatic charger such as this Optimate 4 will bring a discharged battery back to life, unlike the less sophisticated chargers.

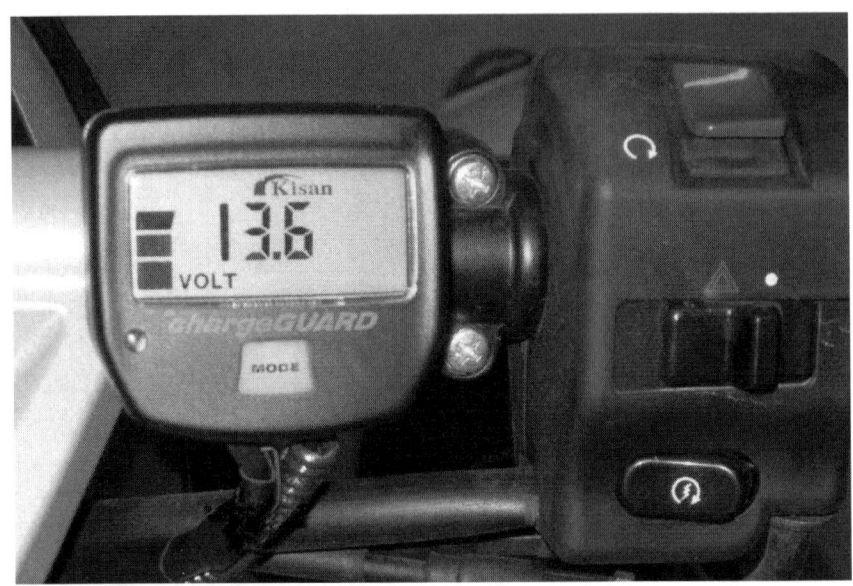

A "float" voltage of 13.6 or 13.7 volts is about right to maintain an AGM battery at full charge. Other types of batteries require different charging algorithms and float voltages. This Kisan ChargeGuard can be installed permanently on the bike, and turns on whenever the battery is receiving a charge. It can also show amperage and ambient temperature.

My suggestion is to get a really good charger-- not one of those cheap versions that promise to charge all types of batteries. The low quality chargers are unlikely to keep your battery at full charge, and very likely won't be able to charge it at all once it starts to go flat. Get something like the Optimate 4 or Battery Doc, or whatever automatic charger is recommended by the manufacturer of the battery on your machine. Just connect a fused pigtail directly to the battery terminals, and get in the habit of plugging in the automatic charger when you park the bike. You can leave the battery plugged into a good automatic charger for months without concern. With a high quality charger you may discover that your bike runs better and your battery lasts twice as long.

A really good charger will not only keep a battery fully charged, but will possibly save a battery that's been allowed to go flat. A lead/acid battery tends to "sulfate" as it discharges. The better chargers have special algorithms and power to cut through the sulfate and bring a discharged battery back to life.

Your motorcycle was designed with a charging system appropriate for a specific type of battery. If you change to a different battery type (say replacing a "wet" lead/acid with an AGM or lithium/iron), your charging system may not be able to get the new battery up to full charge. The bike will still run, and the charging system will work, but the battery never gets up to full charge. However, if you plug in an automatic charger suitable for that battery type whenever the bike is parked, the battery will be kept at full charge for most of its life, and will last much longer.

An automatic charger first charges at a "bulk" rate to get the battery up, then cuts the power for a few minutes to allow the battery to drop to its resting voltage. Then the charger provides a low amperage "float" charge at a voltage suitable for the battery type. Be aware that the ideal float voltage for a battery changes with temperature. Higher ambient temperatures require lower float voltages. For this reason, an automatic charger with temperature compensation is a necessity for hot climates.

If you find your battery terminals corroded, it would be wise to clean the battery and terminals. First, wash the outside of the battery and the battery support with water and baking soda, and rinse with fresh water. Scrape the battery terminals and wire lugs clean, and lubricate with dielectric grease. Connect the wires right on top of the grease, and smear more grease around the exposed metal to help prevent future corrosion.

Whenever disconnecting a battery, remove the ground cable first (usually black or -). When reconnecting a battery, connect the positive cable first (usually red or +). That's to avoid causing a short between the positive terminal and the frame, which would create major sparks.

When disconnecting a battery, remove the negative (black) cable first, then the positive (red). When connecting a battery, connect the positive (red) first, then the negative (black).

Getting More Information

There are a number of online forums where owners of certain brands or types of machines share information. Much of the blather on the forums can be answered by "*RTFM,*" but you can search around a bit and probably find one where the true experts are offering useful advice. With the Internet being worldwide, you may find the best source of information about your bike is from some other country.

Your dealer should be able to order a service manual for your bike. Alternately, you may be able to get one on a CD, or download it from the Internet.

THE GOOD RIDER

Chapter 25: Group Rides

Given my choice of traveling alone or in a group, I'd prefer to ride alone. Life is much simpler when I'm cruising toward the horizon all by myself. I only have to make decisions for one person, and I can change plans instantly without having a roadside conference. Of course, I've had some great canyon rides with small groups of proficient riders.

Statistically speaking, more and more fatal motorcycle crashes are occurring on group rides, at least in the Northwest. And sooner or later you'll be thinking about joining others for a ride, whether a poker run, or a cross-country journey. So, to help avoid disappointments or even crashes, let's consider what's involved in a group ride.

Aggressive Riding

I've been in a number of group rides that were faster than I would have preferred, and I've led a few rides that in retrospect were faster than I should have allowed. There's something about motorcycling that brings out our competitive spirits. *"Boy, those other riders are really aggressive. I'd better crank up the wick so they won't think I'm a wuss!"* It's easy to get stampeded into riding a lot faster than we should. And it's just not macho to say anything about the pace or drop back.

There's something about motorcycling that brings out the competitive spirit.

Some groups are more aggressive than others, whether a matter of wussophobia, or poor leadership. When I realize a group is more aggressive than I'm willing to risk, I'm learning to slow down or even drop out. It's polite to announce to the ride leader that I'm splitting. If there is resistance to my leaving, it's easy enough to make a "wrong turn" in the next few miles and get lost.

I suppose my preference for traveling alone isn't so much that I don't like groups, but that I'm cautious about joining groups that aren't organized well. One group leader turned a simple day ride into a nightmare. Daffy didn't do hand signals, or check his mirrors, or use a radio. Taking off from a stop sign, he would just peel out in front of a line of cars, leaving the rest of us playing catch up. When Daffy instantly decided to make a fuel stop, he slowed in the left lane of an arterial and dove across two lanes of oncoming traffic into a gas station without signaling. After two hours of that nightmare, I abandoned the group after the fuel stop. I just delayed until after everyone else had departed and no one noticed. Looking back, I wonder why I hung in there so long.

Thinking Alike

One assumption that sets a group up for an accident is the idea that we're all on the same wavelength. It's a common misperception that after riding with others for X miles or Y years, we've all learned the same skills and habits.

Two riders are making a cross-country trip together. They are both veteran motorcyclists, and equally skilled. Either one could travel independently, but they enjoy the company and security of another rider. Betty is in the lead today, with Bob following along. Late in the day as they enter another small town, Betty observes a small dog darting around near the street, and rolls off the throttle. As Betty had predicted, the dog darts out into her path, and she pulls off a perfect quick stop to avoid hitting it.

That should be the end of the problem, except that Bob isn't prepared for a quick stop. Before he can reach for the brake, his bike rams into Betty's, fracturing her leg and ending her ride.

That should also be the end of the story, except Bob needs to save face. He argues that Betty should not have made a quick stop just for a small dog. If Bob had been in the lead he would have kept going and swerved around the dog. So, there's a big dispute about who caused the crash. We might also ask Bob, *"Who was in charge here?"*

The idea that we're all thinking alike is an illusion. It's not so much a "group" as several different riders who happen to be on the road together. There's nothing wrong with getting to know your riding buddies and their habits. But it's essential to have some rules. When we're riding down the road in a group, one person is assigned the task of leader, and everyone else is responsible for following and staying in control. And, before we move on, let's agree that a "group" is two or more riders, eh, Bob?

It's an illusion that all the riders in a group are on the same wavelength. It's essential to understand that everyone is responsible for controlling his or her own machine.

Group Leadership

When a group is composed of riders of relatively equal skill and experience, it's customary for everyone to take a turn at leading the ride. Whoever the leader today, it's a good idea to have a meeting before departure to explain what's going to happen. If there are navigation concerns, printed route sheets can be handed out or a GPS route inserted. When I'm leading a group, I may suggest that if anyone doesn't want to ride with the group, they may depart first, and meet us at the next scheduled stop. That way, if they have a problem, we won't leave them stranded.

Clubs who frequently ride in groups often equip their bikes with CB radios or helmet-to-helmet intercoms to maintain voice contact. Riding in traffic, we must expect that a group (even a group of two riders) will get separated by other vehicles or traffic signals from time to time. Without bike-to-bike communications, the plan could be to stop and call the other rider on your cell phone if a certain time period has passed without a visual. For instance, if you haven't seen your riding companion for 30 minutes, stop and call.

Or, if the riders are independently capable, the plan could be for each rider to continue to the specified "meet up" destination, which could be an hour away, a half day away, or at the end of the day's ride. The most hazardous tactic is to double back looking for a missing rider.

Whatever the plan, it should be announced at the riders' meeting. If it's a large group, one basic rule should be that the group will not stop to wait for riders held up by one traffic signal in a string of intersections. If the tail end of the group gets separated by a red light, odds are they will eventually catch up. If not, the leader can pull over on the way out of town to allow the group to reform.

Hey, It's Only Another 300 Miles!

One big factor that sets groups up for crashes is fatigue. Riding all day takes a lot of effort and concentration. Not only do you need to deal with traffic, surface hazards, and weather, you need to keep track of others in the group. After 6 or 8 hours duking it out with traffic, your skills will likely have degraded, you'll be more distracted, and your reaction times will be longer.

A group of three seasoned riders leaves the Seattle area for the 49er rally in Auburn, California. The weather in Washington suddenly turns cold and wet, which slows them down. To stay on their planned schedule, they press on until they are exhausted. The next day in Oregon is also rainy, cold, and windy. All three riders are getting concerned they might not make the rally, but each one keeps that fear to himself, and presses on. After only another 300 miserable miles, they turn in, well short of the planned stop.

On the third day they awake to blue skies. Along with the sunshine, their attitudes get brighter, and all three realize that an aggressive dash through Northern California will get them to the rally on schedule after all. But three hours later one of the bikes spins a bearing in the transmission. The other two riders are frustrated by the delay, but it would be extremely antisocial to leave their buddy stranded. Locating a rental truck puts them another 4 hours behind schedule.

Now the two remaining riders urgently need to make up time, and they press on aggressively. They are just a few miles short of the rally that evening when the two riders collide at a confusing intersection. Both riders are carted off to the hospital, and both bikes are towed away to the impound yard.

As one of the riders admits afterward: *"The underlying cause of the crash was fatigue. We simply pushed too hard and didn't stop often enough. We were focused on getting to the rally on time, and we were unwilling to say anything to each other about how tired we were."*

The Ride Captain

Let's say you are asked to lead a group ride, with a potential for 20 bikes. Hold it! Don't run away just yet. We'll talk you through it. You'll be the leader, or Ride Captain, but you should arrange for another experienced rider to be the "Tail End Charlie" to bring up the end of the group. But don't fire up the engine and zoom into traffic just yet. We have some group dynamics to discuss. First, here's a trick question:

If you immediately pull out onto the highway and accelerate up to 55 mph, how much time will pass before Charlie starts to move, 19 bikes behind you?

Well, if there aren't any other vehicles on the road, and riders manage to follow you exactly two seconds apart, Charlie will be sitting in the same spot for 38 seconds. If Charlie throttles up to 110 mph, he can catch up to the group in maybe 30 seconds. If Charlie is only willing to risk 80 mph, it will take him about a minute and a half to catch up, assuming you hold 55 mph. So you shouldn't be surprised when Charlie approaches you at the first rest stop, hotter than a rear Heritage header.

Think of a group of motorcycles like a train, with the cars hitched together by twenty-foot bungee cords. That's why the sharp ride leader pulls out slowly and creeps along at 30 mph or so, until Charlie finally gets rolling. You can either watch in your mirrors, or listen for Charlie on the radio. Once the entire group is rolling, you can pick up the pace to cruising speed. To avoid holding up other motorists, it's wise to maintain at least the speed limit, or the average speed of traffic if the road is busy. You don't want to hold up traffic, encouraging other motorists to attempt passing the group.

Newbies to the Front, Please

When less experienced riders are invited to a group ride, the tendency is to wait around, watch what everyone else is doing, and fall in at the back of the pack. That way, the others can't see what the novice is doing wrong. But note that the action gets more demanding at the tail end of a group, so you should direct the novices to ride immediately behind you. That also helps you establish a speed that's appropriate for the group, since you can see what the least experienced riders are doing.

The Formation

You've probably seen motor officers (and also big bad bikers) riding side-by-side in two columns. The side-by-side formation looks really impressive, and it's possible because motor officers do a lot of practice together, and learn to trust each other. But even motor officers have had crashes where one bike bumps into the one alongside. My preference is a staggered formation, because it allows more maneuvering room. In a staggered formation, you ride in the opposite wheel track from the rider ahead of you. That is, if the rider in front of you is in the left wheel track, you take the right wheel track. That allows some movement within the lane without bumping into someone. It's the Ride Captain's choice to ride in the left or right wheel track.

In the staggered formation, you alternate wheel tracks.

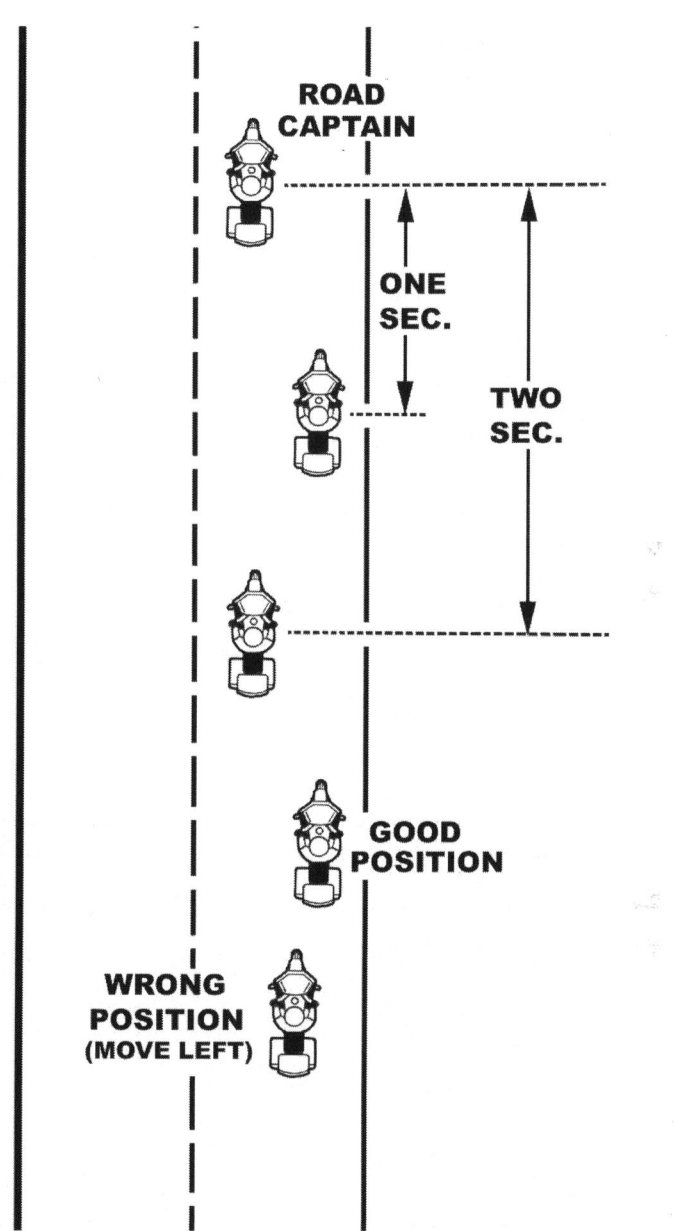

Riding one second behind the bike in the other track puts you two seconds behind the bike directly ahead.

If you follow one second behind the rider in the other wheel track, that puts you two seconds behind the rider directly ahead of you. Two seconds is the minimum distance to provide a space cushion, while keeping the group as compact as possible. If everyone pays attention, it is easy to establish and maintain a staggered two-second formation. If traffic is light, it's advisable to stretch the spacing out to three or even four seconds.

The bad news is that we must be prepared for some less-than-sharp rider to join the group. When you are signaling *start your engines*, Less will probably be nattering with that cutie on the pink Sportster, with his helmet and gloves still parked inside the coffee shop, his keys in an inside pocket, and his gas tank unfilled.

When it's Time to Go, GO!

My suggestion for a Ride Captain blessed with a less-than-sharp participant is to expect everyone to conform to the group, and make that clear at the riders' meeting before the ride. Explain your expectations for the ride, along with any rules you think would help. For instance, you might suggest that if any rider in the group allows following distance to stretch out to six seconds, it is acceptable for following riders to pass. Explain where the group will be stopping, and where the ride is expected to end. Make it clear that when the group stops for fuel, everyone is expected to top up their tanks. Most importantly, take steps to separate alcohol from the ride. My suggestion: if anyone imbibes alcohol during the ride, that's the end of the ride.

When it's time to go, GO! Post some odd start time, such as 8:17 am, and then leave exactly at 8:17 am, to make it clear that you're not kidding. Leave Mr. Thansharp running around in circles back in the parking lot if he's not ready. And keep the rest of the group moving when Less runs out of fuel during the ride. Part of your job as ride leader is to not let one participant ruin the ride for everyone else.

Getting Through the Green Light

When you're leading a group through a controlled intersection in traffic, it is unlikely you'll get everyone through before the light turns amber. There is a temptation for following riders to speed up and run the amber to stay with the group, which encourages riders at the tail end to panic and run the red. Explain at the start that riders are expected to obey all traffic signals, and that you will slow down as necessary to let everyone catch up after a series of intersections.

In practical terms, with a series of signal lights, the leader will get stopped as often as the tail end riders, and everyone will pass through all the intersections at about the same rate. I've been in big groups where some riders are assigned as escorts to pull over and block intersections so everyone can run the red light, but I don't recommend that tactic unless the escorts are on-duty motor officers. If there's a collision, you could be held accountable.

All you usually have to do is keep speed in check as you leave town, to give everyone a chance to catch up before you roll the group up to cruising speed. Once in a while, you may have to creep along in the slow lane, or even pull the group off the road, to wait for riders caught at a long light. With a group of only five or six riders, it is easy to find a place to stop, and also to get rolling again, but with groups of 30 or more it is best to keep going at a slower speed and let the stragglers catch up. If you have radio communication, Charlie will keep you posted on what's happening back there.

Don't even think about stopping a group on the shoulder of a busy highway just because one rider has a problem. I've seen some extremely dangerous stunts, such as a whole gaggle of bikers coming to a screeching halt in the middle of a busy freeway, because one rider dropped a glove. Keep the group rolling and avoid a tragic crash.

Signals

Hand and light signals are quick ways to communicate, with or without radios. My preference for signaling a surface hazard is to tap the brake three times, rather than attempting to point to the hazard with a hand or foot. In other words, alert following riders that there is a hazard, and let them find it. There are various hand signals in use, but there are no standards, and riders tend to forget them anyway. You might demonstrate two or three hand signals during the riders' meeting if you think they could help.

When the group is passing another vehicle, each rider must be responsible for a safe pass. No one should signal the following riders to pass or not pass. You could signal someone to pass, and then realize there's a deer about to leap out.

Getting Stopped

OK, you got the group rolling, you've managed to herd everyone through eighteen signal lights and twenty intersections without losing Less or causing an accident, and it's been a pleasant ride. Now, how do you get a long string of motorcycles stopped and parked for lunch without creating a traffic hazard?

The most important consideration is having a parking area that's big enough for the whole group to ride into. You don't want to get half the group off the road, and leave the other half stranded out there in traffic like sitting ducks. The best scenario is when the group has space to motor into a parking lot and park side-by-side to conserve space. Riders should pull up to the left of each rider ahead, so that everyone can immediately back into the parking space without waiting. With a little experience, the whole group can get parked quickly, which helps move everyone off the road efficiently. It's important to not be creative. Every rider should pull *alongside to the left of the next rider*, and immediately roll back into the parking space.

The larger the group, the more important it is to have specific stops arranged. When I led groups of 80 to 100 riders, I would ride the entire route prior to the tour to identify specific problem areas such as construction zones, to find suitable parking areas, and to make arrangements for a meal. If you are making arrangements for a really big group, you'll need lots of help, and perhaps even a permit.

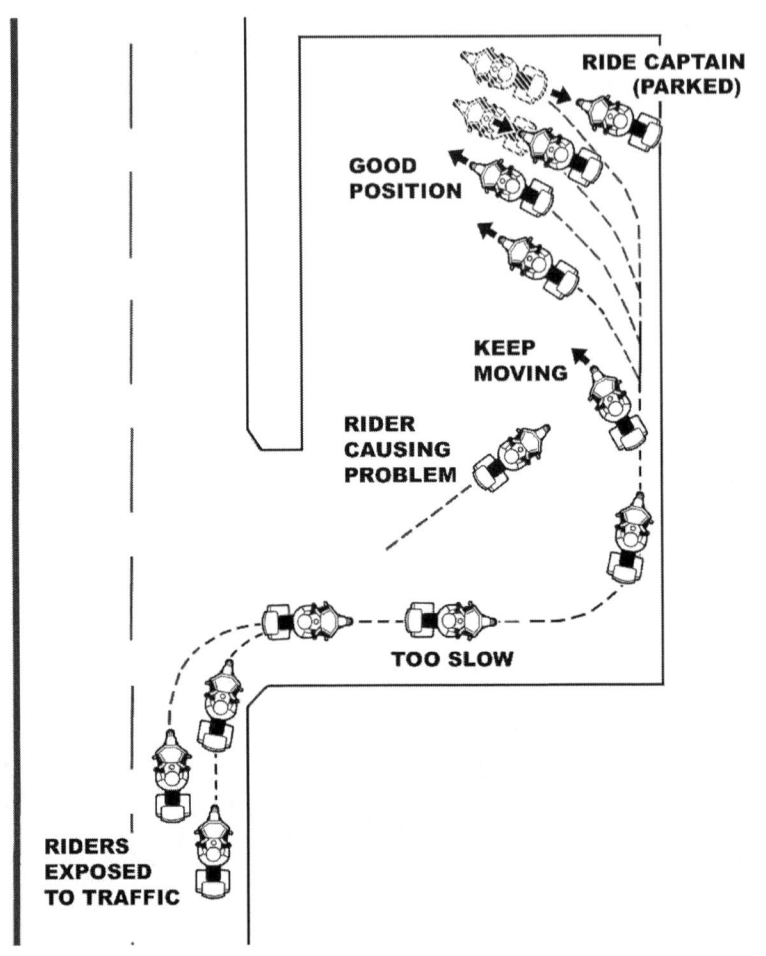

Once riders get used to the parking drill, it can go quickly and smoothly.

Back in the Pack

If you've never ridden in a group, make a point of staying close to the Ride Captain rather than at the back of the pack. It's a lot easier to maintain speed and position if you are no more than two or three bikes from the front. Fill your tank and empty your bladder well before the scheduled departure time. When the leader puts on his helmet and gloves, get your gear on, get your key in the ignition, and get ready to roll.

Once underway, maintain the requested interval and lane position. Try to avoid drifting back and creating a big hole in the formation. If someone ahead suddenly wakes up to being in the wrong track and moves over, immediately signal and re-establish the proper staggered formation. Watch the leader for hand signals. When riders ahead give warning signals, pass the signal back down the line. If another rider has a problem and pulls over, stay with the group and keep rolling unless the leader also pulls over, or asks that you stop to help. It's Charlie's job to deal with the problem.

Alternate Ways to Move a Group

When we think "group ride," we might imagine a long string of bikes in formation, but there are other ways to move a group down the road. One technique I have used is printing up route sheets which detail the route and schedule. It's relatively easy to make up route sheets by snipping pieces out of a state tourist map and adding schedule information alongside. Poker runs and mystery tours are different forms of a group ride, where everyone does their own navigating and rides at their own pace.

One word of caution about complex navigational instructions: avoid written instructions that require a rider to read a half page of small print after every checkpoint. Slow or inexperienced riders are likely to get lost or confused. Even if the instructions are short and clear, some riders simply dawdle so much they run out of time. One reliable tactic for herding in the stragglers is to provide a sealed escape envelope with instructions for a direct route to the destination.

Try It, You Might Like It

If you've been avoiding group rides, consider joining up once in a while as part of your progress toward becoming a good rider. Maybe you'll even discover some fellow enthusiasts you enjoy riding with. And if none of the others measure up to your standards of group leadership, maybe you'll just have to be the Ride Captain and show them how it's done. But remember, riding in a group once in a while doesn't mean you can't go droning off towards the horizon by yourself when you feel like it.

THE GOOD RIDER

Chapter 26: The Second Rider

I've ridden motorcycles in some scary situations. Once, crossing Nebraska, I faced two converging tornadoes. In Colorado during a torrential downpour, I sprinted into a restaurant a few seconds ahead of a lightning bolt. I narrowly avoided a moose collision in British Columbia, and a troop of baboons in South Africa. But the scariest rides of my life were those rare occasions when I had to thumb a ride on the back of someone else's bike:

"Hey! There aren't any handlebars back here—what am I supposed to hang on to? Where's the brake lever? I can't see where the bike is headed! I don't know which way we're going to lean. Uh-oh, I think I'm slipping off the back! Slow down!"

Most motorcyclists I know ride solo much of the time. Sure, there are couples who ride two-up on every trip, but many riders seldom carry a passenger. So when you do ask someone to share the ride, you may forget to explain what they need to know, or remember how the additional load will affect handling. Let's review some of the basic concerns for carrying passengers.

The Safety Briefing

When you board an airplane, you assume the pilot knows what to do, but the passengers may need some coaching about whether the flight includes breakfast, and whether it will arrive in time for the connecting flight. First-time passengers may need some coaching about things like emergency exits, toilets, and seat belts. Similarly, when you have a passenger lined up to ride on the back of your saddle, it's part of your job to provide the necessary riding gear, explain how to climb aboard, discuss what to do when the bike leans, and suggest how to communicate at speed. After a few rides, passengers will know what's expected.

For a novice passenger, you should explain the need for riding gear that is warm and durable, including a heavy jacket that won't flap around, leather boots to prevent burns on hot exhaust pipes, gloves to protect the hands, a helmet to protect the brain, and a face shield or goggles to protect the eyes. You don't need to bring up the possibility of rain, if the weather that day looks sunny. You should discourage any potentially harmful clothing, such as a long, floppy scarf that could wrap around a helmet in a cross-wind, a long drover coat which could snag in the rear wheel, boots with dangly things which could catch on a foot peg, or spiked heels which could melt down on your mufflers.

For first-timers, it's also helpful to explain that you will saddle up first and get the bike balanced, and then the passenger can stand up on the left passenger peg and swing onto the saddle. Mention that motorcycles lean into corners, that leaning over is normal, and that the passenger should lean the same as the rider. There are a number of other little points you could cover, such as the passenger keeping feet on the pegs when stopping, and that you will do the traffic signals, thank you. New passengers want to do the right thing, and will probably appreciate some coaching.

Expect Handling Changes

What's most important for the rider is that a second person on the bike not only increases the total weight, but also relocates the Center of Mass (CoM) and adds sail to the rear of the bike. Those changes affect your control of the machine. Acceleration, braking, and cornering tactics all change, not just because of the additional mass and where the weight is loaded on the bike, but also because the second rider's weight can shift around when you're not expecting it.

Quick Stops

For example, consider what happens during hard braking: there is more total mass to stop, so you can expect a somewhat longer stopping distance. With more weight on the rear wheel, more rear braking can be used in a quick stop, or on slick pavement. On a machine with integrated brakes, you won't notice much difference, except that it takes harder braking and more distance to stop quickly. More weight means increased traction, so you might think the limiting factor would be brake efficiency. But what you will discover when you try a quick stop is that the passenger slams forward during hard braking, limiting how much brake effort you're willing to apply.

When you brake aggressively carrying a passenger, the passenger's mass slams into your back. You may have to ease off the brake just to keep from being pushed up onto the tank.

Once when riding with my wife on the back, I observed what appeared to be a brown log in the left ditch. But as we got closer, the "log" suddenly raised up its antlers, leaped up onto the pavement, and clattered into a U-turn. I immediately squeezed on the brakes, but my wife wasn't prepared for a quick stop, and slammed into my back, pushing me forward onto the tank. Even though she is a relative lightweight, I had to modulate the brakes well short of maximum, just to keep from being pushed into the handlebars. We managed to miss the deer by inches, but the lesson to me was clearly that I must always allow more stopping distance when carrying a passenger. Remember, the passenger can't see ahead as well as you can, doesn't know when you are going to suddenly squeeze the lever, and during a stop doesn't have much to brace against except you.

If you regularly carry a passenger, you might consider practicing quick stops with the passenger aboard. Some training sites allow passengers to be carried during the practice exercises. The typical drill is for the rider to take the course with no passenger, and then repeat the same exercises with a passenger the next day. Passengers may find it helpful to listen to the classroom presentations, too. It helps them to understand why you're doing what you're doing, and why you must concentrate so much on traffic and surface hazards.

Acceleration

When accelerating, you have more control over the situation, because you can roll on the gas smoothly to help the passenger stay put. Heavyweight touring machines with top boxes and passenger backrests provide a relatively secure perch for the second rider, but many machines don't offer much in the way of passenger hand holds. Those silly straps that manufacturers used to stretch across the middle of the saddle were supposed to be grab handles for passengers, but no one ever explained how a human being might have braced against acceleration or deceleration with their hands between their knees. Some machines provide solid grab handles around the rear of the saddle, but it is still difficult to hold on if the bike is accelerating quickly.

Just remember that your passenger may not have much except you to hold onto. You can suggest that they grasp you lightly around your waist. If your passenger gives you a little squeeze while riding along into a beautiful sunset, the message is probably *"Gee honey, I'm glad you brought me along."* But if your passenger suddenly strangles you in a bear hug as you roll on the gas, it's probably a sign you are getting a little too aggressive with the throttle. If you want to enjoy the company of a second rider, you've got to make them comfortable, which really means riding more conservatively than if you were all by yourself.

Cornering

When you are carrying a passenger with little or no motorcycle experience, you shouldn't be surprised when they panic as you lean the bike over into the first sharp turn. Of course it will be your turn to panic if the passenger manages to lean toward the outside while you're trying to get the bike leaned over toward the inside. The wise rider takes corners sedately for the first hour or so, to allow the novice passenger some time to adapt to this leaning business, and for you to adapt to cornering with the additional mass.

If your bike already has limited lean-over clearance, don't be surprised when the bike starts making sparks while cornering with a passenger. That's because the additional weight of the second rider compresses the rear suspension more, reducing lean-over clearance. You can reduce the touchdown problem by following a larger-radius cornering line, by reducing entry speed more than for solo riding, and by rolling on the throttle more as the bike is leaned over. But if your machine makes sparks too easily, that's a message to get the bike jacked up off the pavement a little more.

First of all, check your tire pressures. When carrying extra weight, your tires need extra pressure. Typically, the tire chart for your bike will suggest 3 to 6 psi more pressure in the rear tire. If you've already been lazy about checking your rear tire pressure, you could easily be 10 psi under "passenger" specs.

While you're checking the bike, take a close look at the rear suspension. The springs on your shocks may have been on the weak side right off the showroom floor, and most springs sag a bit as the mileage builds up. If you have an agile and cooperative passenger, you can check the shock preload by measuring the travel with a tape measure. With the bike unladen, measure the spring length. Then measure again with both rider and passenger weight on the machine. Ideally, the springs should compress only about halfway to the limit with the full load supported on the wheels.

If the shocks are close to bottoming out just sitting there, jack the spring preload to maximum, and check again. If that doesn't get the preload back into an acceptable range, it's time for stronger shock springs. Shock suppliers can usually provide similar-looking but stronger springs, or dual rate springs. There are also specialty shocks with multiple springs for a wider range of preload adjustment, and spring spacers for front forks. The suspension specialists are always willing to offer advice. Talk to your parts man, or call the aftermarket suspension people directly. Be prepared with the model number and year of your bike, and the weight you intend to carry, including rider, passenger, and typical baggage. Don't settle for off-the-shelf suspension just because it's described as "heavy duty."

Hills

Hills can provide some surprises, too. Consider where a passenger's weight is positioned on the bike. Typically, the second rider is sitting over the rear axle. On level pavement that means the rider's weight isn't applying any load on the front wheel. But when the front end is pointed downhill, more of the passenger's weight is transferred to the front wheel.

When you are braking on a downhill section, the weight shift forward will increase front wheel traction. Obviously, the brakes have to overcome the forward energy of both riders and machine. What's less obvious is that when pointed downhill, the riders' weights are being pulled downhill by both forward energy and gravity. And kinetic energy increases dramatically with increased speed.

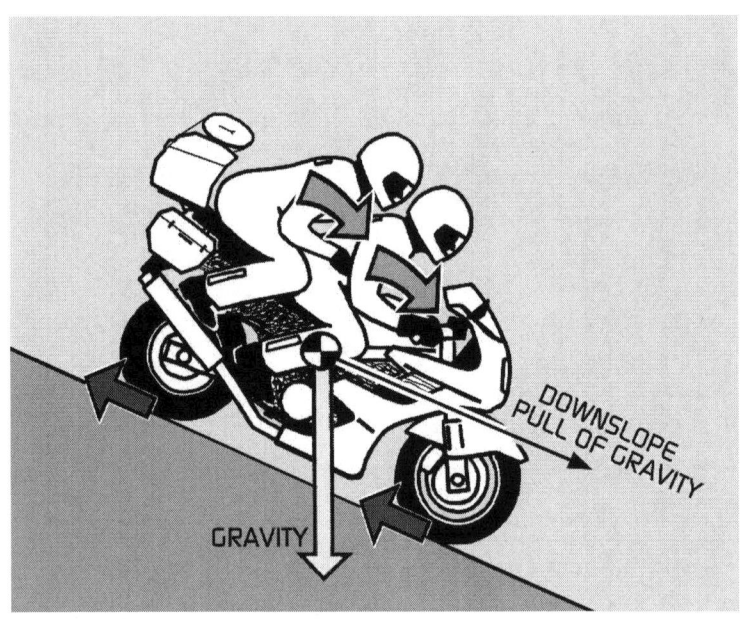

When braking downhill, the brakes have to overcome both forward energy and the downslope pull of gravity.

If you're approaching a steep downhill turn, you don't want to delay braking until the last second, and then find you can't get the bike slowed to an acceptable entry speed for the corner. More than a few riders of heavy touring machines have made sight-seeing excursions into the weeds when they discovered they couldn't get the overloaded bike down to speed on the available pavement.

When pointed uphill, it's a different ball game. Remember, if the passenger is perched over the rear axle on the level, then on an uphill slant the passenger's weight may actually be centered *behind* the rear axle. And the rider's weight will also be carried more on the rear wheel. That's why a bike with a passenger aboard wants to do a wheelie when you're trying to get started uphill, especially a short wheelbase sport bike.

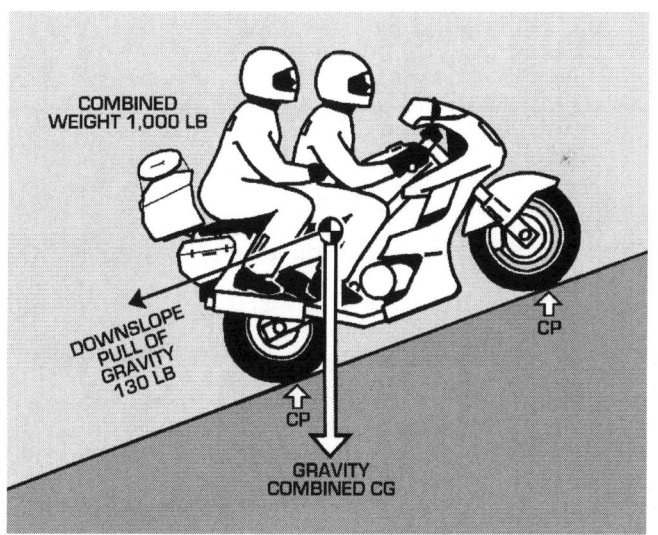

With a passenger aboard, the weight is biased toward the rear, and when starting uphill a bike with a short wheelbase may tend to wheelie. You'll need to be very smooth with the clutch to keep the front wheel on the surface.

The wheelie problem can be even worse when there is a heavy load carried behind the passenger. If you find yourself in a situation where the front wheel starts to float as you ease out the clutch, try to get some weight shifted forward. You can try standing on the pegs and leaning up over the tank, but that's not easy when balancing the bike with a passenger. If you encounter this situation more than occasionally, you should take steps to unload the rear of the bike, one way or the other.

For instance, consider what you're carrying in the top box or saddlebags. Perhaps heavier objects could be moved to the front of the saddlebags, or to a tank bag. Maybe you don't really need to carry that set of ½"- drive sockets strapped over the taillight. Or maybe it's time for a bike with a longer wheelbase.

Even if the bike doesn't show any air under the front wheel when the bike is climbing uphill, be aware that the weight shift rearward unloads the front tire, and that decreases traction. In an uphill turn, the front wheel has more of a tendency to drift wide.

You can help maintain front tire traction in uphill corners by entering at a slightly higher speed than in a comparable level corner, so that the machine's forward energy continues to pull it uphill. Remember, rolling on the gas tends to lift the front end, so you don't want to roll on just where you're also leaned over. If the machine's inertia can carry it uphill, you won't have to roll on the gas in mid-turn. That's a good tactic when riding by yourself, but when carrying a passenger it is much more important.

Whether you're intending to carry an occasional passenger, or your significant other wants to go along on every ride, the experience is bound to be more fun if everyone understands what's needed, and there aren't any hazardous surprises. If your life has been getting a little boring recently, I highly recommend a ride on the back of someone else's saddle, to gain a little experience and a lot of feeling for what it's like to be the second rider. After that, you'll probably appreciate a conservative rider who takes off gradually, stops smoothly, and corners uphill or down without any unplanned sight-seeing excursions off the road.

Carrying Children

If you're suddenly faced with the dilemma of choosing between children and a motorcycle, the obvious win/win situation is to take the kid along on the ride. The problem with that is that children younger than perhaps 9 or 10 years old tend to be not equipped physically or mentally to stay put on the back of a motorcycle at speed. The potential problem for the adult rider is that even a minor injury to a child from motorcycling will probably spell the end of the ride for another ten or fifteen years. Statistically speaking, very few children under age twelve are injured in motorcycle accidents, but if you're the unfortunate parent or grandparent holding onto the handlebars when the kid gets hurt, you're going to receive more trouble than you bargained for.

A variety of imaginative approaches have been invented for carrying children on the back of a motorcycle, but none of them are foolproof. The most obvious hazard is that the child can fall off. So, there are belts with passenger handles for the child to hold onto, and belts which strap the child to the rider. Providing a belt with handles for the child, you have to assume the child can stay awake and hang on tightly enough to stay put. If the approach is to belt the child securely to the rider, the child gets dragged along with the rider if the bike goes down. Either way, there is the potential for serious injury.

The safer approach to carrying children is to go for a sidecar outfit. Not only is it unlikely a child will fall out of a sidecar after they fall asleep, but in the event of an accident, the child has some protection by the sidecar body and chassis. Most importantly, a three-wheeler is much less likely to take a spill if the tires lose traction on a surface hazard, so there is much less risk of anyone taking a tumble. If you aren't quite willing to risk carrying a child on your two-wheeler, but you're willing to learn how to drive a three-wheeled motorcycle, maybe it's time to look into a sidecar.

If you are faced with the dilemma of making a choice between children and motorcycling, the win-win situation is to add a sidecar.

Be aware that driving a three-wheeler is an entirely different experience, but fun in its own way. There are no statistics available from the insurance industry, the federal government, or the motorcycle industry in the U.S. which give us any conclusions about the lowered risk of sidecars, but veteran sidecar-ists believe that outfits are inherently less risky than two-wheelers. Be aware that there are sidecar/trike training courses where you can learn the appropriate driving skills.

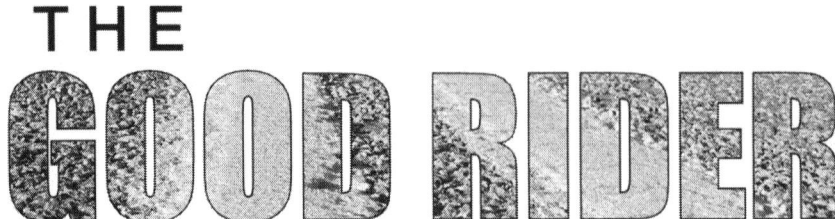

Chapter 27: Let's Get Loaded

A few decades ago, while on a gypsy tour of Northern California, our group was temporarily delayed by a road construction project. Since the road would be closed for an hour or so, most of us took advantage of the break to do laundry and bike maintenance. I was standing around kicking tires with Hawgbone Hal. Hawgbone was snorting about the extra "junk"

his "old lady" felt were necessities on a motorcycle tour: hair dryer, travel iron, portable radio, high-heeled shoes…

I understood his concerns. The amount of weight a motorcycle can carry is limited. My wife and I had wondered whether we should bring our heavyweight raingear in addition to the load of camping gear and clothing. We were already pushing the weight limits on our Moto Guzzi Ambassador. Hawgbone had a home-made top box the size of a steamer trunk on the back of his Harley Davidson.

While we were waiting for our significant others to finish the laundry, Hawgbone decided it would be a good time to adjust his drive chain. From the bottom of his monster top box, he started extricating tools, included a full set of ¾"-drive sockets, an impact driver, a large size locking pliers, a monster adjustable wrench, a selection of drift pins, and a hydraulic jack. My jaw dropped open. Peering over his shoulder, I could see he still had a three-jaw bearing puller, a serious ball-peen hammer, and a full set of combination wrenches in there.

Here I'd been concerned about an extra 5 pounds of raingear—and this XXL-size rider had brought along an extra 50 or 60 pounds of serious tools! I don't know what the suggested weight limits were for his H-D, but Hawgbone was so far over any reasonable limits he gave new meaning to the term "gross."

If you ride a sport or sport touring bike, you'll have to work hard to exceed the Gross Vehicle Weight Restriction (GVWR) for your machine, because sport bikes don't provide a big enough platform to attach much luggage, and a heavy passenger probably won't become a regular on a tiny "pillion pad." You, your tank bag, and your throw-over saddlebags will probably be within the limits, even if you are 6'6" and 240 lb. But if you often carry a second rider plus a pile of camping gear, you can be close to the limits. And if you or your passenger are packaged in the XL or XXL sizes, you may be well over the GVWR for your bike, even with empty saddlebags.

Gross Vehicle Weight Restriction

Motorcycle manufacturers determine the maximum weight they'd like to see you carry on a specific machine. *Gross weight* is the total load of motorcycle, passengers, fuel, and gear, as you would get riding across a truck scale. The permissible gross weight or GVWR is determined by such things as frame and wheel strength, steering geometry, suspension damping capacity, braking systems, and tire load ranges.

Carrying Capacity

The GVWRs are a quick way to compare different motorcycles, but GVWRs aren't the bottom line. You need to subtract the "wet" weight of the motorcycle from the GVWR to get the maximum load that you, your passenger, and your gear can share. The wet weight includes battery, fuel, oil, and fluids, but not passengers or baggage. For example, the GVWR of the 1996 Harley-Davidson FXDS Convertible is listed as 108 pounds. Subtract the wet weight of 675 pounds., and that leaves you a Carrying Capacity (CC) of 411 pounds. That's the maximum load for you, your passenger, and your gear, including the hair dryer, tent, hydraulic jack, and whatever else you intend to carry on board.

That 411 pounds may sound like a lot of CC, but it gets used up very quickly when you add a second rider. Without getting too precise, let's say my weight is ...*ah*... around 200 pounds wearing leathers and helmet, and my wife is maybe 135 pounds. So, we add up to 335 pounds. Subtract that from the CC for the bike, and we can strap on an additional

76 pounds. If we stuff 20 pounds. of clothing into each saddlebag, we can pile on another 36 pounds of camping gear, tools, etc. before we exceed the limits set by Harley-Davidson.

FXDS Convertible, GVWR	1086 lbs
Minus net weight	675 lbs
Maximum CC	411 lbs
Big Dave	200 lbs
Little Diana	135 lbs
Clothing	40 lbs
Remaining CC	**36 lbs**

For comparison, let's check the CC for a few other bikes.

Machine	GVWR (lbs)	CC (lbs)
2006 BMW K1200GT	992	324
2007 H-D FLHRS Road King	1259	515
2007 Honda VTX1800T	1219	362
2008 Kawasaki KLR 650	788	360
2007 Suzuki GSX-R750	840	403
2007 Triumph Tiger 1050	941	434
2006 Yamaha FJR1300AE	1109	427

Just looking at motorcycles parked next to the curb, you'd think the giant killer Honda VTX would be the champion weightlifter, eh? Does it surprise you that the Suzuki GSX-R750 has 40 pounds more CC than the VTX? Or that the FJR1300 can carry 100 pounds more than a BMW K1200GT?

I'm not trying to step on anyone's toes here. I'm merely pointing out the significance of comparing the GVWR and CC numbers when you go shopping for a bike, especially if you intend to do a lot of long-distance touring, two-up or with heavy camping loads.

How Much Can I Overload?

Obviously, as Hawgbone Hal demonstrates, you can overload some machines and still keep them more-or-less under control. But you'll have to accept some responsibility for exceeding the limits. First of all, overloading will affect reliability. Hawgbone *has* to adjust his drive chain more frequently because that chain wasn't designed to handle the full-throttle power required to push an overloaded machine up steep hills and through gnarly detours. His wheel bearings, fork sliders, shock absorbers, and brakes are all stressed more than the designers intended.

Second, overloading effects handling. Hawgbone barely managed to keep his groaning machine from wallowing into a mud bath as we struggled through the detour. And, after we got through the dirt, the bottomed-out machine would make sparks if leaned over even modestly in the corners.

"*Big deal,*" you may be thinking. "*I can live with a little less cornering speed, and a few more jolts!*" But the ride might turn into a *big deal* if the corner ahead happens to be one of those decreasing-radius killer corners where reduced ground clearance makes the difference between staying on the pavement and bouncing off a stone retaining wall.

What's more, suspension helps maintain traction. Obviously, the springs will sag more under a heavy load, eating up ground clearance in the corners, and bottoming once in a while on sharp bumps. Shock/spring suspension systems are designed to maximize traction with the shock absorber piston in the middle of the suspension range. What I mean by *maximize* is that the tires can keep a constant grip on a bumpy road. If the tires can't get down into holes or up over bumps quickly enough, they can't maintain constant traction.

For instance, if the shock piston is already up at the end of the cylinder when the wheel hits a bump, it can't absorb the jolt. The wheel can only try to lift that end of the bike. The resulting shock can bounce the tires right off the pavement, reducing traction to zero for a moment. So, I'm not talking just bouncing kidneys here, I'm talking bikes levering themselves off the pavement, tires losing traction, maybe even axles or shock rods bending, or the frame cracking. I could go on, but you probably get the idea that GVWR and CC are important numbers you ignore at your own peril.

Staying Within the Limits

There are several techniques for staying within the weight limits. First, pay enough attention to the CC when buying a motorcycle to be confident it will handle the loads you expect it to carry. If you weigh less than 250 pounds and primarily ride alone and with maybe just a tank bag of extra gear, you won't have to worry about the limits. But if you and your passenger add up to some impressive weight, and your style of motorcycling leans toward long distance touring, you ought to be as concerned about the GVWR as you are about the horsepower and torque charts. *Motorcycle Consumer News* includes GVWR and Carrying Capacities in motorcycle reviews to help readers make informed decisions. You'll also find the GVWR on the machine, usually on a decal under the seat.

Prioritize, Downsize

When I'm getting ready for a long trip, it is easy to take too much. Wise trip advice: *take twice the money and half the gear*. One tactic for piling less gear on the bike is to prioritize. Make a list, or even better, put everything you think you *must have* in one pile on the floor. Put the items you think you *might need* in a second pile. Put the *nice to have along* items in a third pile. Of course, if you will be carrying a passenger, each rider will have separate piles of gear.

Now take a good look at those gear piles, starting with the *must have*. What can you reduce in size and weight? Bikers and hikers are faced with the same problem: weight. If you're not a hiker, you might consider spending some time in an outdoor store looking at compact, lightweight tents, sleeping bags, and cooking utensils. If you'll have a second rider aboard, compare the items and see if you can eliminate duplicates.

For example, maybe toothpaste is a *must have* item, but you may not need to carry two economy-sized tubes. And do you really need two full camera outfits with 600 mm telephoto lenses, or can you get along with one little shirt-pocket rangefinder camera? Does a weekend trip require the six man *stand-up-to-put-your-pants-on* tent, or can you make do with a cramped little two man tent? If you can reduce the size and weight of the items in the *must have* piles, you may have room for a few more *might need* and *nice to have along* items.

Tom Mehren has a clever little book called *Packing Light, Packing Right* that helps you choose the most compact gear for traveling on a motorcycle. It's available from *http://www.soundrider.com*.

When you have pared down the gear, weigh the load on the bathroom scale. Don't forget to include the extra tools, spare parts, motor oil, and tie-down straps. You should have some idea of the CC of your motorcycle. If you are stretching the limits, you can forget the *nice to have along* things, and start paring down the *might need* piles. Of course, the next question is: how you are going to pack it all on the bike?

Packing the Bike

When you begin stacking everything on the bike, *where* you pack it is important. Loading extra weight far from the motorcycle's Center of Gravity (CoG) will contribute to sluggish handling. You could tie a big suitcase on the back hanging out over the taillight, but saddlebags are a better location for heavy objects, because they are closer to the bike's CoG. A tank bag is an excellent place to carry weight, but be smart about what you put in it, because you may have to get up close and personal with whatever is in the bag should you become involved in a crash.

Big touring machines often have a capacious box over the rear end, called a touring case, top box, or scoot boot. You may also have big racks attached to the top of the saddlebag and top box lids, to which you can tie even more gear. Hold on, though! If you check the suggested weight limits for bags, boxes, and racks, you may find the limits surprisingly low. One familiar chrome rack for Honda Gold Wing top boxes lists a 3 pound limit. What the manufacturers are trying to tell you is to keep the weight down, even if the volume is large. Load heavier objects in the saddlebags, lighter things in the top box, and only the lightest gear strapped on the bag racks.

Tie One On

If you're a novice motorcycle traveler, consider how you're going to pack the load to carry it on the bike. You don't want to have your underwear falling off on the freeway or getting soaked in a rain shower. If you don't want to install hard bags, take a good look at the various fabric bags on the market. Whatever system you choose, be sure it can be secured in place and doesn't get tangled in the running gear or sag down onto the mufflers.

If you're traveling without a passenger, the rear half of the saddle is a good location for larger, heavier gear, because the bike is designed to carry passenger-sized loads there. When I'm riding by myself I often strap a heavy fabric bag over the back of the saddle. Some travelers prefer an upright pack that secures over a vertical rack, but of course that creates a sail that contributes to instability in cross winds.

The standard device for holding loose items on a motorcycle is the elastic bungee cord. I've learned to dislike bungees because of their bad habits and limitations. For example, a long bungee stretches as the bike goes over a whoop-de-do, allowing something on the bottom of the pile a chance to slip out. Worse yet, when the hook on a loose bungee strap gets snagged by a wheel spoke it suddenly whangs back in your direction.

You need to have straps of the correct length, and suitable places to attach them. ROK straps are a clever design that joins two pieces in the middle with a buckle which can be quickly unlatched to gain access to the bag. (available from SoundRider.com, Aerostich.com, and WhitehorseGear.com) You pull the closed loop around a rack or frame tube and pull the rest of the strap through the loop to secure it. There's nothing to scratch your paint, and it can't detach itself when you're not looking. The loose ends of the straps can be tucked underneath the tight part to keep them from flapping around.

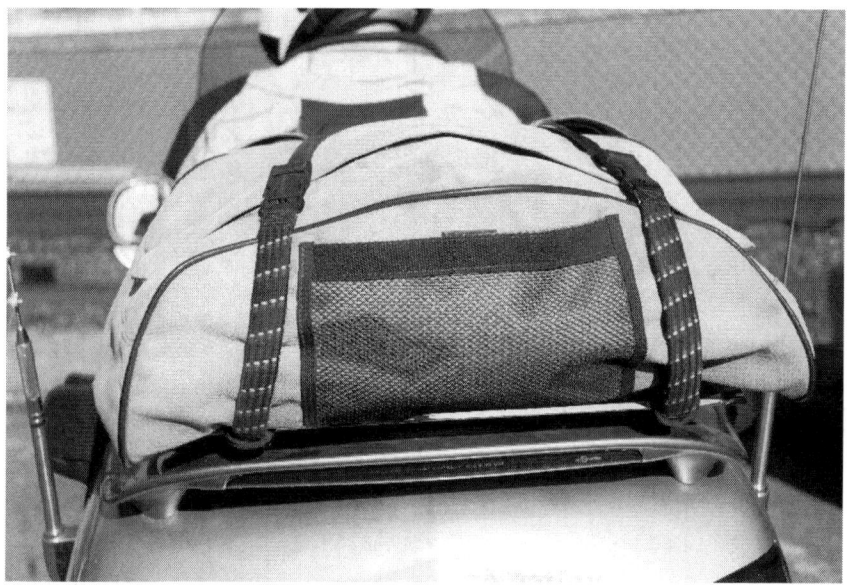

ROK straps are a clever design that joins two pieces in the middle with a buckle which can be quickly unlatched to gain access to the bag.

Luggage

If your motorcycle didn't come with factory luggage, you may want to add some bags. The most obvious choice is throw-over fabric bags. But hard bags (usually cast plastic) have several advantages over fabric. Hard bags can be rigidly mounted to the machine so they don't sag into the mufflers or flap in the wind. They are reasonably water resistant, and are usually equipped with locks to help keep your stuff *your stuff*. The disadvantages of hard bags are the extra width on the motorcycle, and the difficulty of removing luggage if it is permanently installed.

The Europeans have focused more on removable (quick-detach) luggage systems, which combine the security of hard bags and the ease of being able to grab everything off the bike and hustle it up to a hotel room. Quick-detach bags also make maintenance much easier. Quick-detach luggage systems usually depend upon a clever bag carrier that attaches to different motorcycles with different brackets. If you don't like what your dealer has available, check out the European luggage.

Adventure travelers typically look for bags that are even more durable than what motorcycle manufacturers offer. Aftermarket aluminum panniers are available in various sizes and configurations, and can be fit to many different machines with appropriate mounting racks. Aftermarket suppliers include Jesse Luggage Systems, Happy Trails, and Touratech, Plastic hard bags are available from GIVI, and there are reinforced Pelican cases with mounting systems from Caribou.

The aftermarket Happy Trails aluminum panniers on this BMW are powder coated black inside and out to prevent the oxide from rubbing off on gear. Each bag is secured with two large screw knobs inside, making them easily removable. The lids have special gaskets to make them dustproof and waterproof. (Photo courtesy of Happy Trails)

Wind Turbulence

As you add gear to your bare bike, be aware that it all affects wind turbulence. The shade tree rule for untested luggage is to avoid speeds above 85 mph, whether it's hard luggage, throw-over fabric bags, or strapped-on duffels. Generally, the closer you can tuck everything in toward the bike, the less wind turbulence you'll encounter. That 85 mph maximum speed is a precaution against turbulence that could cause the bike to wobble. But when carrying passengers or adding accessories, consider that anything on the bike carried above the CoG will act as a sail in cross winds. That's something to remember when you are thinking about stacking a tall pack behind the sissy bar, or strapping bulky sleeping bags on the top box rack.

Chapter 28: Sidecars and Trikes

Photo courtesy of EZS Sidecars

When you hear the word *motorcycle*, do you picture in your mind a cruiser, a sport bike, a heavyweight tourer, a dual-sport, or a dirt bike? Whatever the style of motorcycle that comes to your mind, it's probably a two-wheeler. Sure, you may have seen a sidecar outfit in the movies, but it may not have registered that sidecar outfits and trikes are motorcycles, too.

Mainstream motorcyclists may look down on three-wheelers with both curiosity and disgust, cracking jokes about training wheels and old guys, and questioning why anyone in their right mind would screw up a perfectly good motorcycle by attaching a third wheel. Of course, automobilists wonder why anyone in their right mind would ride a two-wheeler, so maybe it's just a matter of prejudice.

To be sure, three-wheeled motorcycles have some negative points. Dragging an extra wheel around eats up horsepower, makes the motorcycle handle all funny, and adds extra stresses to the frame, suspension, and wheels. To add insult to injury, a sidecar or trike conversion will probably void your new bike warranty. Considering all that bad news, why do so many motorcyclists take the big plunge?

One practical reason for a sidecar is to carry children in reasonable comfort and safety. When you're young and free, kids are someone else's problem. But when kids arrive in your family, there is an immediate crisis of the bike vs. the children. A caring parent realizes there is really no safe way to carry small children on the seat of a two wheeler. So, what are the options?

Some parents ignore the risks, pack the kid on the back of the saddle, and hope for the best. Others sell the bike or let it gather dust until the kids grow up. Some parents leave the kids with a sitter and accept the guilt of traveling without them. But adding a sidecar allows the whole family to travel together without taking any unnecessary risks, accumulating any guilt, or giving up the motorcycle.

Converting a motorcycle to a three-wheeler allows people with missing or incapacitated legs to participate fully in motorcycling. A sidecar or trike holds the bike up at slow speeds or when stopped, so it's not necessary to have fully functional legs. The motorcycle can be fitted with special controls such as an electric shifter, or a relocated clutch lever.

Passengers who are not comfortable riding on the back of a motorcycle saddle may find that riding in a sidecar is a practical option. And a sidecar is really the only safe way to carry children on a motorcycle

One recent trend in motorcycling is dual-sport sidecars like this KLR/DMC Enduro that are not only fun to drive, but very capable on dirt, loose gravel, or even snow.

For people with physical limitations, a three-wheeler conversion allows a way to keep on motorcycling. After losing his left leg below the knee, Mike Paull continues to lead GlobeRiders adventure tours from the seat of his sidecar.(Photo courtesy of globeriders.com)

Another practical reason for a three-wheeler is extending the riding season into winter. The threat of dropping your speedy two-wheeler on a patch of black ice is a very real concern. In northern climates, motorcyclists tend to put the bike away for the winter, because it's just too scary trying to keep a two-wheeler upright on a slippery road. The addition of a third wheel provides a way to keep on motorcycling even when the roads are slippery wet or icy slick. Even in good weather, a motorcyclist may be so concerned about dropping the bike that it stays in the garage more and more. When the day comes that you are reluctant to take the bike out because you're concerned about dropping it, that's a sign that it's time to stop chortling at three-wheelers and start looking at them.

Although there are certainly practical reasons for three-wheelers, the simple truth is that a lot of motorcyclists get into sidecars or trikes just for the entertainment value. Just about everyone is friendly toward a sidecar. It's fun to motor through a neighborhood on your outfit and have people smile and wave—the same people who normally sneer at motorcycles.

Yeah, but it doesn't lean around corners!

Riders who have limited themselves to two-wheeled motorcycles up to now may think that not leaning around corners would take all the fun out of riding. Over the years, various sidecar outfits have been built with connections that allow the motorcycle to lean, even with a sidecar attached. You might wonder why *leaners* aren't more popular. The short answer is that driving a rigid outfit is just as much fun as riding a two-wheeler, but in a different way. A leaner has the same liability of a two wheeler: it falls into a heap if traction is lost. It's a real kick in the pants to hang off and slide an outfit around a sharp turn, or drift down a gravel road without the fear of taking a tumble.

Most importantly, some of us enjoy challenges. Once we've learned how to ride two-wheelers, we're ready to try something more challenging. Sure, a sports car would be fun, but it's pretty ho-hum compared to a sidecar rig. A trike or an outfit is still a motorcycle. You're still out in the breeze, hanging onto handlebar grips, and rolling on the throttle. Sure, it's a big challenge to figure out how to handle these strange, three-wheeled vehicles that are like no others, but some of us are willing to learn.

One point to remember about three-wheelers is that you don't have to give up your two-wheeler just because you learn how to handle a hack, too. A sidecar gives you a good reason to have more than one type of motorcycle. Why not set up one bike as a sidecar rig, and have a two-wheeler for those occasions when you want to enjoy leaning into curves?

There are all sorts of three-wheelers available, from antique sidecar rigs to low-slung trikes that corner like a sports car. Some of the European sidecar rigs will corner with the best of today's two-wheelers, without the risks of taking a tumble. The most tip-resistant layout for a three-wheeler is with a single drive wheel in the rear, and two steerable front wheels. There are also some four-wheeled motorcycle-like vehicles being built, commonly called *street quads*. But since laws generally differentiate between *motorcycle* and *automobile* based on the number of wheels, I'm going to take the role of curmudgeon here and refuse to accept four-wheeled quads as *motorcycles* until the laws are changed.

Trikes

Motorcycle-based trikes are similar to sidecar outfits in many ways, and handle much like a sidecar rig of comparable size. The most popular type of trike today is built by replacing the single rear wheel of a big bike such as the Honda Gold Wing with a two-wheel rear axle/differential. A trike corners as well as or better than the typical sidecar rig, with surprisingly good tip resistance, but tends to bounce more over pavement ripples because of the greater unsprung weight of the single rear axle. A trike provides symmetrical handling, which can be a plus for a driver who is overweight or someone with lower body paralysis, but a passenger must ride "motorcycle style" behind the driver.

While a sidecar outfit provides better passenger accommodations, and the possibilities for custom sidecar bodies are endless, the choices in motorcycle-based trikes are more limited. The cost to convert a bike to either a trike or a sidecar rig is approximately the same for a package of equivalent quality and features.

There are also three-wheelers with the two-front, one-rear configuration, such as the Liberty Ace, being produced by Liberty Motors in Seattle. The Ace is a contemporary reiteration of the old British Morgan, but the Ace uses a Harley-Davidson V-twin engine. The Ace handles more like a sports car than a motorcycle-based trike.

Motorcycle-based trikes such as this Gold Wing conversion are surprisingly tip-resistant, and require less skill to drive than a sidecar rig.

Most of today's motorcycle-based trikes replace the single rear wheel with a modified automobile axle/differential. Typically, a large trunk is built into the space between the two wheels.

The Can-Am Spyder is a new three-wheeled motorcycle with the two-front, one-rear wheel layout.

The Liberty Ace is a contemporary three-wheeler reminiscent of the old British Morgan, with the two-front, one-rear wheel configuration. The Ace is powered by a Harley-Davidson V-twin engine, and has an automobile transmission with a reverse gear. (Photo: Liberty Motors)

Three-wheeled motorcycles have been around since the beginning of motorcycling. But very few motorcycle-based trikes were produced prior to about 1990. During the 1970s and 1980s, a number of auto-based trikes were built by attaching a motorcycle front end to the rear engine/transaxle of a Volkswagen Beetle or Chevrolet Corvair. Then in the 1990s, the motorcycle-based trike was created by swapping the single rear drive wheel of a Honda Gold Wing to a modified automobile rear axle/differential. That leaves most of the motorcycle stock, simply adding an automotive rear axle/differential and some integrated bodywork. The two rear wheels with automobile tires are driven by the motorcycle's shaft just as in a rear-drive automobile.

There are arguments over who designed the first motorcycle-based trike, but today there are several manufacturers who convert two-wheeled motorcycles to trikes. Normally, the bike owner will deliver the two-wheeler to an authorized conversion facility, the entire conversion to a trike will be completed, and the owner will take delivery and drive it home.

Building an Outfit

Building a sidecar rig is more like a treasure hunt because there are so many options. You can't just run down to your local Honda or Kawasaki dealer and pick out a sidecar rig you like. The sidecar-ist must be ingenious, curious, and persistent to solve all the riddles and find all the pieces. There are a few sidecar manufacturers and installers in the US who can make the conversion for you if you have the right bike. There are also sidecar installation specialists who will attach the sidecar of your choice to the motorcycle you have selected. They either know where to find the needed bits and pieces, or can custom-fabricate whatever special clamps or adapters are required.

If you're thinking about attaching a sidecar to your current motorcycle, be aware that the sidecar should be matched to the motorcycle in size and weight. Perhaps you found a good deal on a lightweight sidecar at a swap meet, but if your bike is a heavy-duty cruiser, putting them together will produce a poor-handling rig. In very general terms, the empty sidecar should weigh approximately 30 percent of the bare motorcycle.

Sidecar Attachment

Attaching a sidecar isn't as simple as dropping a trailer onto a ball hitch. The connections between the motorcycle and sidecar must be strong enough to handle the stresses of cornering and braking. The standard approach to sidecar attachment is four mounting points, two along the lower frame rail of the bike, and two at the top.

To facilitate alignment, some sidecar manufacturers build sidecars to fit specific brands and models of motorcycles, and the result, like this Liberty sidecar on a Harley-Davidson, is a well matched combination with a foolproof connector system and excellent handling.
(Photo courtesy of Liberty Sidecars)

Learning to Drive

The most important lesson about sidecars and trikes is that a three-wheeler has very different handling dynamics from a bike. Sure, it's almost the same motorcycle, with the same license plate. But having a tricycle footprint changes the way it steers and corners, and that can be a real mental shock for the experienced motorcyclist who hops on a three-wheeler for the first time. Trikes are a little easier to handle, because they are symmetrical.

There are a number of special skills involved in piloting a sidecar outfit, and it may take a few errors before the correct skills settle in between your ears. If you haven't driven a rig before, it makes a lot of sense to practice some specific exercises away from traffic and fire hydrants before you take an outfit out on public roads. Once the novice sidecar-ist acquires the new skills, an outfit magically gets a lot easier to control.

Before you take a sidecar out to the street for the first time, you should spend a few hours practicing exercises in a wide open parking lot free of obstructions. Better yet, take the Sidecar/Trike Education program and get two full days of training under the watchful eye of a certified instructor.

Remember that two-wheelers must lean to turn, and leans are initiated by counter-steering: to turn left, you steer right. A sidecar rig doesn't have to lean first before turning, so to turn a rig to the left, you just point the front wheel toward the left. For motorcyclists with years of practice on two-wheelers, steering a sidecar combination tends to confuse the brain until it switches off the two-wheeler balancing habits. That mental confusion is the major reason why a veteran motorcyclist may initially dislike the feel of a three-wheeler, and why it's a good idea to learn how to control the rig before hitting the street. And in case you're wondering, it's relatively easy to switch back and forth between a two-wheeler and a three-wheeler, just as you can switch between a car and a bike.

What about rider training courses?

Until recently, state rider training sites have focused on a basic "learn to ride" course that was designed by the Motorcycle Safety Foundation. What is seldom noted is that MSF courses are for two-wheeled motorcycles only. The Sidecar Safety Program developed a sidecar driving course to fill the gap which was subsequently adopted by the Evergreen Safety Council in Seattle, who assumed responsibility for three-wheeler training nationwide, parallel to two-wheeler training.

The three-wheeler course is called the Sidecar/Trike Education Program (S/TEP). Some states are just starting to think about three-wheeler training, and both Virginia and Washington already include sidecar/trike courses in their motorcycle safety programs. One big advantage of S/TEP is that you can get some hands-on experience with a sidecar or trike before you spend a lot of money.

"Driving a Sidecar Outfit" Textbook

The Sidecar Safety Program has a textbook available, *"Driving a Sidecar Outfit,"* which includes both theory and practice exercises. It is a complete do-it-yourself text, very similar in content to the S/TEP course. If you're curious about sidecars, *"Driving a Sidecar Outfit"* explains the skills in detail. It's available from Printwerk Graphics and Design. Although specific to sidecars, much of the book is applicable to driving a trike.

Not the Bottom Line

I wouldn't want you to believe that the above is all you need to know about sidecars or trikes. The need-to-know list is about twice as long as for other motorcycles, and I've barely scratched the surface. Now, if all this stuff about building a strange handling vehicle, sliding the tires, and riding around in the wintertime leaves you colder than a frozen mackerel, you probably aren't ready to move beyond two wheels yet.

But if something I've said has triggered your imagination, let it simmer for a while. However, I advise you to use caution when looking at three-wheeled motorcycles, or talking with sidecar or trike enthusiasts. The third wheel virus is contagious, and there is no known cure.

THE GOOD RIDER

Summary

We started out on this journey by suggesting that while lots of us look up to successful racers as being the epitome of good riders, there's a lot more to motorcycling than competition. I've shared my thoughts about what I think defines a good rider, and then helped explain not only where I think we should be headed, but also how we might get there. If you don't agree with my definitions, that's OK; feel free to write your own. The purpose here is not to build a fence around my thoughts, but to help you become a better motorcyclist in your own way. If you're happy with your ability to control the bike and the situation, don't feel that I'm pressuring you to become something you don't want to be.

I know a number of very experienced instructors, and I don't know anyone who believes that there are quick, easy fixes that will suddenly make you a smart and skillful rider. If you feel that you have completely mastered something, that's a clue that you're ready to ascend to the next level of understanding. If you think you know how to ride skillfully, try mentoring a less experienced rider. You'll probably discover that you learn more than your "student."

If you have difficulty with some skill or tactic, I suggest you go to work resolving it, not just so that you'll be less likely to embarrass yourself, but so that you'll gain more enjoyment from being more skillful. For example, if your bike seems to go wide across the centerline making a simple right turn, or it keeps making little nervous corrections going around a turn, it's time to your work on accurately controlling roll and direction. Whatever you find difficult is what you should be practicing.

Let's note that whatever we're trying to do, we're either getting better, or we're getting worse. We don't just stay the same. And that applies as much to mental skills as to physical skills. If you typically put the bike away during the winter months or can't ride for long periods of time, you will likely find that your mental skills have degraded. You may have to think harder about such things as car drivers getting in your way, or surface hazards you've forgotten about. A book such as this may help you review what you're doing. Lots of riders use books to jack up their skills when the motorcycle is parked for months at a time.

I've found it curious that more than a few people seem to have forgotten how to read. I've gotten feedback from motorcyclists who have apparently scanned through one of my books in a few minutes and then proclaimed it too simplistic or not sufficiently advanced. "Where's the secret information?" "Where are those advanced techniques that will instantly make me faster?" "Where's the secret information the experts are hiding from me?" Disrespectful or ignorant comments don't stimulate me to rewrite something to make it more complex. Rather, I know that a reader who studies rather than scans will typically discover more knowledge, and even more will be revealed the second or third time around.

Motorcycling is a bit like health care. No one can make you healthy or skillful. But if you take an active role in your health or your motorcycling, you'll steadily get better and better. If this book triggers some additional curiosity about motorcycling, be aware of the other books that are available, including my own books Proficient Motorcycling and Mastering the Ride. And there are training courses where an instructor can help you eliminate bad habits. In other words, continue to learn. Use the resources on the next pages to continue your learning. *You never need to graduate from the school of motorcycling.*

David L. Hough

Resources

National Training Programs

- *BMW Motorrad USA* - www.bmwusa.com
- *Ride Like a Pro* - www.ridelikeapro.com
- *Sidecar/Trike Education Program* - www.esc.org
- *STAR Motorcycle School* - www.starmotorcycle.com
- *Total Control Advanced Rider Clinic* - www.totalcontroltraining.net
- For localized training search the internet for your state.

Books

- *A Twist of the wrist*, Keith Code
- A Twist of the Wrist II, Keith Code
- *Blood, Sweat and Second Gear*, Flash Gordon
- *Mastering the Ride,* David L. Hough
- *Motorcycle Handling & Chassis Design*, Tony Foale
- *Motorcycle Suspension Bible*, Paul Thede with Lee Parks
- *The Motorcycle Touring Bible*, Fred Rau
- *Packing Light/Packing Right*, Tom Mehren
- *Proficient Motorcycling,* David L. Hough
- *Sport Riding Techniques,* Nick Ienatsch
- *Street Strategies,* David L. Hough
- *Total Control*, Lee Parks
- *The Upper Half of the Motorcycle*, Bernt Speigal

Periodicals and Newsletters

- *American Motorcyclist* - www.americanmotorcyclist.com
- *BMW Motorcycle Magazine* - www.bmwmcmag.com
- *BMWMOA News* - www.bmwmoa.org
- *City Bike* - www.citybike.com
- *Friction Zone* - www.friction-zone.com
- *Motorcycle Consumer News* - www.mcnews.com

- *Rider* - www.ridermagazine.com
- *RoadBike* - www.roadbikemag.com
- *Road Runner* - www.roadrunner.travel
- *Sound RIDER!* - www.soundrider.com

Gear

- *Aerostich Rider Wearhouse* - www.aerostich.com
- *RoadGear* - www.roadgear.com
- *Sound RIDER!* - www.soundrider.com/store
- *Touratech USA* - www.touratech-usa.com/
- *Twisted Throttle* - www.twistedthrottle.com
- *White Horse Gear* - www.whitehorsegear.com

Biography

David L. Hough (pronounced "huff") is a motorcyclist and motorcycle journalist who has been riding for 45 years and ridden more than a million miles on several different continents, both on two wheels and three. Dave and his wife Diana live near Port Angeles, Washington, about 80 miles northwest of Seattle.

Dave has contributed to a number of motorcycle magazines over the years, including the "Proficient Motorcycling" and "Street Strategies" columns in *Motorcycle Consumer News*. He contributed the "Between the Ears" column in *BMW Owners News* for a decade. He currently contributes to *Iron Butt Magazine* and *BMW Motorcycle Magazine*, and generates online columns for *http://www.soundrider.com*.

Hough started commuting to work by motorcycle in 1965, and learned to negotiate Seattle traffic by trial and error. But the lessons learned from commuting led to writing. Over the years, Dave has written several books, including *"Proficient Motorcycling: The Ultimate Guide to Riding Well," "Street Strategies: A Survival Guide for Motorcyclists," "Mastering the Ride: More Proficient Motorcycling,"* and *"Driving a Sidecar Outfit."*

Dave has taught both two-wheeled and three-wheeled motorcycle training courses. He continues to offer riding skills seminars at various motorcycle events in the Northwest U.S. He has received awards for his riding skills articles, including special awards from the Motorcycle Safety Foundation and the BMWMOA Foundation. In recognition of his lifetime efforts toward motorcycle safety, he was inducted into the AMA Motorcycle Hall of Fame in 2009.

The GOOD RIDER